AF594547

Dante Gabriel Rossetti

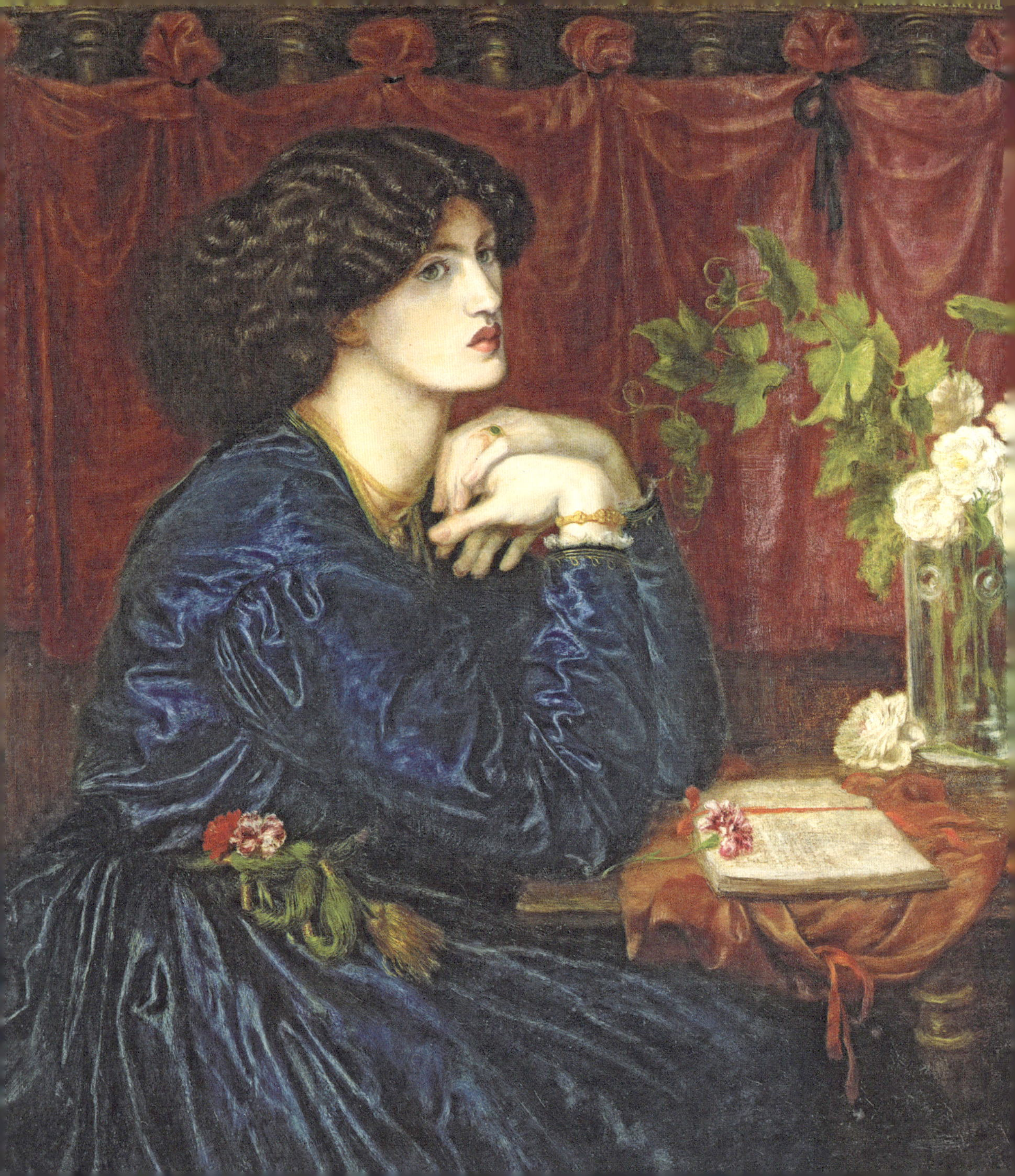

Dante Gabriel Rossetti

PORTRAITS OF WOMEN

Debra N. Mancoff

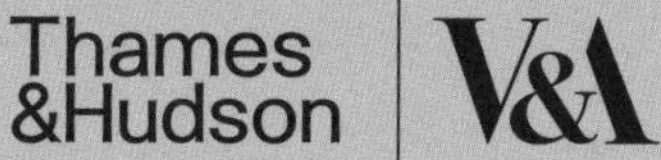

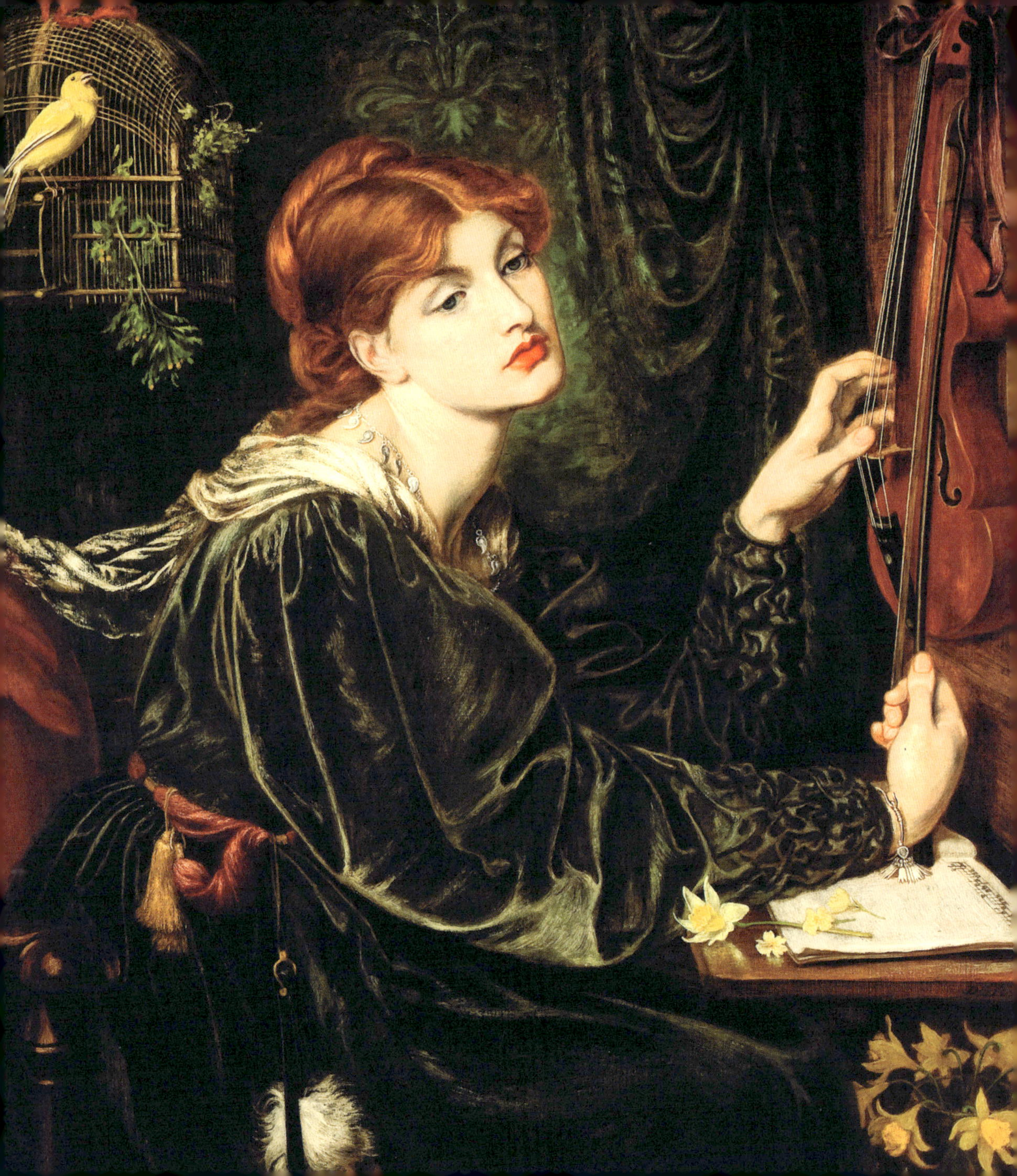

Contents

6 Preface
8 Introduction
32 Plates

138 Notes
140 Picture Credits
141 Selected Bibliography
143 Acknowledgments
143 Author's Biography

Preface

While working on *The Day Dream* (1880; **plate 85**), Dante Gabriel Rossetti wrote to Jane Morris, 'I think you look very much like yourself in the picture.'[1] The distinctive features of his longtime muse – her brooding violet eyes, her ivory complexion, the dark lustre of her hair, her long, graceful neck – are readily recognizable in what would be his last finished painting. At the same time, Jane's image in *The Day Dream* was much more than a straightforward likeness. It bore witness to Rossetti's enduring affection for her, but also to his memories of the other women who had inspired him and his lifelong romantic conviction that the highest expression in art is love inspired by beauty.

Throughout his life as an artist, Rossetti sought meaning and motivation for his art in the portraits he painted of women. Whether as a heroine or villainess, in a portrait or personification, as a character from literature or the love of his life, no subject held for him a greater fascination. As a young artist, Rossetti cultivated the belief that the right model would animate his imagination. But he sought more than a model, he sought his muse, and over the decades this essential fixation guided his path as a painter and a poet. To paint beauty was to possess it, and he saw beauty in difference; countering the decorous and compliant contemporary Victorian standard, he portrayed women as self-absorbed, sensuous and aware of their own allure. His sometimes unsettling approach, in which admiration grew into obsession, synthesized the unmistakable faces of his favourite sitters into a singular icon – the Rossetti woman – as a metonym of the timeless power of love.

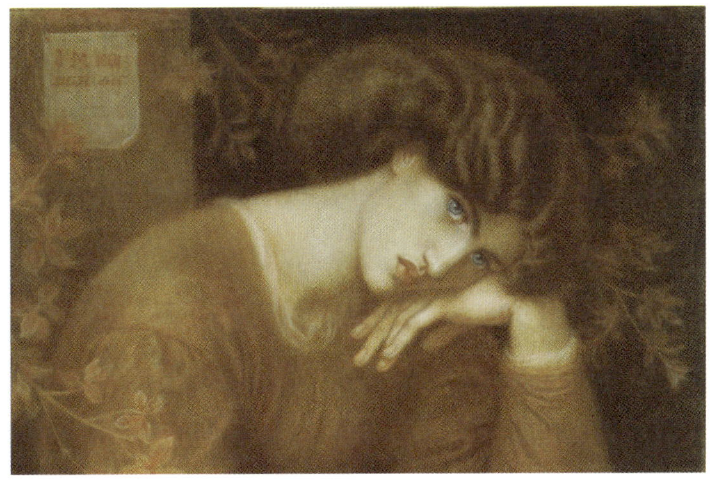

Fig. 1 Detail of *Reverie*, 1868
Ashmolean Museum, Oxford
(WA1939.9)

Dante Gabriel Rossetti: Portraits of Women explores Rossetti's central artistic motif from his youthful years as a founding member of the Pre-Raphaelite Brotherhood to his last days working in seclusion. Drawing on the rich and varied collections of the Victoria and Albert Museum, this journey features works in every media, from his earliest portrait sketches and illustrations to his watercolours, oils and decorative-arts designs, as well as photographs of his models and the poetry that he wrote in conjunction with his art. In his signature subject, Rossetti intertwined the events of his life and the purpose of his art, looking to find fulfilment for both in the compelling faces of women.

Introduction

'They that would look on her must come to me.'

In his sonnet 'The Portrait' (1870), Dante Gabriel Rossetti (fig. 2) describes painting the image of his beloved as an act of reverence.[2] Harking back to classical practice, he opens with an invocation – not to the muses, but to a special divinity ('O Lord of all compassionate control,/ O Love! let this my Lady's picture glow'), whom he asks to guide his brush as he delineates the woman's comely features, endearing glances and alluring smiles in the hope that he will convey the 'very sky and sea-line of her soul'. Although Rossetti defines the portrait as a tribute to her ('Her face is made her shrine'), his final declaration is a testimonial to the scope of the painter's power: 'Let all men note/ That in all years (O Love, thy gift is this!)/ They that would look on her must come to me.'

Throughout his career, Rossetti painted portraits of women. Whether in the conventional sense of portraiture, within a literary narrative or as an allegorical motif, he emphasized a distinctive type of female beauty to the extent that even now it is possible to recognize what a contemporary visitor to his studio called the 'well-known Rossetti type'.[3] He often exaggerated the appearance of his favourite models to conform to his personal preferences, but within the amalgam of their features he sought fine differences, looking for affinities between them and the heroines, goddesses and femmes fatales of his imagination. He intertwined his artistic ambitions and romantic desires, seeking inspiration in heightened

Fig. 2 Lewis Carroll (Charles Lutwidge Dodgson; 1832–1898)
Dante Gabriel Rossetti
Albumen print
13.4 × 9.8 cm (5³⁄₈ × 3⁷⁄₈ in.)
Victoria and Albert Museum, London (V&A 814-1928)

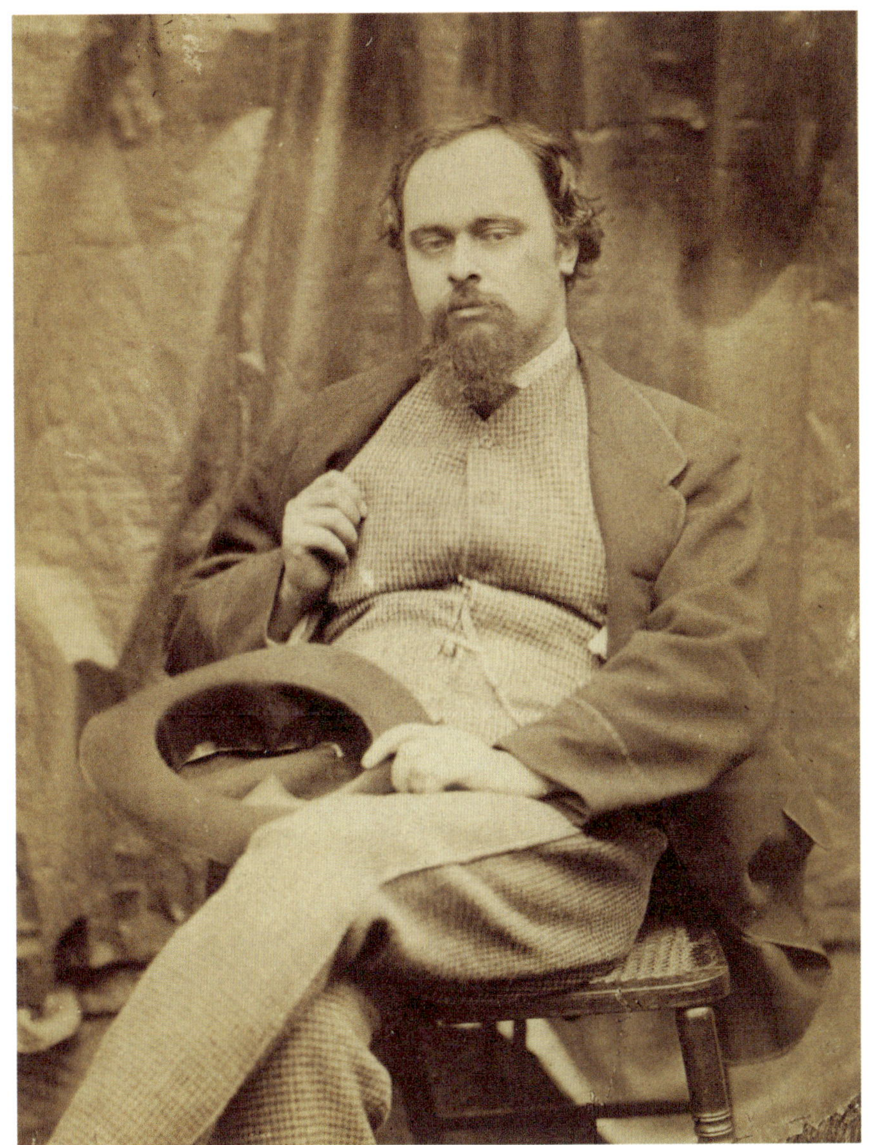

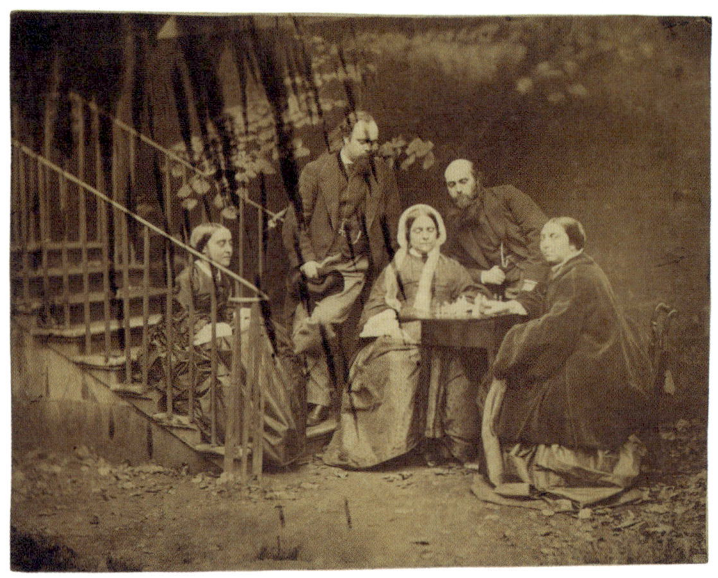

states of emotion and developing passionate attachments that blurred the boundary between his life and his art. Although he regarded the female face as his lodestar and his touchstone, as a painter of women's portraits Rossetti revealed more about himself than about the women he portrayed.

***

Gabriel Charles Dante Rossetti (1828–1882) grew up in an intellectual Anglo-Italian household in Fitzrovia, London.[4] His mother Frances, the daughter of an Italian-born translator and an English governess, and his father Gabriele, a literary scholar from Vasto in the Kingdom of Naples, encouraged their four children to read widely, write freely and speak fluent Italian. Near in age, the Rossetti siblings – Maria (1827–1876), Gabriel, William (1829–1919) and Christina (1830–1894) – remained close throughout

Fig. 3 Lewis Carroll (Charles Lutwidge Dodgson; 1832–1898)
The Rossetti Family, October 1863
Albumen print
17 × 21 cm (6¾ × 8⅜ in.)
Mark Samuels Lasner Collection, University of Delaware Library, Museums and Press

their lives (fig. 3). Frances took charge of the children's early education, emphasizing the study of literature and languages; Gabriele held a position as Professor of Italian at King's College, London (1831–47), and carried out his interpretative research into the work of Dante Alighieri at their Charlotte Street home.

The young Rossetti studied in the junior department of King's College (1837–41) and possessed a precocious talent for the visual arts. A favourite family legend describes how as a four-year-old his drawing prompted a milkman to declare, 'Imagine such a baby making a picture!'[5] Throughout his childhood Rossetti designed sets and costumes for his siblings' home theatricals. Influenced by his favourite writers – William Shakespeare, Sir Walter Scott and Matthew Lewis (author of *The Monk*) – he wrote and illustrated his own stories. In 1842 Rossetti entered Sass's Academy, with a curriculum that prepared students to attend the prestigious Royal Academy Schools. He was accepted as a probationer in December 1845, beginning with the study of ancient casts in the Antique School, which he briefly supplemented with private lessons in the spring of 1848 from the painter Ford Madox Brown (1821–1893), who became a lifelong friend.

With a passion for sensational romances and supernatural tales, Rossetti favoured subjects that allowed imaginative interpretation; his tight, detailed approach was charged with heightened emotion (5) and mysterious suggestion (6). Two keenly observed portrait drawings from this time – a self-portrait (fig. 4) and a portrait of his sister Christina (2) – demonstrate Rossetti's natural ability to capture likeness. His interest in writing remained strong; he composed poems and began to translate late-medieval and early Renaissance Italian poetry into English. By 1849 he completed his first rendition of *La Vita Nuova* (*c.* 1294), Dante's courtly romance in prose and poetry. As Rossetti put the tale of Dante's chaste yet passionate devotion to Beatrice into his own words, the belief that love ignited inspiration took root in his imagination.

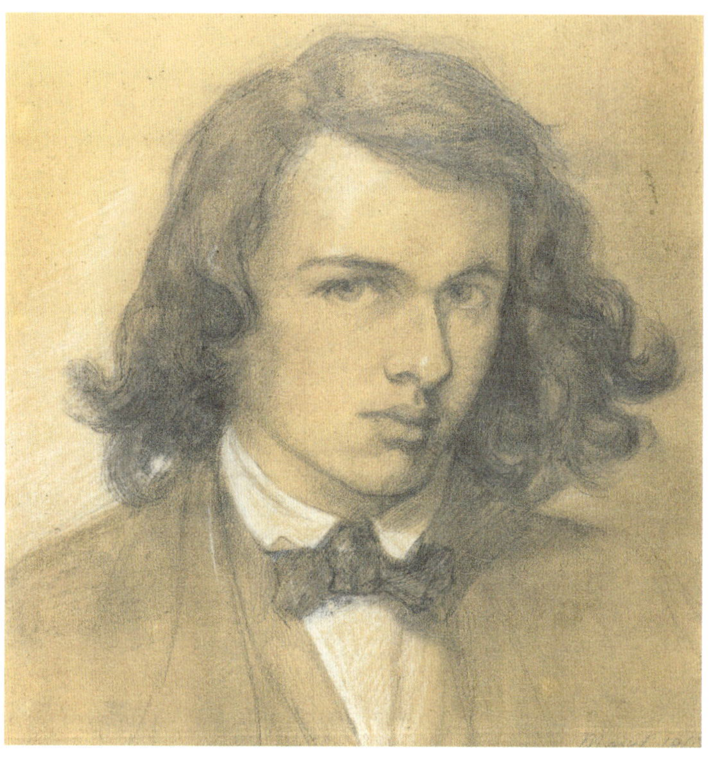

Fig. 4 *Self Portrait*, 1847
Pencil and white chalk on brown paper
20.7 × 16.8 cm (8⅛ × 6⅝ in.)
Inscribed, lower right: *March 1847*
National Portrait Gallery, London
(NPG 857)

This deep engagement with Italian medieval poetry was further enhanced by a fascination with the Middle Ages. Rossetti formulated his understanding of medieval art from an idiosyncratic collection of sources – prints reproducing Trecento (fourteenth-century) frescos, illustrated costume books, illuminated manuscripts – developing a vision of the medieval period that was based on romantic ideals, rather than historical events or archaeological artefacts. Rossetti conflated his burnished view of medieval art with his objectives as an artist; rejecting what he judged as artificial in the present art world, he embraced an idealized standard crafted from a fantasy of the past.

Keen on finding fellowship, Rossetti shared his ideas with two new acquaintances, William Holman Hunt and John Everett Millais, rising students at the Royal Academy Schools. Over the autumn months of 1848, they drew others into their circle – Frederic George Stephens, Thomas Woolner, James Collinson and Rossetti's brother, William – and before the year ended, they had founded the Pre-Raphaelite Brotherhood. Their youthful enthusiasm gave the endeavour the aura of a secret society. The name 'Pre-Raphaelite' linked them to the arts of the late Middle Ages, before the time of Raphael (1483–1520). They formulated principles to guide their efforts: '1. To have genuine ideas to express; 2. To study Nature attentively, so as to know how to express them; 3. To sympathize with what is direct and serious and heartfelt in previous art; 4. To produce thoroughly good pictures and statues.'[6] Their assiduous attention to nature derived from the art critic John Ruskin's advice to young artists in the first volume of *Modern Painters* (1843) to go to 'Nature in all singleness of heart ... rejecting nothing, selecting nothing, and scorning nothing', and to rejoice in 'the truth of that instruction'.[7] The Brothers made the exact rendition of landscape, setting and material objects part of their distinctive aesthetic.

For his first 'genuine' subject, Rossetti chose an enduring theme in Italian art: scenes from the life of the Virgin Mary (1). He posed his sister Christina as Mary and his mother as the Virgin's mother, St Anne. The Pre-Raphaelites often sat for one another; it was an expedient way to avoid professional models' fees. Their belief in the meticulous observation of nature also extended to the effect of a person's character and experience on their appearance. Rossetti enthusiastically embraced this idea of a 'character' model and, in doing so, he made portraiture a significant carrier of meaning in his narrative subjects. Likeness meant more to Rossetti than the rendering of recognizable features, it was the means to unleash the agency a model brought to the composition, and it bound artist and model in creative reciprocity. He also composed two sonnets under one title, 'Mary's Girlhood (For a Picture)' (1848–9), which he conceived as a parallel interpretation of his theme, rather than explanatory text. Throughout his career Rossetti would create these dual works of art, establishing a self-identity as a poet-painter.

While the concept of the character model added a resonance of reality to Rossetti's art, he yearned to meet the woman who, in the manner of Dante's Beatrice, could kindle both his love and his imagination. His prose romance *Hand and Soul* (1849), published in the first issue of the short-lived Pre-Raphaelite journal, *The Germ* (1850), follows the fate of a fictional aspiring Trecento artist. Chiaro dell'Erma is young, handsome and supremely talented, but feels that neither fame nor fortune – nor even faith – can validate his artistic endeavours. One night, delirious with fever, Chiaro has a vision of a beautiful woman with a veil of golden hair. She soothes him with comforting words and reveals that she is the image of his soul ('Paint me thus as I am, to know me'), showing Chiaro his distinctive path to truth and purpose in his art.[8] In this tale, Rossetti asserted a spiritual, as well as a romantic, bond between the artist and model, and the convergence of model, muse and beloved remained an evocative theme in his art (7).

While translating *La Vita Nuova*, Rossetti kept a running list of potential subjects, but he did not find an appropriate model for Beatrice until 1850, when Elizabeth Siddal (1829–1862) was introduced into the Pre-Raphaelite circle by Rossetti's friend Walter Deverell.[9] Lizzie, as she was known, proved to be a talented model; the daughter of a working-class family with limited opportunities, she may have seen modelling as a means to nurture her own interest in the arts. She posed as various characters for Deverell, Hunt and Millais, but Rossetti, who would later claim that when he saw her, he 'felt his destiny was defined', came to monopolize her time.[10] He was enthralled by her striking appearance – heavy-lidded grey eyes and copper-red hair, with a serious demeanour – and her passion for the arts made her an engaging

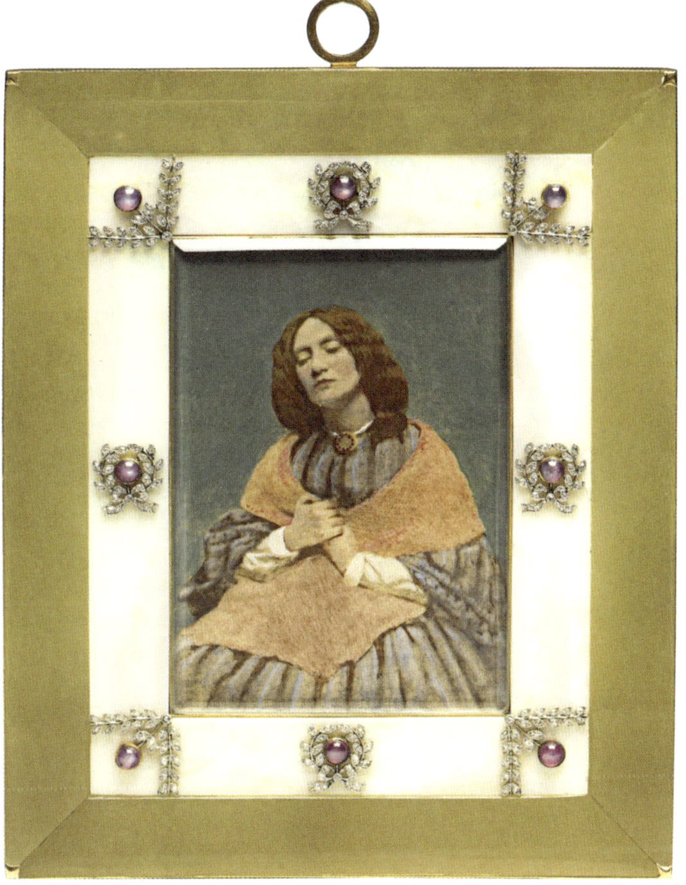

Fig. 5 *Mrs Rossetti*, by an unknown photographer Albumen print (?), overpainted with gouache (by Rossetti?); frame: gold, opal, sapphires and diamonds (added 1906 by J. Pierponzt Morgan) Image: 5.1 × 7.6 cm (2 × 3 in.); frame: 13.2 × 10.8 (5¼ × 4⅜ in.) Walters Art Museum, Baltimore (38.416)

companion (fig. 5). Rossetti saw in Lizzie his soulmate, and he made her face the template for beauty in his work. As her first appearance in a subject from *La Vita Nuova*, Rossetti portrayed her as Beatrice, refusing to acknowledge Dante's humble greeting, in a jewel-toned watercolour that highlighted her bright hair and pale skin (8). By 1852 Lizzie modelled solely for Rossetti and, although there seems to have been no formal agreement, they regarded themselves as engaged.

Late in life, Rossetti would dismiss the original Pre-Raphaelites' aspirations as the 'visionary vanities of half-a-dozen boys', and despite their enduring influence on British art, the Brotherhood itself was never more than a loose and changing association of friends.[11] By 1853 all of the original members had gone their separate ways.[12] Rossetti had already turned his focus to Lizzie; her nascent talents as a painter and poet widened her role in the studio beyond that of a model. In a series of pencil drawings made between 1854 and 1855 (**9** and **10**), Rossetti portrayed her sitting, standing, reading and working at an easel. They offer a testament to his unrelenting observation of her, rather than of their relationship; her gaze rarely meets his. Brown recorded in his diary that Rossetti showed him a 'drawer full' of such sketches, calling them 'matchless in beauty'.[13] Lizzie's face also reigned in Rossetti's paintings, as his sister Christina observed in her 1856 poem, 'In An Artist's Studio'. But even though 'One face looked out from all his canvases', he portrayed her as a character, 'Not as she is, but as she fills his dream'. In fact, their life together was hardly ideal. Rossetti's gregarious nature overshadowed Lizzie's diffidence. She developed a neurasthenic temperament and suffered from neuralgia and respiratory disease, the latter made chronic after posing for hours in a cold bath for Millais's *Ophelia* (1851–2). She sought remedies in rest cures and painkillers. Despite Rossetti's claim of devotion, he always put his own interests first, and their relationship frayed. Lizzie, constant but frustrated, followed her own path as best she could, and in 1857 left London to study at the Sheffield School of Art.

Disinclined to exhibit his work, Rossetti cultivated private patrons and sought commissions for illustration (**12**). Along with more than two dozen other artists, including Hunt and Millais, Rossetti was invited by the publisher Edward Moxon to create designs for a deluxe illustrated edition of Alfred Tennyson's most popular work, which was published in 1857 and became known as the 'Moxon Tennyson'. Rossetti complained about the subjects

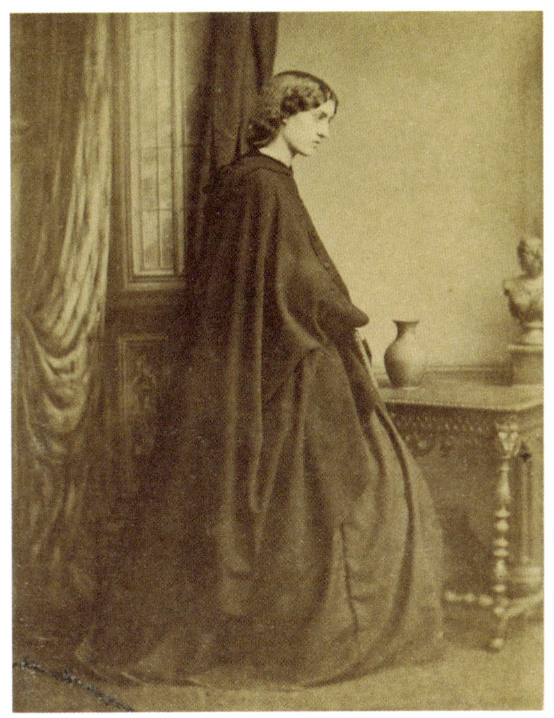

Fig. 6 *Jane Morris*, by an unknown photographer, *c.* 1858
Albumen print
8.5 × 5.9 cm (3³/₈ × 2³/₈ in.)
Victoria and Albert Museum, London (V&A 1736-1939)

he was assigned and was chronically late with submissions, but his designs for the woodcut illustrations presented perfect worlds in miniature (13–15). Even on this small scale, Rossetti was attentive to facial expression, charging his figures – particularly the women – with an emotional and dramatic power rarely matched in this medium. On the strength of this endeavour, he persuaded Alexander Macmillan to publish an edition of Christina's new poems, promising to supply illustrations and to design the cover. Although Christina was reluctant to present her work to the public, *Goblin Market and Other Poems* (1862) established her reputation (37 and 38).

In the summer of 1857 Rossetti convinced a group of young artists, including his new friends William Morris and Edward Burne-Jones, to join him at Oxford to decorate the Debating Hall in the university's new Union with murals based on the Arthurian legend. Most of the painters were inexperienced, and the so-called 'jovial campaign' was better remembered for the antics of the artists than the quality of the results.[14] The funding only covered materials, so the painters sat for one another as the Knights of the Round Table, and they sought out local 'stunners' (Pre-Raphaelite slang for beautiful women) to pose as the legend's heroines. One evening in autumn, Rossetti and Burne-Jones caught sight of two young women leaving a theatre. Jane Burden (1839–1914) and her sister Bessie were the daughters of a stablehand and a washerwoman, but Rossetti saw in Jane the potential to impersonate a queen (fig. 6). After she agreed to model for him, he sketched her in poses that emphasized her sharp profile, hollowed cheeks and aureole of dark, rippled hair. Rossetti's compulsion

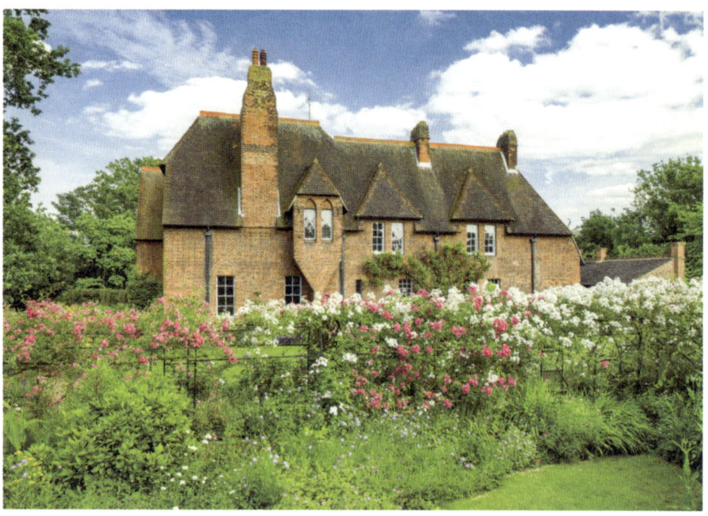

to draw his new muse was cut short in November when he left Oxford to join Lizzie in Matlock, Derbyshire, where she had taken ill. He encouraged Morris to draw Jane; soon afterwards, Morris proposed to her and they married in 1859.

After nearly a decade of plans and broken promises, as well as estrangements and illness, Rossetti and Lizzie themselves wed on 23 May 1860. A brief honeymoon was curtailed by Lizzie's condition, and they returned to their London flat in Chatham Place. They often visited the Morrises' new home Red House (fig. 7) in Bexleyheath, now southeast London but what was then the Kent countryside. Built by Morris's friend Philip Webb, Red House provided the setting for camaraderie and collaboration, as Rossetti and his friends painted the walls with murals and filled the house with their own designs for tiles (fig. 8), stained glass and furniture. As before they sat to one another, and now the women of the circle took an active part in painting and embroidering decorative textiles. Skilled in sewing, Jane helped to develop an innovative approach to embroidery design based on traditional techniques,

Fig. 7 Red House, built 1859–60
Bexleyheath, London
Designed by Philip Webb and
William Morris

Fig. 8 Edward Burne-Jones (1833–1898)
and William Morris (1834–1896)
Geoffrey Chaucer, 1863
Earthenware, painted by Morris
in enamel colours and covered
in clear lead glaze
15.3 × 15.3 cm (6⅛ × 6⅛ in.)
Victoria and Albert Museum, London
(V&A C.61-1979)

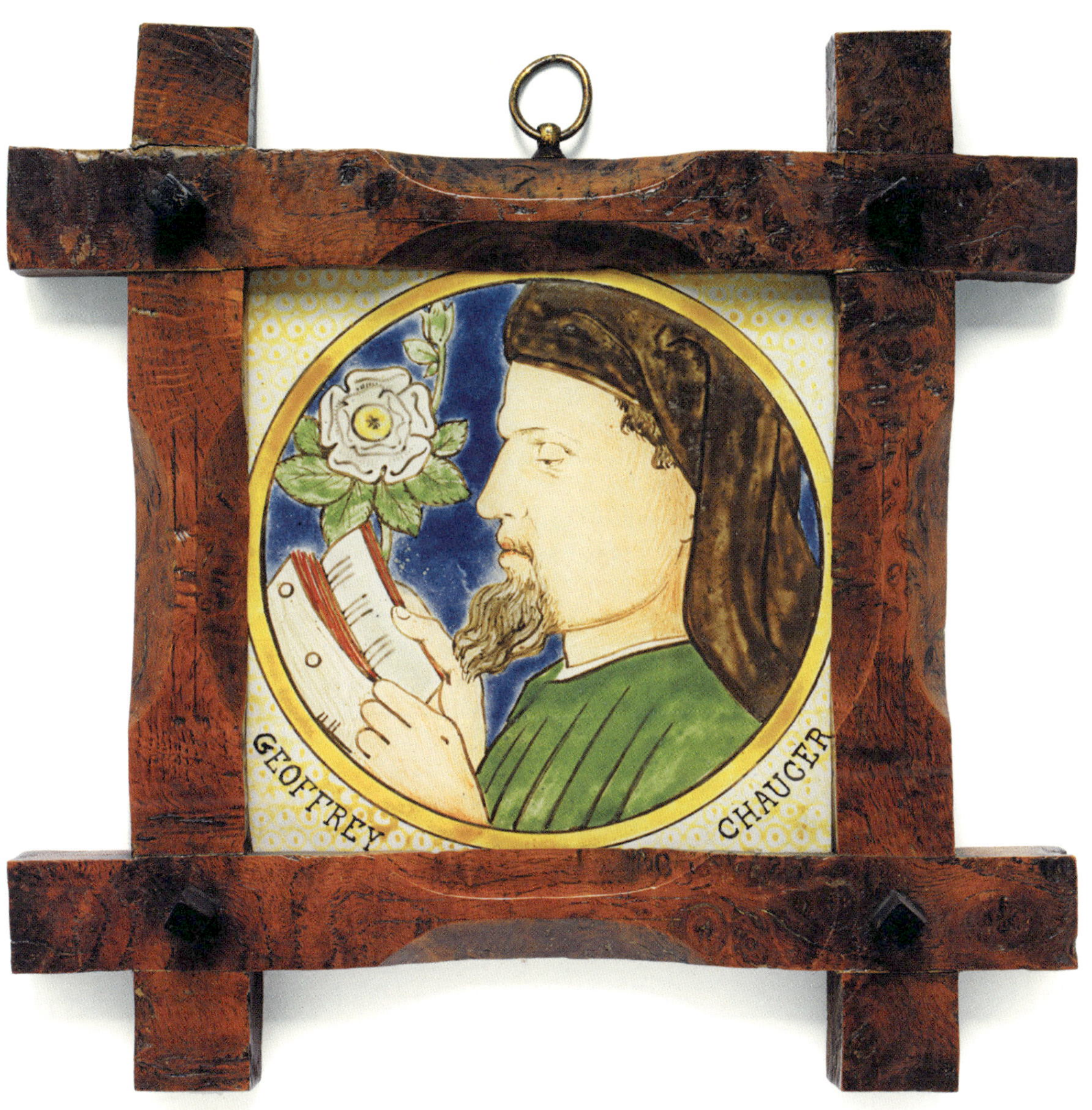
GEOFFREY
CHAUCER

and worked on vintage fabrics. Pleased with the results of their creative labours, the men decided to found a communal enterprise specializing in tiles, stained glass and painted panels, as well as furniture loosely based on medieval prototypes and embellished with figurative painting (20–5). The choice of narrative subjects often featured women, linking the artists' vision of romantic medievalism with the domestic domain (36). Everything produced by Morris, Marshall, Faulkner & Co. – generally known as 'The Firm' – reflected Morris's ideals of medieval craftsmanship, with the artists and artisans working in a seamless collaboration (26).[15]

Barely a year into the marriage, Lizzie delivered a stillborn child. For several years she had relied on laudanum – an opiate tincture widely used as a sleeping aid – to cope with her chronic pain and insomnia, and now, deeply depressed, she increased her doses. On 11 February 1862, Rossetti returned from an evening out to find her unconscious with an empty bottle near the bed; despite efforts to revive her, by morning she was dead. Whether the overdose was intended or accidental can only be speculated. Rossetti tucked the only copy of his original poems in her coffin, lamenting to Brown: 'I have often been writing at those when Lizzie was ill ... and now they shall go.'[16]

Unable to return to the shared flat in Chatham Place, Rossetti stayed briefly with his mother before moving into an eighteenth-century house on Cheyne Walk in Chelsea, near the Thames Embankment. Built on the site of Sir Thomas More's residence, it was called Tudor House. By year's end he had begun painting Lizzie as Beatrice envisioning her own impending death, while in the shadowy background Dante and his companion, Love, can neither soothe her nor save her (19). Subsequent correspondence reveals that Rossetti had planned to take on the subject of *Beata Beatrix* well before Lizzie's death, and that he based the exacting likeness on previous studies of her (18 and 21).[17] Now a tribute, the subject sanctified the loss of both the woman he loved and the incarnation of his artistic ideal.

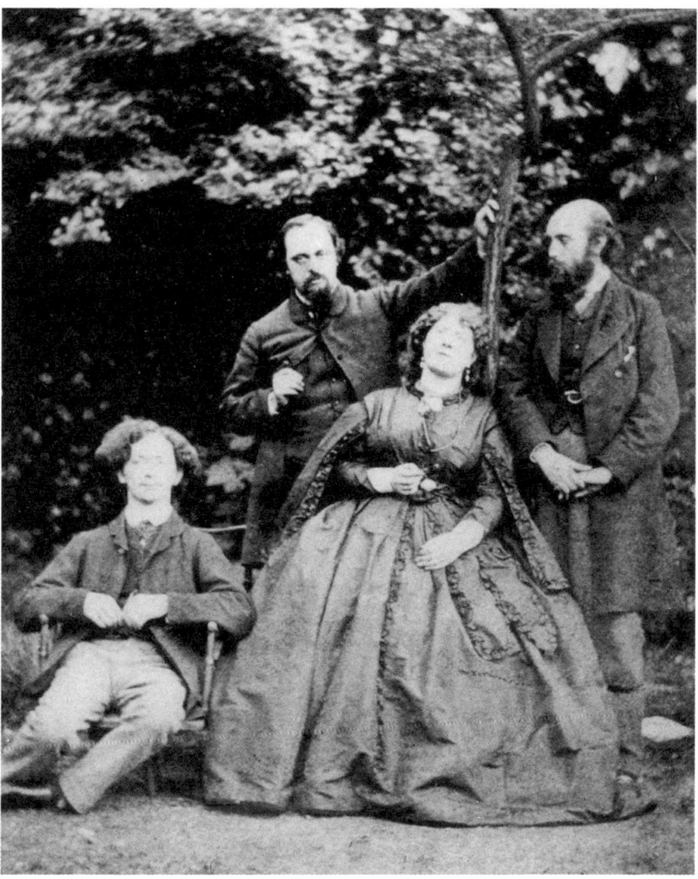

Fig. 9 W. & D. Downey
Algernon Charles Swinburne, Dante Gabriel Rossetti, Fanny Cornforth and William Rossetti, c. 1863
Albumen carte-de-visite
National Portrait Gallery, London

During the years that Rossetti envisioned Lizzie as medieval damsels, angels and his cherished Beatrice, he turned elsewhere to find inspiration for more worldly characters. From 1854 into the 1860s he painted Annie Miller (1835–1925), a young working-class woman brought into the circle by Hunt, in a range of roles from 'fallen woman' to Helen, whose beauty catalysed the Trojan War (40).[18] In 1858 Fanny Cornforth (1835–1909) caught Rossetti's attention in a chance encounter, and he cast her as sexualized characters and as femmes fatales (**39**).[19] Within a year of meeting Fanny, Rossetti's portraits of women took a startlingly new direction. *Bocca Baciata* (**33**) – the title taken from a seductive line in Giovanni Boccaccio's *Decameron* (*c.* 1348–50): 'The mouth that has been kissed loses not its freshness,/ Still it renews itself even as does the moon' – depicts a woman with parted lips and unbound hair. Rossetti painted it in oil, rather than watercolour, emphasizing the lustrous surfaces of Fanny's velvet robe and gleaming ornaments. The result was sensuous, rather than soulful; earthy, rather than ethereal. Rossetti also found Fanny to be a lively companion, matching his energy and appetites; her presence in his life was likely one more source of discord in his relationship with Lizzie. Fanny lived with Rossetti for a number of years at Tudor House (fig. 9), where she was his companion and housekeeper. She also made costumes for the studio and continued to model into the 1870s (**44**).

The pose and composition links *Bocca Baciata* to fifteenth-century Florentine portraits, including one by Botticelli that Rossetti acquired in 1867 (fig. 10).[20] The overall aesthetic, however, mirrors the tactile and tonal richness of such later Venetian masters as Giorgione and Titian. In correspondence, Rossetti referred to subsequent paintings in this mode as his 'Venetian pictures' for their emphasis on material luxury and physical beauty.[21] Whether a figure from literature, history or his imagination, Rossetti portrayed each woman in a confined yet opulently appointed space, inviting the viewer's admiring gaze. Rather than tell a story, the Venetian portraits stir the senses through colour and texture. Rossetti used many different models for them, including professional models Agnes Manetti (**31**) and Marie Ford (**42**). Above all, Rossetti favoured Alexa Wilding (1847–1884) and paid her a retainer to keep her readily available (**46**). Stately, with large, regular features, Alexa had an enigmatic quality; studio assistant Henry Treffry Dunn compared her to a Sphinx (fig. 11).[22]

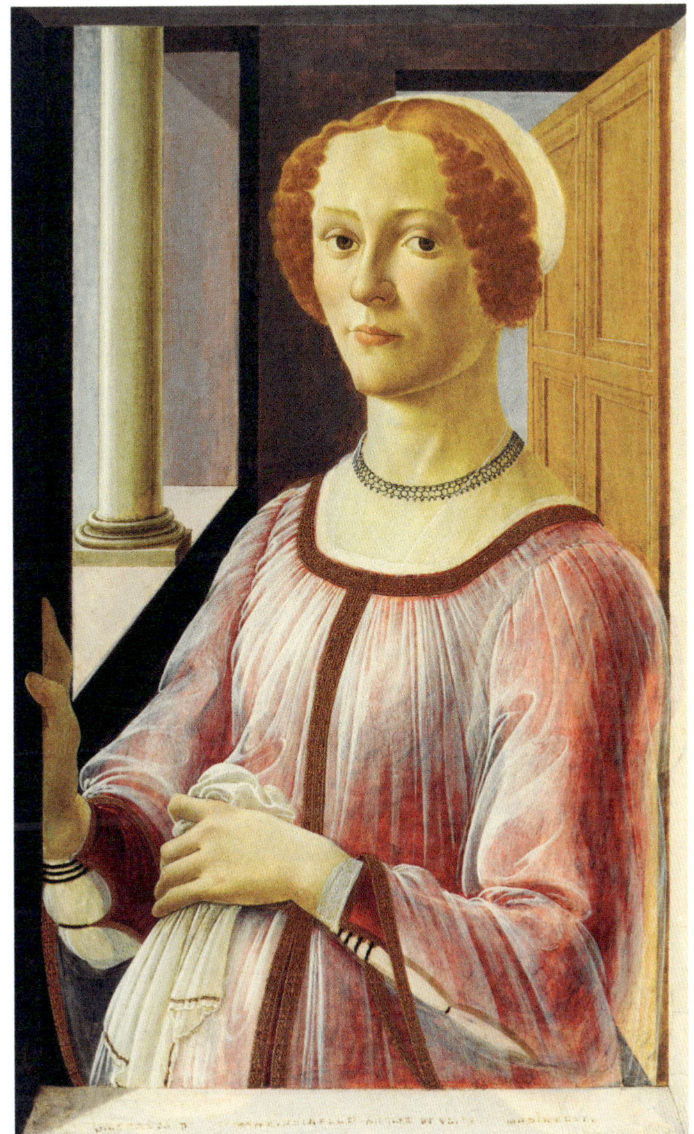

Fig. 10 Sandro Botticelli (*c.* 1445–1510)
Portrait of a Lady known as Smeralda Bandinelli, *c.* 1470–5
Tempera on panel
65.7 × 41 cm (25⅞ × 16¼ in.)
Inscribed, on windowsill: *Smeralda de... Bandinelli moglie di Vi... Bandinelli*
Victoria and Albert Museum, London
(V&A CAI.100)

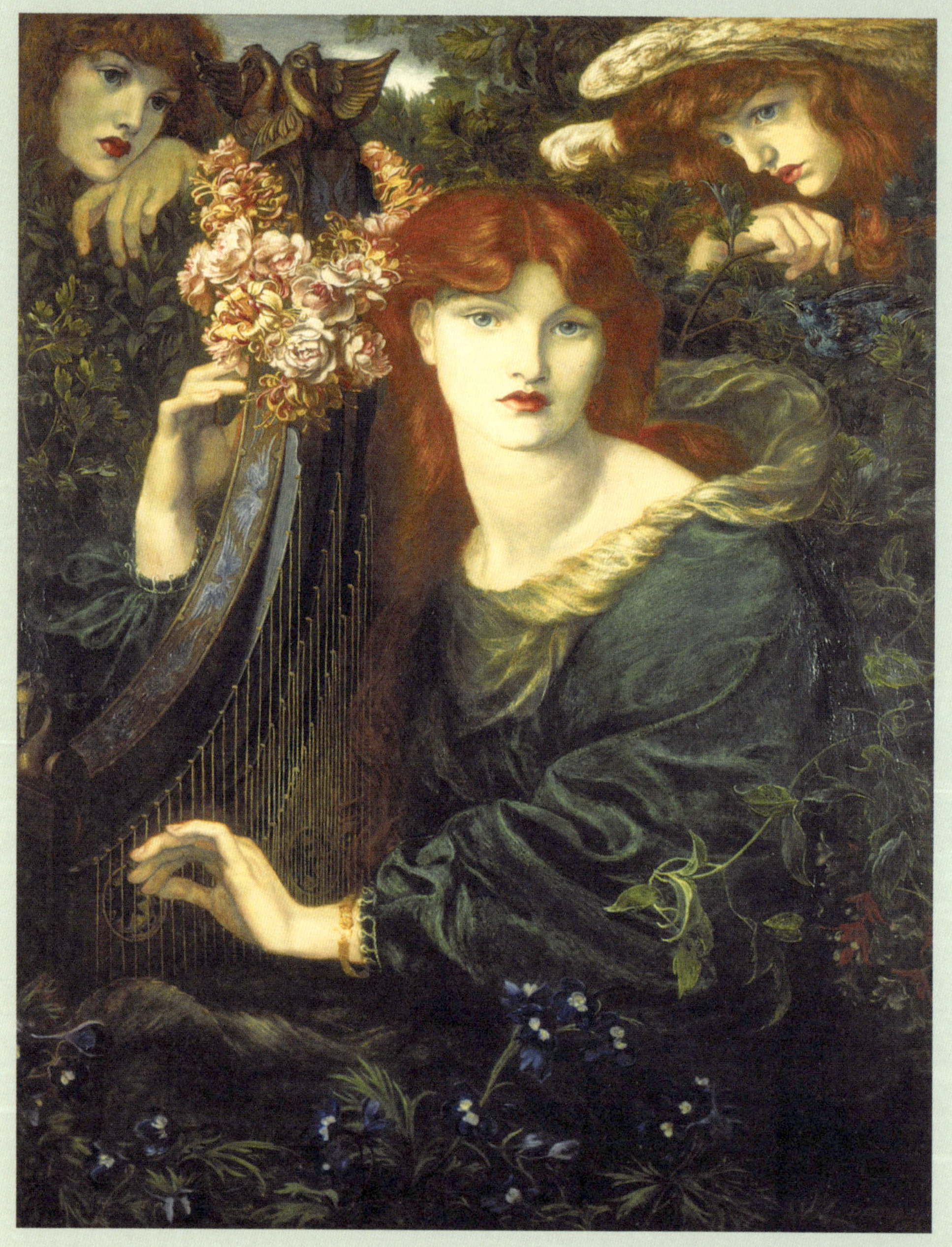

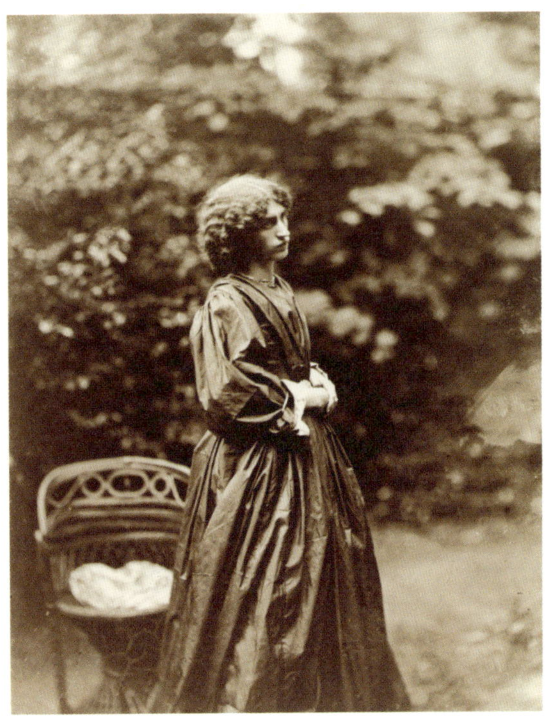

Her placid beauty and often expressionless face became essential elements in Rossetti's most exquisite Venetian ensembles (49).

In 1863 Rossetti wrote to his patron Ellen Heaton that it was difficult to find a 'suitable model' for a portrait of Beatrice: 'The only one I know is Mrs Morris', but he hesitated to impinge on her time.[23] By this time Jane was the mother of two young girls and, in addition to running the Morris household, continuing her artistic work in embroidery and making her own dresses and those of her daughters, was also an active reader, enjoying poetry, literature and plays. From the time he had first met her in Oxford, Rossetti had been captivated by Jane's appearance (56). In the years following Lizzie's death, his feelings towards Jane – and fascination with her – deepened. On 12 July 1865, he invited her to Tudor House to be photographed by John Robert Parsons, whom Rossetti had hired to create a set of *aides-mémoires* (fig. 12). He selected her garments and set her in poses, which would soon appear in his paintings (64). The photographs proved more than a reference tool, however; Rossetti conceived them as a portrait series through which he consecrated Jane as his reigning muse.

Fig. 11 *La Ghirlandata*, 1873
Oil on canvas
124 × 85 cm (48⅞ × 33½ in.)
Guildhall Art Gallery, London
(1059)

Fig. 12 John Robert Parsons
(*c.* 1826–1909)
Jane Morris, posed by Rossetti, 1865
Albumen print from wet
collodion-on-glass negative
25.5 × 20.5 cm (10⅛ × 8⅛ in.)
Victoria and Albert Museum, London
(V&A 1753-1939)

The Morris family had moved to London in 1865, and even though Rossetti had his photographs, Jane became a regular visitor to his studio and they grew close. Rossetti came to regard her as the embodiment of every character that he desired to create, whether as a doomed mythological heroine (77) or as his beloved but unattainable Beatrice (75). Unlike his Venetian pictures, in which the subject's appearance was often an amalgam of various models, Rossetti wanted Jane to be recognizable as the sitter.

He compared her 'sovereign face' to the spark of inspiration that ignited artistic powers, declaring in a sonnet that 'Beauty like hers is genius'.[24] Rossetti often created deft chalk and pencil portraits of other female friends and acquaintances (69–74), but his need to render Jane's likeness had a different motivation. He confessed to her that he wanted to 'feel sure I had painted you once and for all so as to let the world know what you were'.[25]

But these images of her were hardly biographical, and they revealed more about Rossetti's passion for her than about Jane's individuality. The portraits were his way to pursue and possess her, and he believed that Jane's idealized image embodied the ultimate expression of his art. In 1868 he finished *The Blue Silk Dress* (65), a portrait commissioned by William Morris. It hung in their home, and when Henry James visited the following year, he described it as 'strange and unreal', but when compared to the actual sitter he had to admit that it was 'an extremely good likeness'.[26] Rossetti's infatuation with Jane became a ripe topic of gossip in his circle (fig. 13); poet William Bell Scott claimed Rossetti behaved like 'a perfect fool' in his overt display of attention.[27]

Throughout this time, Rossetti devoted as much energy to his poetry as to his painting. Fuelled by his feelings for Jane, he composed sonnets that praised the allied forces of love, art and beauty.[28] It had been nearly a decade since his collection of translations, *The Early Italian Poets* (1861), had appeared, and he felt it was time to publish a volume of his own compositions. Along with his recent poetry, Rossetti wanted to feature his early poems, but had placed the final revisions of such works as 'The Blessed Damozel' (78) in Lizzie's coffin. He made the difficult decision to have her body legally exhumed to retrieve them, and the resulting collection of old and new poems was published in 1870. The unorthodox retrieval of his manuscript remained secret, but a scathing critique in *The Contemporary Review* (October 1871), which characterized the poems as 'fleshly', set him on a downward spiral of paranoia.[29] Starved for sleep owing to chronic insomnia, Rossetti

Fig. 13 Edward Burne-Jones (1833–1898)
Rossetti Carrying Cushions for Jane Morris, *c.* 1868
Pencil on paper
17.8 × 11.5 cm (7⅛ × 4⅝ in.)
Mark Samuels Lasner Collection, University of Delaware Library, Museums and Press

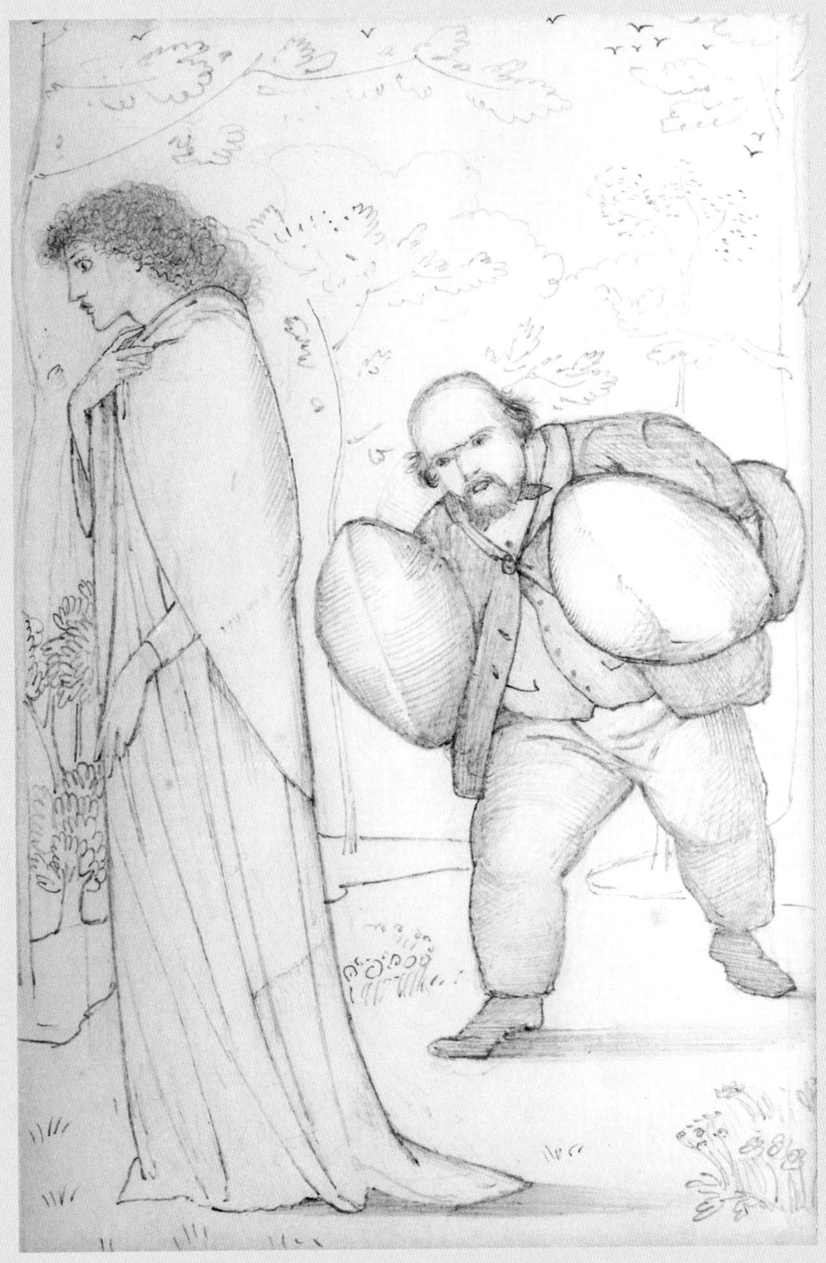

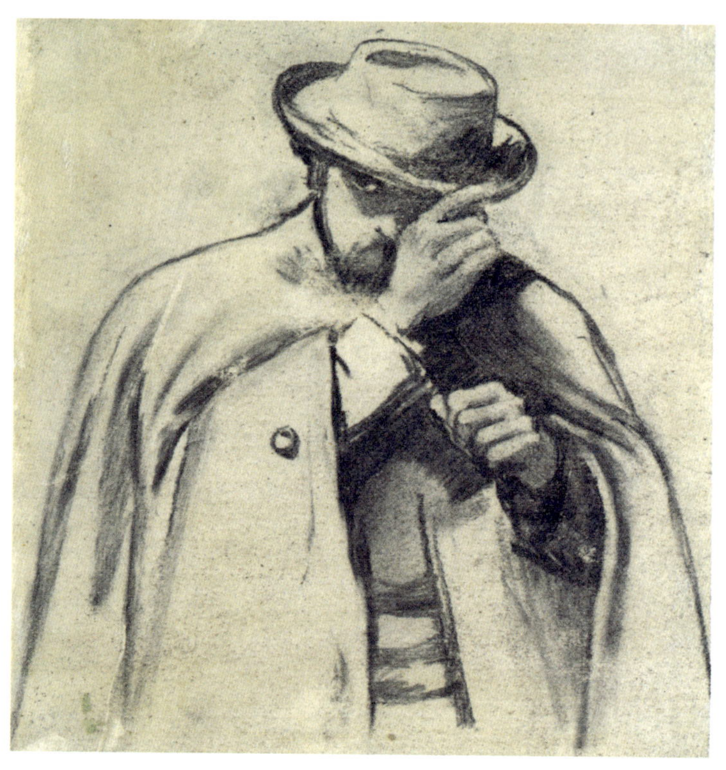

Fig. 14 Charles Keene (1823–1891)
Dante Gabriel Rossetti, n.d.
Charcoal on grey paper
13.3 × 11.7 cm (5¼ × 4⅝ in.)
Ashmolean Museum, Oxford
(WA1950.178.311)

began taking whiskey dosed with chloral. Over the months that followed, he heard taunting voices and experienced delusions; on 7 June 1872, he imbibed a bottle of laudanum. After nearly two days in a drug-induced stupor, his physician managed to revive him and over the summer Rossetti slowly convalesced in the care of his friends and patrons. He never fully recovered (fig. 14).

As Rossetti returned to his painting, Jane resumed her role as his muse. During the winter of 1875–6 she made two trips to Bognor Regis in Sussex, where Rossetti had gone for a cure, to pose as a Babylonian deity (80). But during the second visit, she discovered the extent of his dependency on whiskey and chloral and refused future invitations. They remained fond friends – Jane's visits became short and social – and they kept up a lively correspondence, discussing art and literature, as well as trading gossip and remedies for their chronic ailments. Jane's image remained central to Rossetti's art. He drew from studies of her, reprising old themes and seeking out new subjects from *La Vita Nuova* to portray her as the embodiment of compassion (82). Decades later, William Rossetti reflected upon the vital role Jane's likeness played in his brother's art: 'It seemed a face to fire his imagination and quicken his powers', and that in following his muse, Rossetti 'did some genuine justice to this astonishing countenance'.[30]

Throughout his career, Rossetti had consulted older studies and revived abandoned ideas for new inspiration. He first mentioned his desire to depict a 'Lady seated in a tree with a book in her lap' in a letter to Ford Madox Brown in 1872.[31] It is not known if he began the composition then, but six years later the motif took form in a chalk drawing featuring a naturalistic and recognizable likeness of Jane (83). He called the study *Vanna Primavera*, loosely linking the figure to the Lady Giovanna in *La Vita Nuova*, whose fresh beauty reminded Dante of spring. After visiting Rossetti's studio in 1879, the collector Constantine Alexander Ionides commissioned a large-scale oil version of the subject; Rossetti shared the news with Jane, writing: 'It is a pleasure to me to think that luck generally comes through drawings of your dear face.'[32] As Rossetti worked on the painting, he conferred with her about the type of flower in the woman's hand, the dress the figure would wear and the pleasure he took in achieving her exact likeness, except for 'the dangling foot, which alas! I did from someone else'.[33]

By August 1880, he had renamed the painting *The Day Dream*, and by December it was finished (fig. 15 and 85). To accompany the work, he wrote a poignant poem on the sublimity of a reverie that haunts the dreamer even as the seasons change. Rossetti's final completed painting – and his last dual work of art – paid tribute to his chosen muse as essential to his art. As certain as the exquisite yet mutable beauty of Nature that Rossetti alludes to in the poem, the artistic imperative of painting his muse had permeated his life from the potential of his youth to the fullest expression of his waning days.

Over the following year, Rossetti's health steadily declined, and he died of uremia on 9 April 1882. Reflecting in his diary upon the loss of his brother – 'My dear Gabriel' – William described him as 'the pride & glory of our family'.[34] Through his portraits of women, Rossetti had sought to praise them and possess them, and ultimately his legacy reversed the bold proclamation of his sonnet, 'The Portrait'. To know him, we must look at his portraits of women.

O Lord of all compassionate control,
O Love! let this my lady's picture glow
Under my hand to praise her name, and show
Even of her inner self the perfect whole:
That he who seeks her beauty's furthest goal,
Beyond the light that the sweet glances throw
And refluent wave of the sweet smile, my know
The very sky and sea-line of her soul.

Lo! it is done. Above the lithe throat
The mouth's mould testifies of voice and kiss,
The shadowed eyes remember and foresee.
Her face is made her shrine. Let all men note
That in all years (O Love, thy gift is this!)
They that would look on her must come to me.

'The Portrait', from 'The House of Life', *Poems* (1870)

Fig. 15 Detail of *The Day Dream*, 1880
Victoria and Albert Museum, London
(V&A CAI.3)

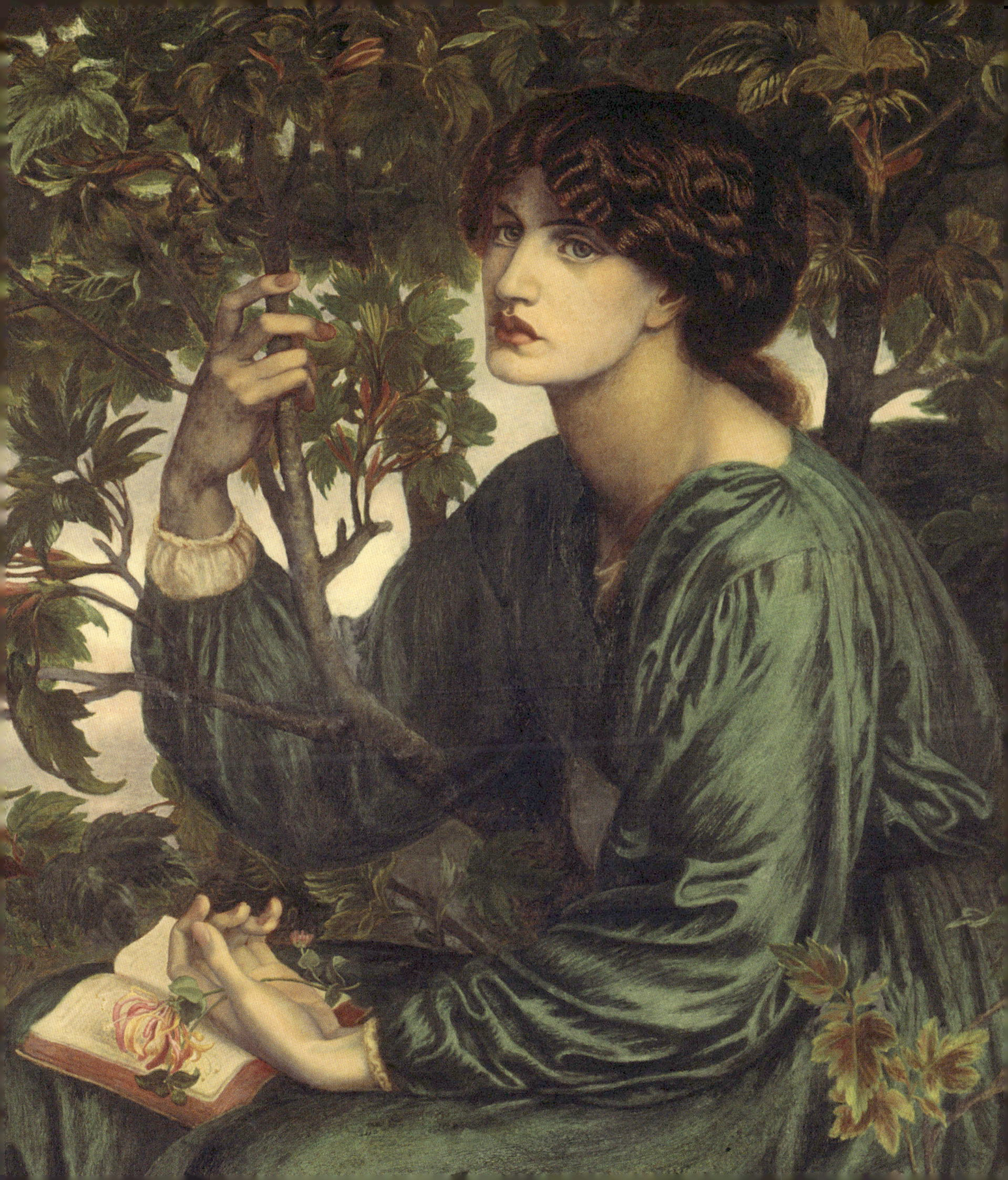

Plates

I
This is that blessed Mary, pre-elect
God's Virgin ...
Her gifts were simpleness of intellect
And supreme patience. From her
  mother's knee
Faithful and hopeful; wise in charity
Strong in grave peace; in duty
  circumspect

II
These are the symbols ...
The books (whose head
Is golden Charity, as Paul hath said)
Those virtues are wherein the soul is rich;
Therefore are wherein the soul is rich:
Therefore on the lily standeth, which
Is innocence, being interpreted.
The seven-thorned briar and the palm
  seven-leaved
Are her great sorrows and her
  great reward

'The Girlhood of Mary Virgin' (1849–50)

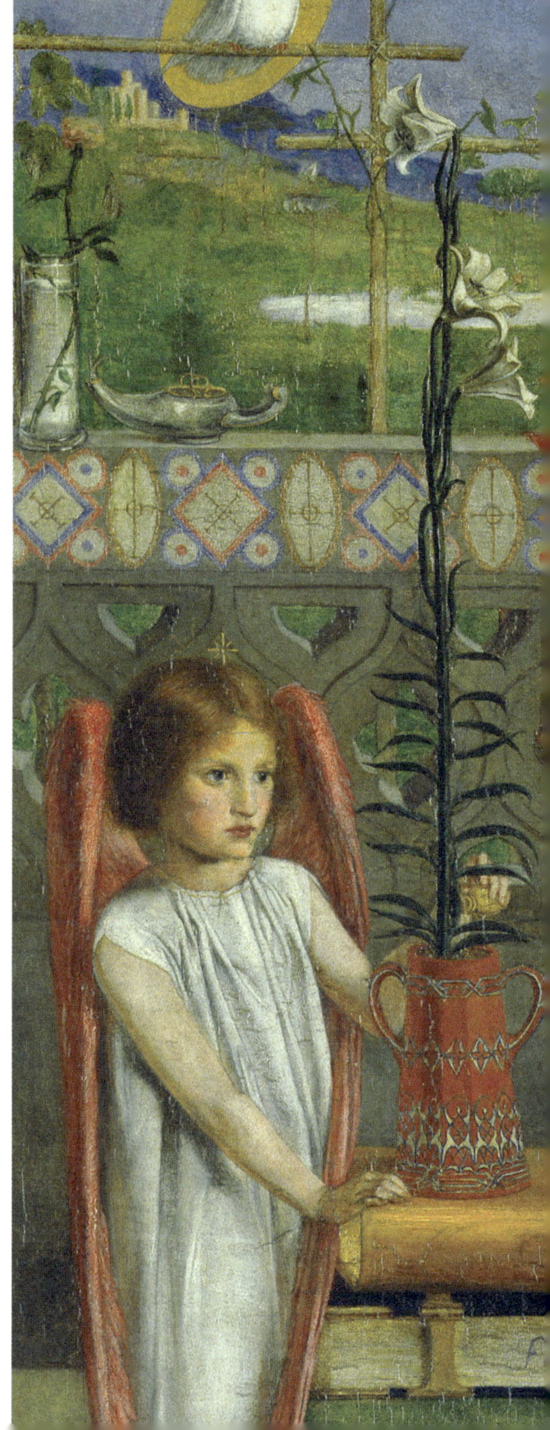

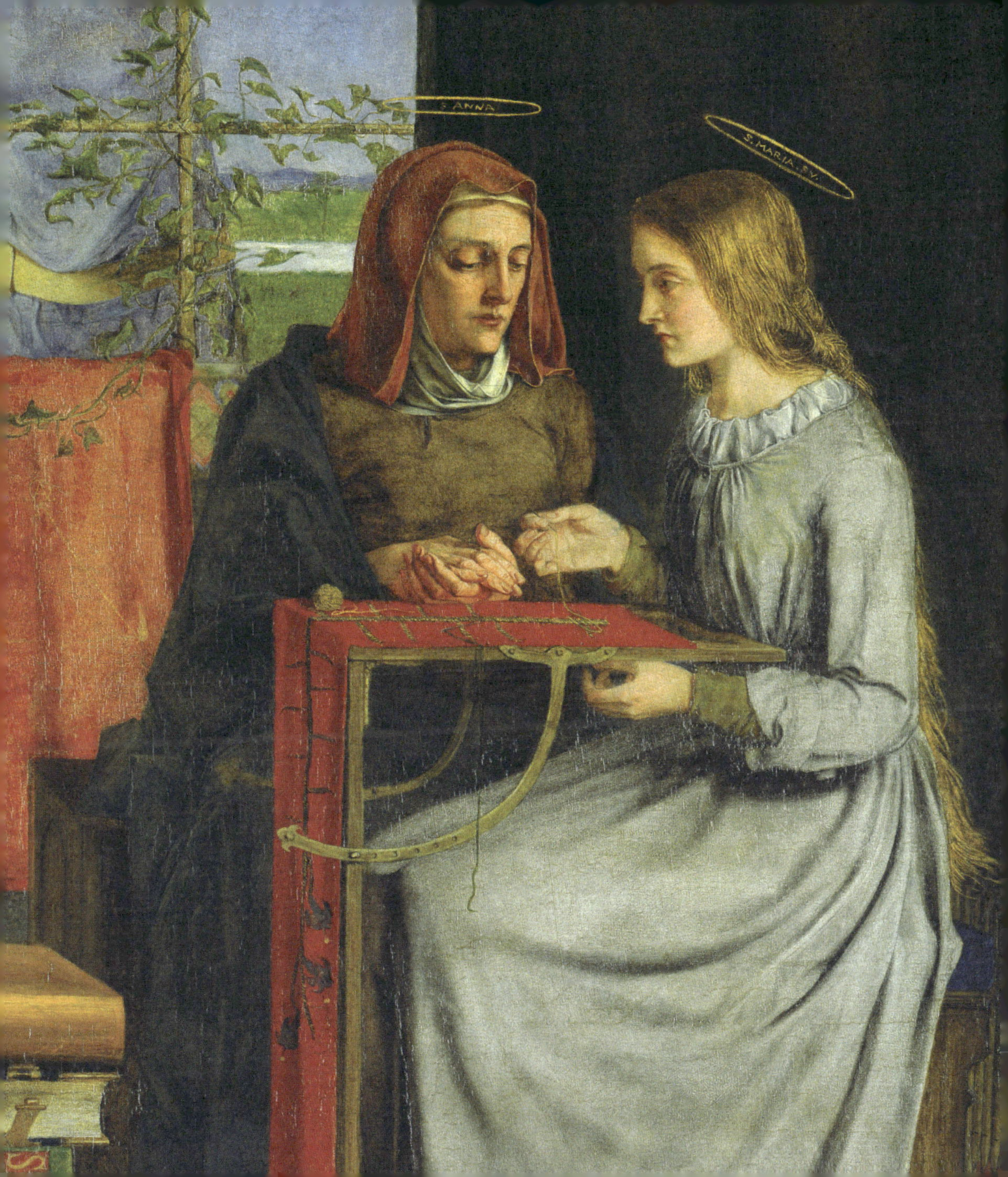
S ANNA
S. MARIA. S.V.

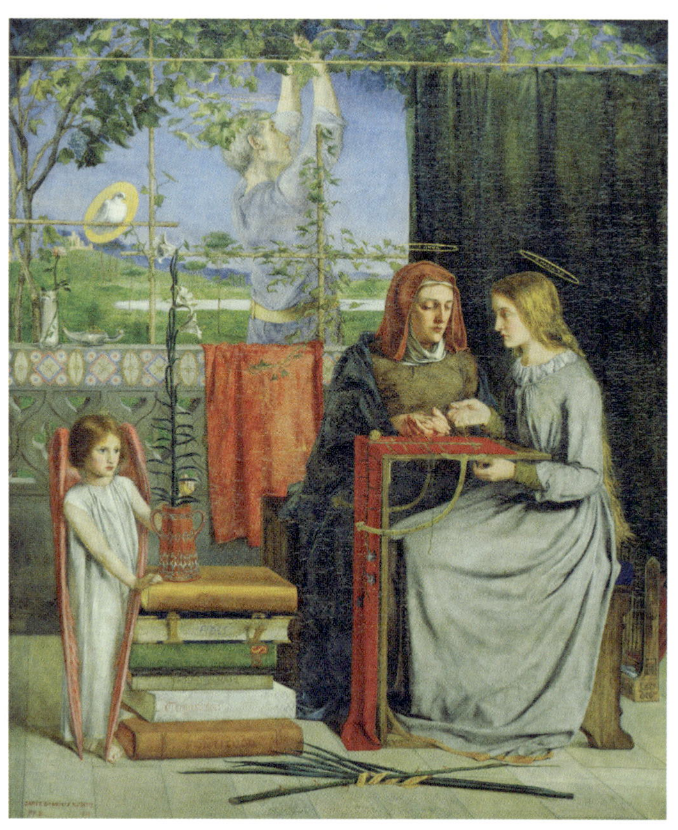

1. *The Girlhood of Mary Virgin*, 1848–9
Oil on canvas
83.2 × 65.4 cm (32⅞ × 25¾ in.)
Tate Gallery, London
(Tate N04872)

Rossetti cast this imagined scene from the Virgin's youth with his younger sister Christina as Mary and their mother Frances as St Anne. Choosing the right model was part of the Pre-Raphaelite pursuit of 'absolute, uncompromising truth', an idea that shaped Rossetti's concept of portraiture.[35] In Rossetti's eyes, Christina's chaste demeanour and religious devotion made her the ideal sitter.

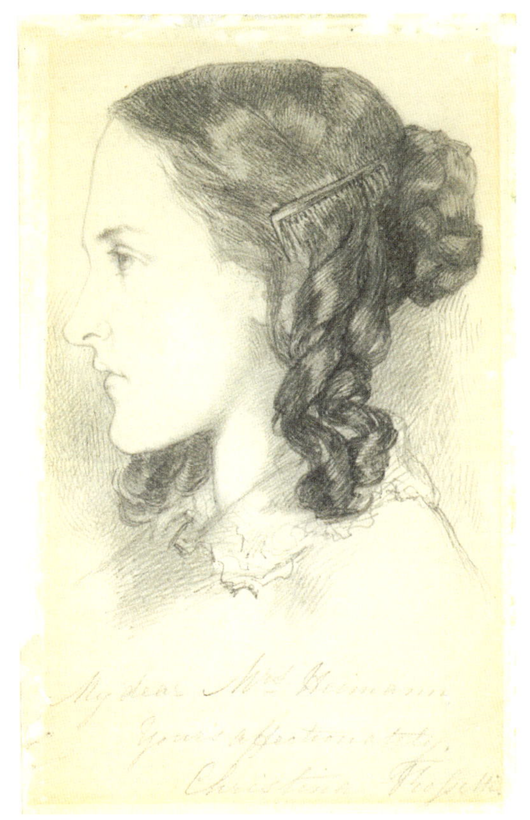

2. *Portrait of Christina Georgina Rossetti at the age of 16*, 1847
Pencil on paper
11 × 8.4 cm ($4\frac{3}{8} \times 3\frac{3}{8}$ in.)
Inscribed by the sitter: *My dear Mrs. Heimann, Your's affectionately, Christina Rossetti*
Victoria and Albert Museum, London
(V&A E.146-1928)

This precise profile drawing of Christina, the youngest of the Rossetti siblings, captures her intense temperament and penetrating intelligence. The portrait was drawn during a visit to the home of their German instructor, Adolf Heimann; Christina dedicated it to Heimann's wife Amelia, who was a close friend. For her first printed collection of poems, *Verses* (1847), Rossetti replicated the drawing as the frontispiece for a presentation copy for their mother.

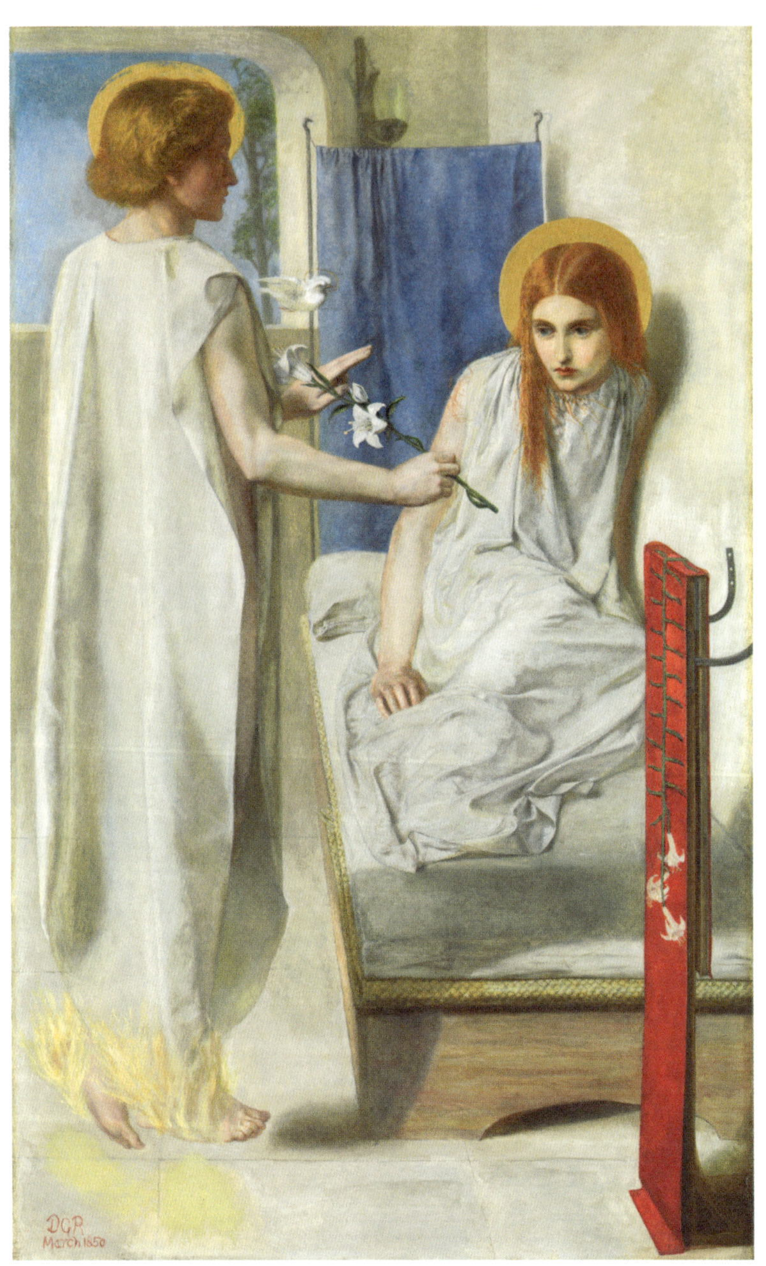
DGR
March 1850

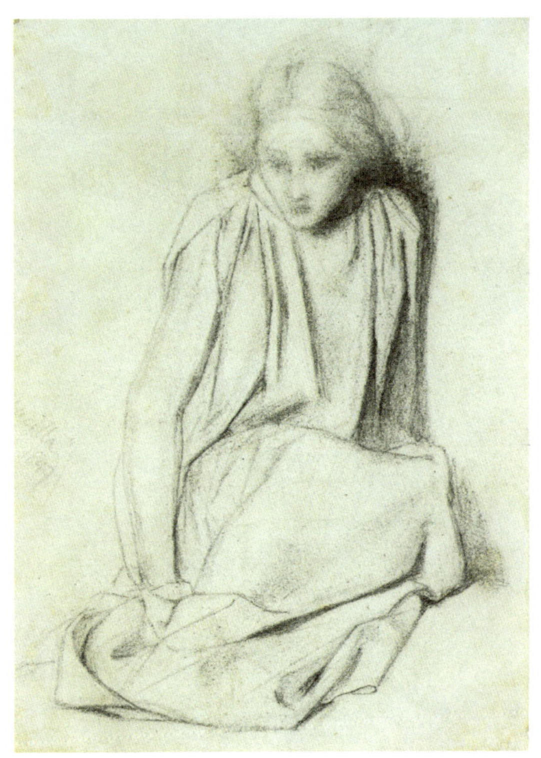

3. *Ecce Ancilla Domini! (The Annunciation)*, 1849–50
Oil on canvas
72.4 × 41.9 cm (28⅝ × 16½ in.)
Tate Gallery, London
(Tate N01210)

4. *Study for Ecce Ancilla Domini! (The Annunciation)*, *c.* 1849
Graphite on paper
19.4 × 13.7 cm (7¾ × 5½ in.)
Tate Gallery, London
(Tate T00287)

Although Christina Rossetti posed for the face of the Virgin Annunciate, Rossetti used a professional model named Miss Love for her gleaming, red-gold hair. Transforming his sister from a brunette to a redhead enforced the iconographic palette: white for chastity, blue for the heavens and red for sacrificial blood. Startled by the appearance of the archangel Gabriel, Mary accepts her fate with the declaration, 'Behold, I am the handmaiden of the Lord' (Luke 1:38).

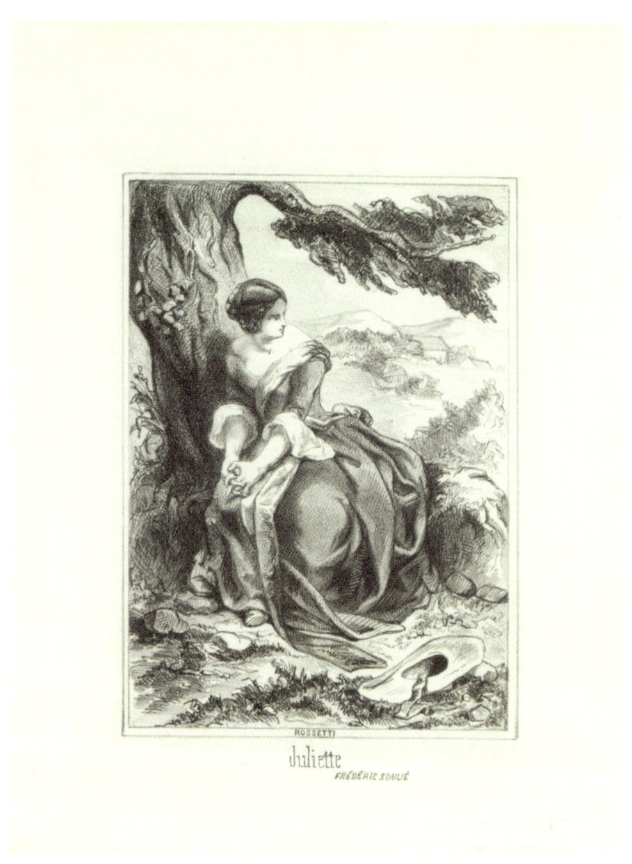

5. *Juliette*, illustration for Frédéric Souliés, *Les Mémoires du Diable*, *c.* 1845–6
Lithograph on paper
22.7 × 15.7 cm (9 × 6½ in.)
Victoria and Albert Museum, London (V&A E.149-1928)

This rare example of Rossetti's work in lithography is an illustration for Frédéric Souliés's 1838 tale of Count Armando de Luizzi's deal with the devil, cited by William Rossetti as one of his brother's favourites. Such tales of diabolical temptation captivated Rossetti, particularly when the male protagonist's transgression affected the virtue of a young woman; two years later, he would illustrate the tragic fate of the trusting Gretchen in Goethe's *Faust*.[36]

Then, methought, the air
grew denser, perfumed
from an unseen censer
Swung by Seraphim whose
foot-falls tinkled on the
tufted floor

Edgar Allen Poe, 'The Raven'
(1845), ll. 14.1–2

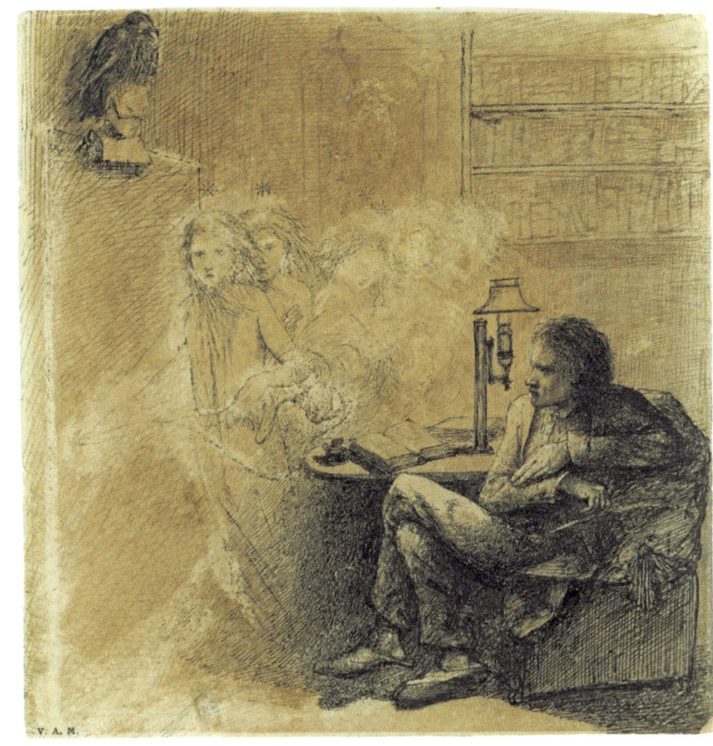

6. *The Raven*, *c.* 1848
Pen and ink on paper
22.9 × 21.6 cm (9⅛ × 8⅝ in.)
Victoria and Albert Museum, London
(V&A E.3415-1922)

Rossetti was fascinated by Edgar Allen Poe's dark imagination. In this illustration for 'The Raven', the narrator's mournful reverie is broken by the ominous bird's fluttering wings and the soft steps of Seraphim, whose burning censers scent the chamber. A faint rendering of a portrait, not mentioned in the poem, can be seen on the wall above the cloud of perfumed smoke; perhaps it depicts his lost love, Leonore.

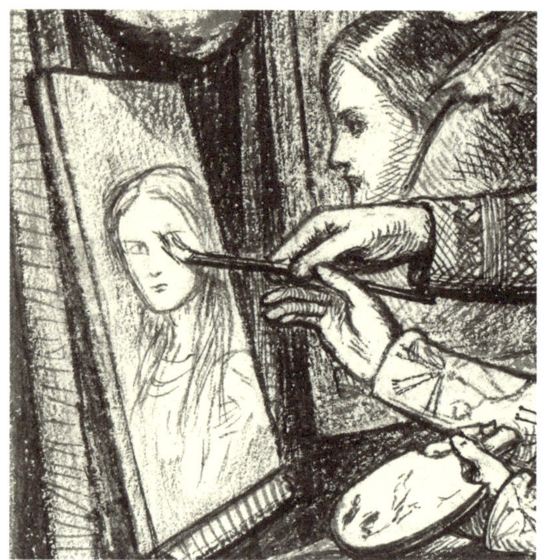

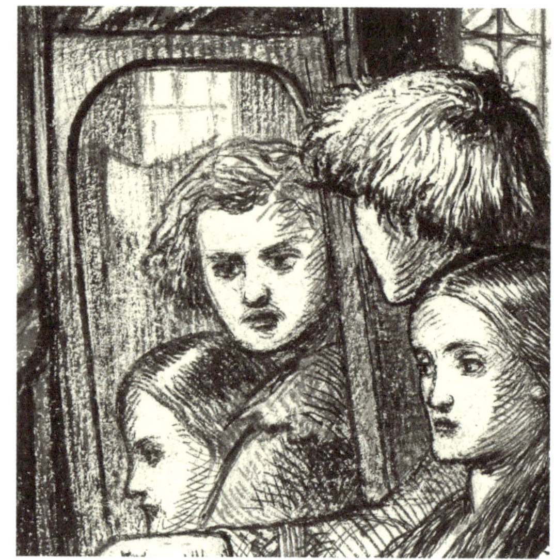

7. *Love's Mirror, or A Parable of Love*, *c.* 1850–2
Black pen and ink over pencil, with ink wash on paper
17.5 × 19.5 cm (7 × 7¾ in.)
Birmingham Museums and Art Gallery (1904P491)

No literary source can be found for this 'parable'. As the man guides the woman's hand, their eyes do not meet; he gazes at her reflection in the mirror in which she is studying her own likeness. Who is painting this portrait: the woman at the easel, or the man whose fingers displace hers to control the brush? And which is the more truthful mirror of love: their reflected image, or the portrait they create together on the canvas?

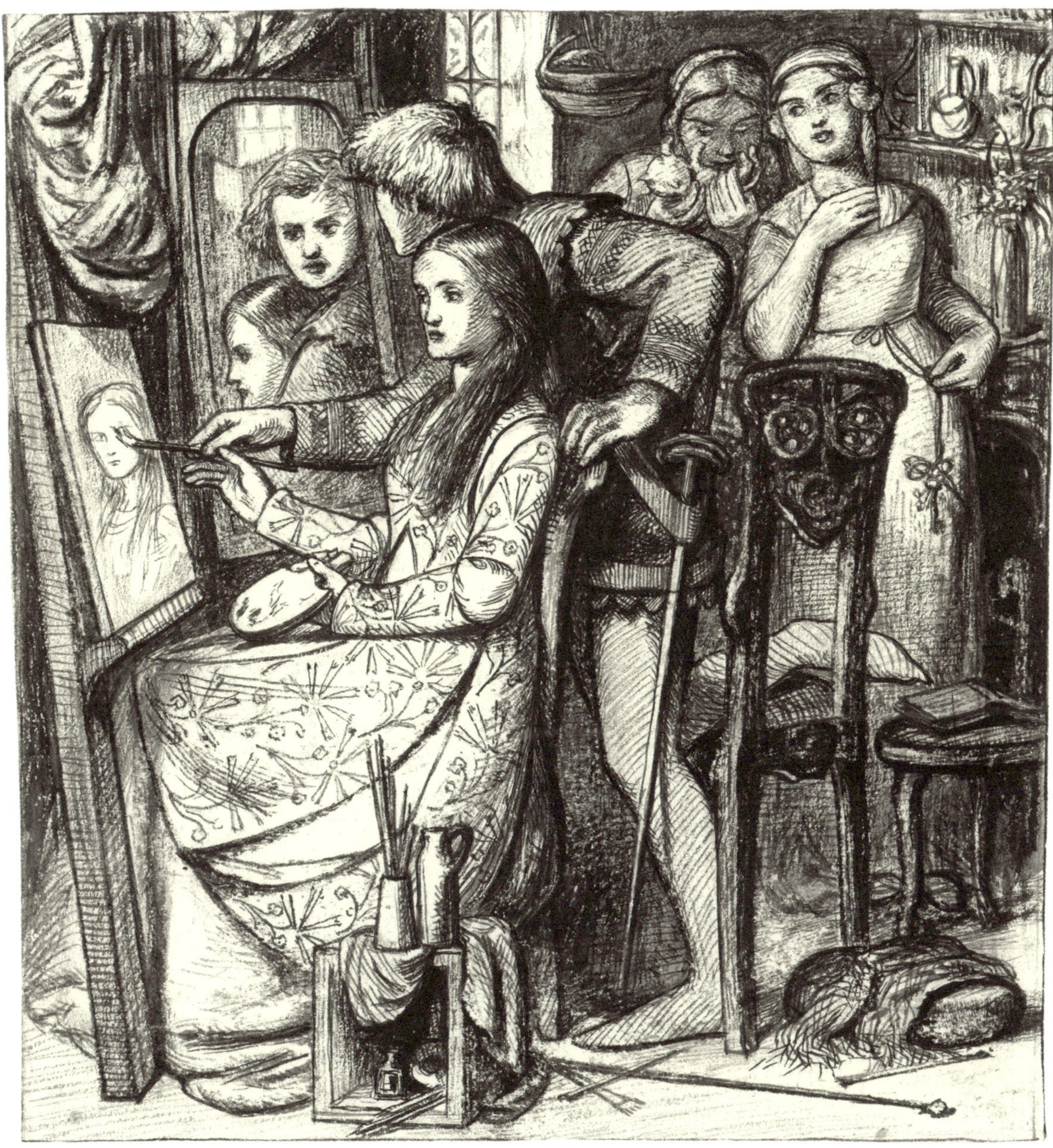

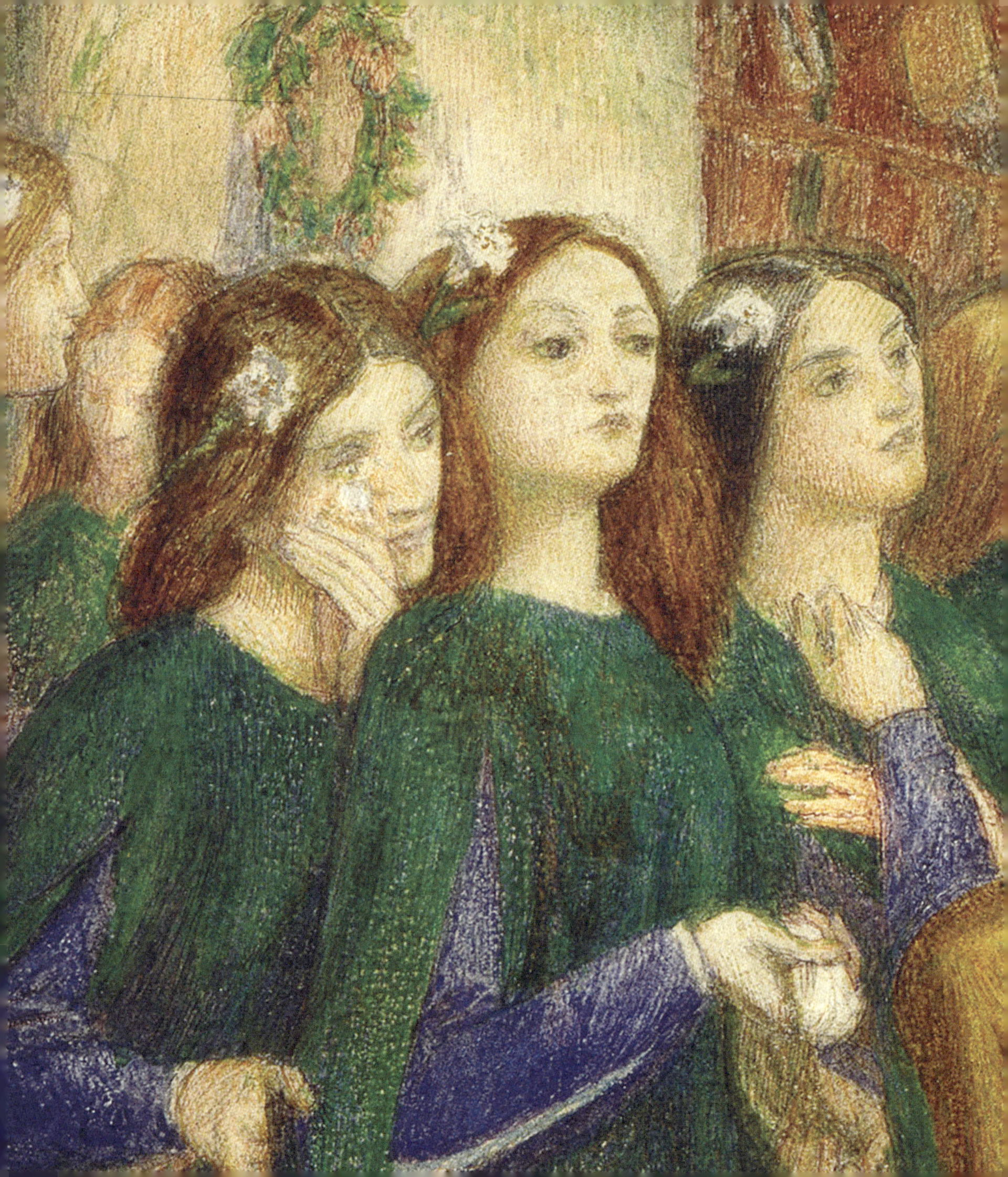

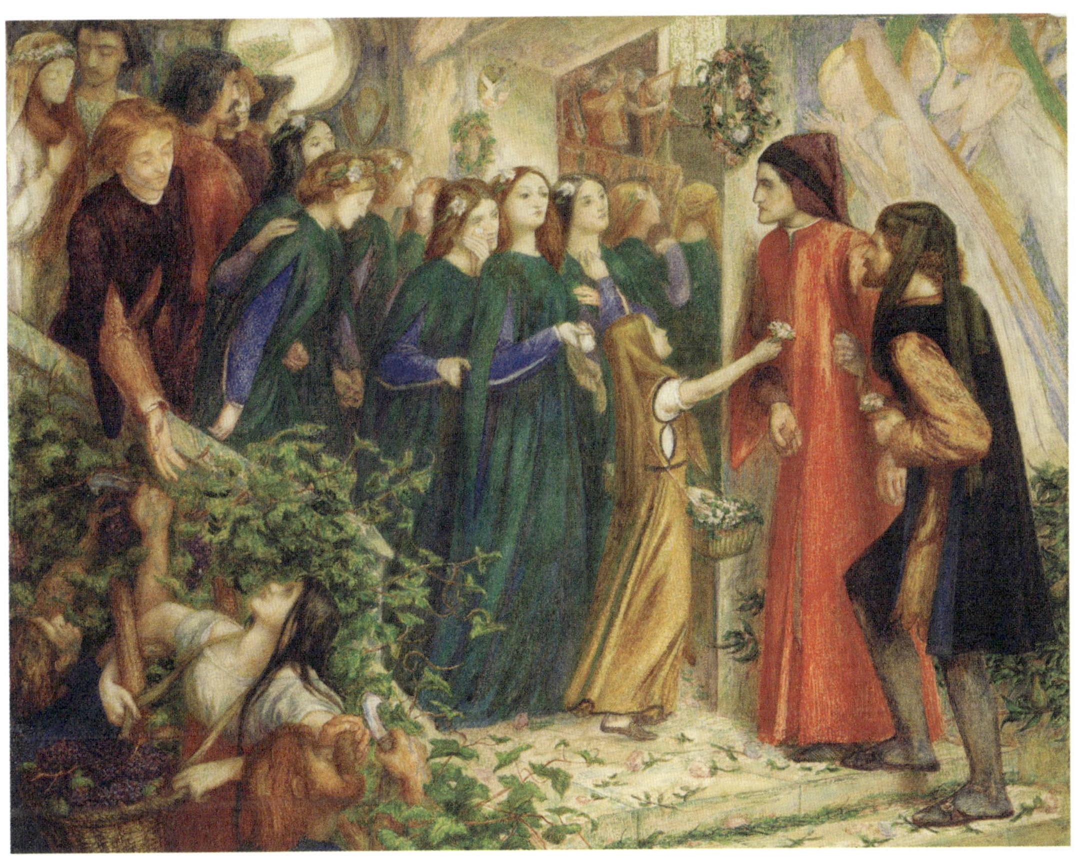

8. *Beatrice at a Marriage Feast, Denying her Salutation to Dante*, 1855
Watercolour and pen
34.1 × 42.2 cm (13½ × 16⅝ in.)
Ashmolean Museum, Oxford
(WA1942.156)

Rossetti embraced his identification with Dante in the poem '*Dantis Tenebrae* (In Memory of My Father)' from 1861: 'And didst thou know indeed, when at the font/ Together with thy name thou gav'st me his/ That also on thy son must Beatrice/ Decline her eyes according to her wont.' Here, in a scene from Dante's *La Vita Nuova*, Rossetti portrays Elizabeth Siddal for the first time as Beatrice, as a member of a wedding entourage.

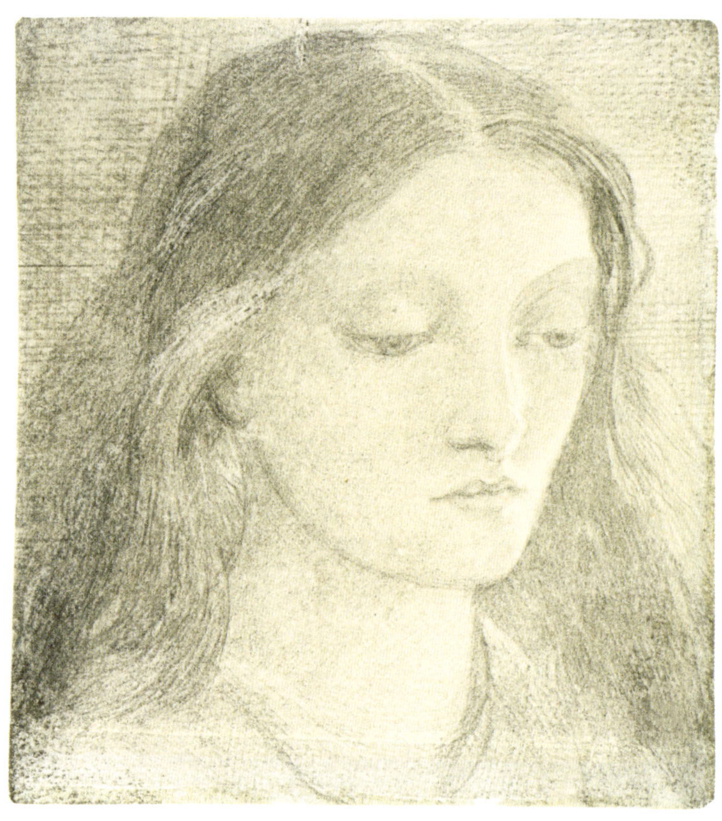

9. *Head of Miss Elizabeth Siddal*, *c.* 1854–5
Pencil on paper
12.1 × 11.4 cm (4⅞ × 4½ in.)
Victoria and Albert Museum, London
(V&A 492-1883)

With her grave demeanour, heavy-lidded eyes and veil of straight, coppery hair, Lizzie Siddal's beauty differed from the popular preference for girlish prettiness and coy charm. Rossetti found her appearance so compelling that during the first years of their relationship he repeatedly sketched her likeness for pure pleasure, rather than just in preparation for planned paintings. After seeing countless such drawings in his friend's studio, Ford Madox Brown characterized Rossetti's fascination as a monomania.

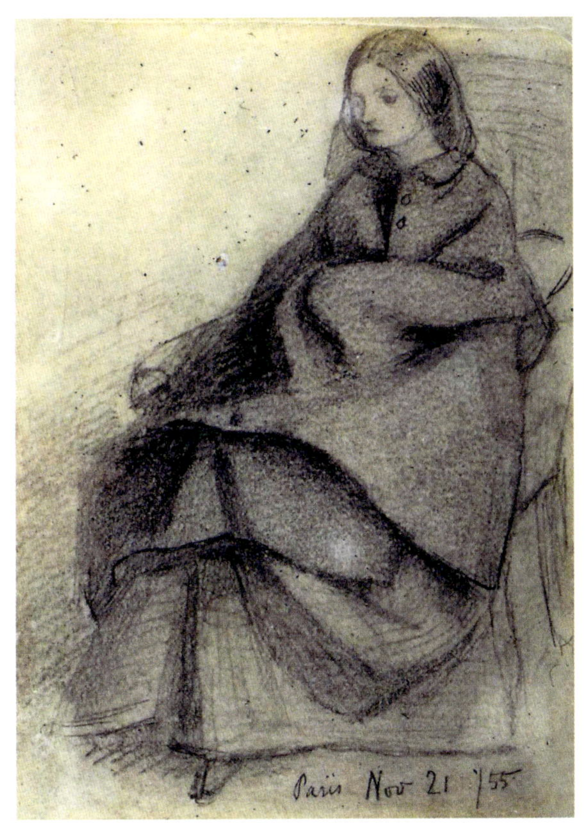

10. *Elizabeth Siddal*, November 1855
Pencil on paper
12.1 × 8.3 cm (4⅞ × 3⅜ in.)
Inscribed, lower right: *Nov 21 1855*
Mark Samuels Lasner Collection, University of Delaware Library, Museums and Press

Lizzie and Rossetti were constant companions between the years 1852 to 1856. Rossetti encouraged her to draw, paint and compose poetry, regarding her as a fellow artist as well as his model, muse and fiancée. He also fretted about her health, urging her to try treatments and rest cures. In their circle, Lizzie's fragility became part of her identity; on one visit Ford Madox Brown noted that she looked 'thinner & more deathlike & more beautiful & more ragged than ever'.[37]

One face looks out from all his canvases
One selfsame figure sits or walks or leans:
We found her hidden just behind those screens,
That mirror gave back all her loveliness.
A queen in opal or ruby dress,
A nameless girl in freshest summer-greens,
A saint, an angel – every canvas means
The same one meaning, neither more or less.
He feeds upon her face by day and night,
And she with true kind eyes looks back on him,
Fair as the moon and joyful as the light:
Not wan with waiting, not with sorrow dim;
Not as she is, but was when hope shone bright;
Not as she is, but as she fills his dream

Christina Rossetti, 'In An Artist's Studio' (1856)

11. *Elizabeth Siddal*, May 1854
Pen and ink on paper
23.8 × 11.2 cm (9⅜ × 4½ in.)
Inscribed, upper left: *Hastings May 1854*
Victoria and Albert Museum, London
(V&A 491-1883)

Lizzie spent the spring of 1854 in the seaside town of Hastings in Sussex to improve her health. During his repeated visits, Rossetti made a series of drawings that were as intimate and affectionate as his favourite nicknames for her: Lizzie, Guggums, the Dove.

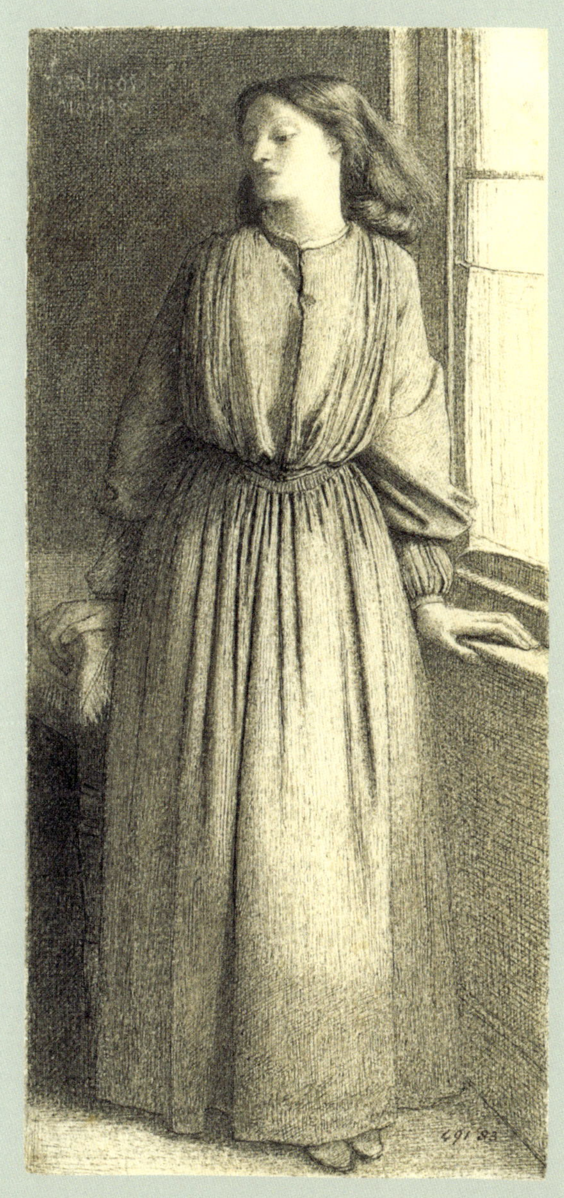

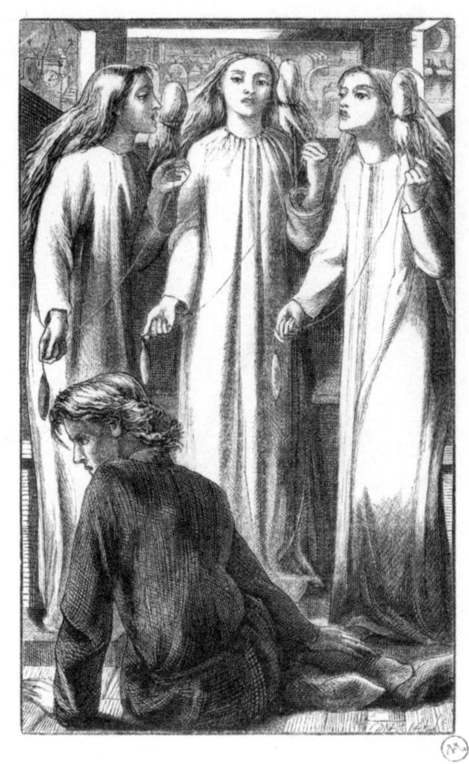

12. *Maids of Elfen-Mere*, illustration for William Allingham, *The Music Master: A Love Story, and Two Series of Day and Night Songs*, *c.* 1855
Engraved by Brothers Dalziel, after a design by Rossetti
Wood engraving on India paper
Image: 12.8 × 7.8 cm (5⅛ × 3⅛ in.); Sheet: 15.1 × 10.2 cm (6 × 4⅛ in.)
Victoria and Albert Museum, London (V&A E.2923-1904)

The Irish poet William Allingham asked Rossetti to illustrate his version (published in 1855 by Routledge) of an old German tale about a pastor's son bewitched by a trio of mysterious maidens. They would appear each night, singing and spinning thread, only to disappear when the village clock tolled eleven. To delay their departure, the lovesick youth turned back the clock's hands, but his extra hour of pleasure cost him dearly. After that night, they never appeared again.

Or, in a clear-wall'd
  city on the sea,
Near gilded organ-pipes,
  her hair
Wound with white roses,
  slept Saint Cecily;
An angel look'd at her

Alfred Tennyson, 'The Palace of Art' (1832), ll. 97–100

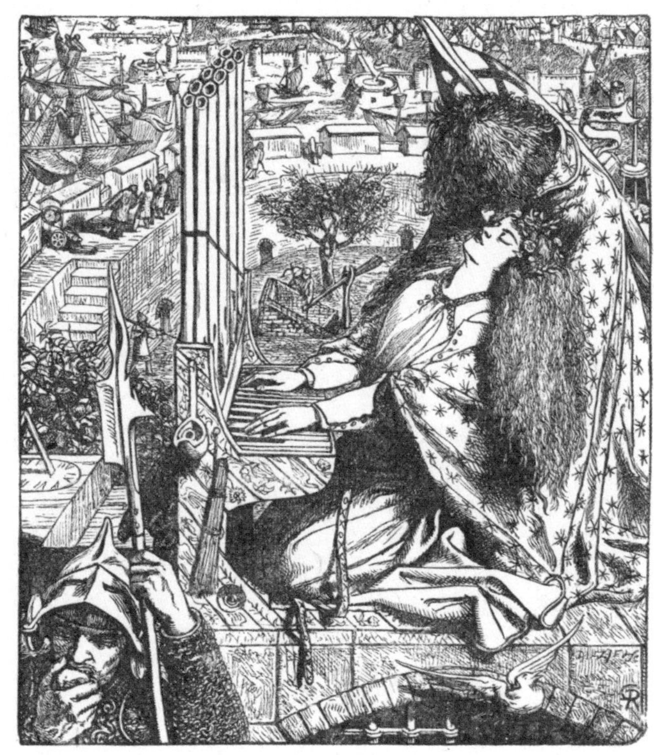

13. *St Cecilia*, illustration for Alfred Tennyson, *Poems*, 1857
Wood engraving on India paper
Image: 9.3 × 7.9 cm (3¾ × 3⅛ in.); Sheet 12.2 × 10.9 cm (4⅞ × 4⅜ in.)
Victoria and Albert Museum, London (V&A E.29-1910)

When commissioned to produce illustrations for the Moxon Tennyson, Rossetti chafed under the guidance of both poet and publisher and declared his preference for subjects that allowed him to 'allegorize on one's own hook'.[38] For 'The Palace of Art', he depicted St Cecilia in an ecstatic pose, her neck extended and her face radiating pleasure in a passionate knight's embrace, although Tennyson described her sleeping 'near gilded organ-pipes' and watched over by an angel.

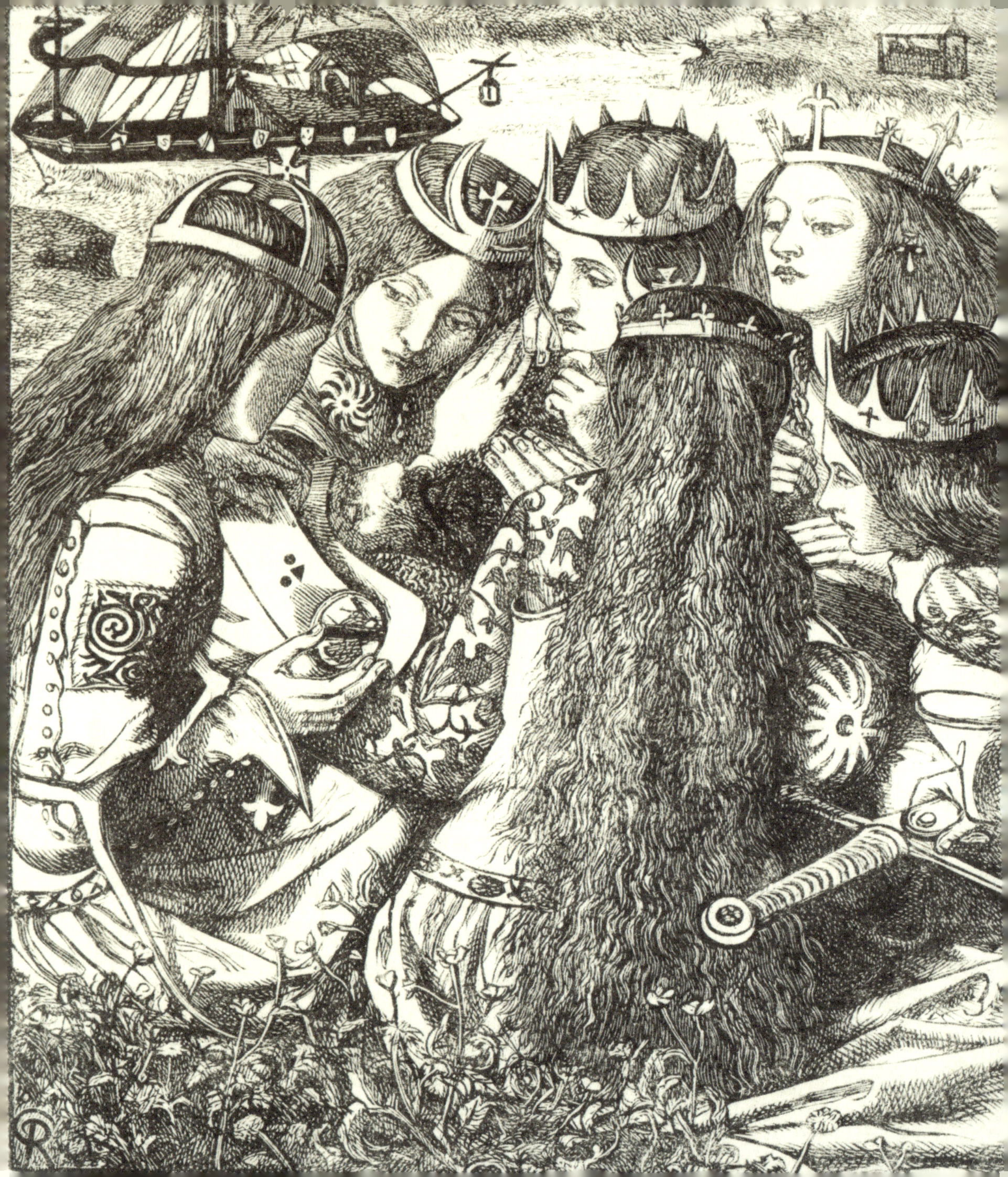

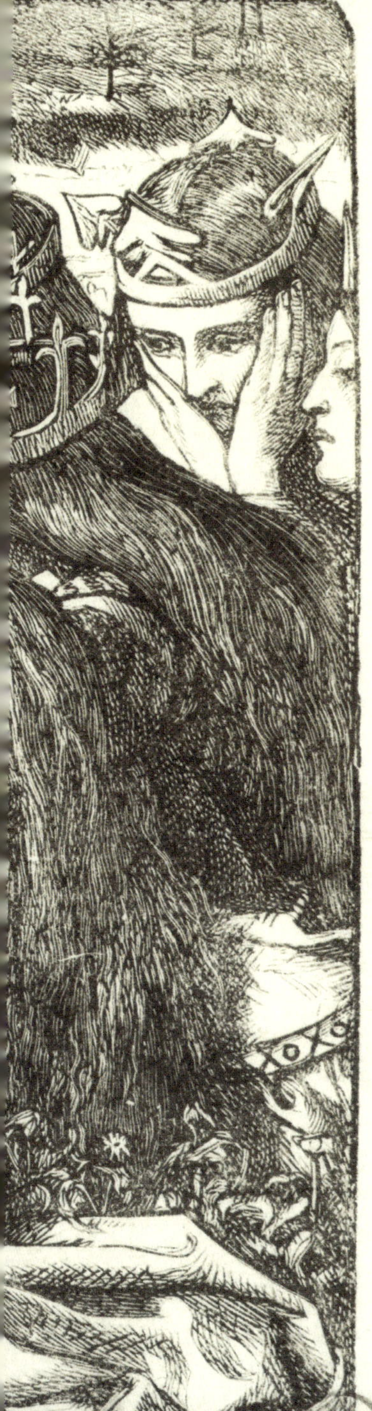

14. *The Death of King Arthur (Arthur and the Weeping Queens)*, illustration for Alfred Tennyson, *Poems*, 1857
Printing ink on paper
Image: 8 × 9.5 cm (3¼ × 3¾ in.);
Sheet 10.9 × 12.2 cm (4⅜ × 4⅞ in.)
Victoria and Albert Museum, London
(V&A E.286.23-1893)

Or mythic Uther's deeply-wounded son
  In some fair space of sloping greens
Lay, dozing in the vale of Avalon,
  And watch'd by weeping queens

Alfred Tennyson, 'The Palace of Art' (1832), ll. 115–18

Keeping close to Tennyson's text in his second illustration for 'The Palace of Art', Rossetti surrounded the wounded King Arthur, resting in Avalon, with a tight circle of compassionate queens. Their resemblance to one another creates an otherworldly atmosphere, but close inspection reveals a slight variance in the set of their eyes and the length of their noses. Rossetti used two models: his sister Christina and Lizzie Siddal.

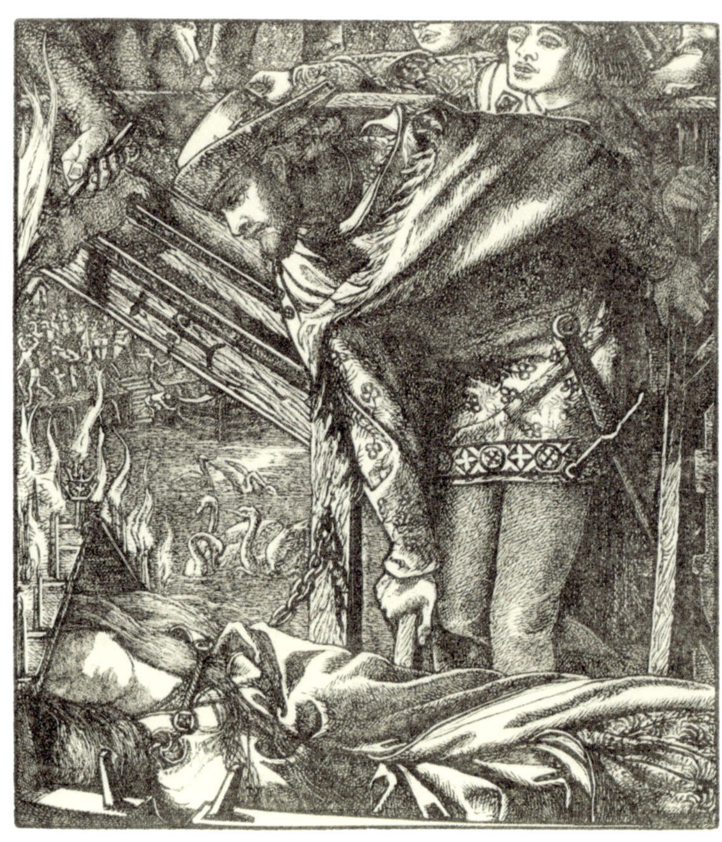

15. *The Lady of Shalott*, illustration for Alfred Tennyson, *Poems*, 1857
Wood engraving on India paper
Image: 9.4 × 8.1 cm (3¾ × 3¼ in.); Sheet: 14.7 × 12.7 cm (5⅞ × 5 in.)
Victoria and Albert Museum, London (V&A E.1284-1912)

Rossetti had hoped to provide both illustrations for 'The Lady of Shalott', declaring it the subject he cared for 'most of all'.[39] But Hunt had already drawn the climactic moment when the Lady glimpses Lancelot riding beneath her window (opposite); her desire triggered a curse that drew her out of her sanctuary tower and to her demise. Rossetti depicted the end of the story (above), when the Lady arrives at Camelot, and Lancelot, unaware that he caused her death, muses, 'She has a lovely face.'

Who is this? and what
is here?
And in the lighted palace near
Died the sound of royal cheer;
And they crossed themselves
for fear,
All the knights at Camelot:
But Lancelot mused
a little space;
He said, 'She has a lovely face;
God in his mercy grant
her grace,
The Lady of Shalott'

Alfred Tennyson, 'The Lady of Shalott' (1832), ll. 164–71

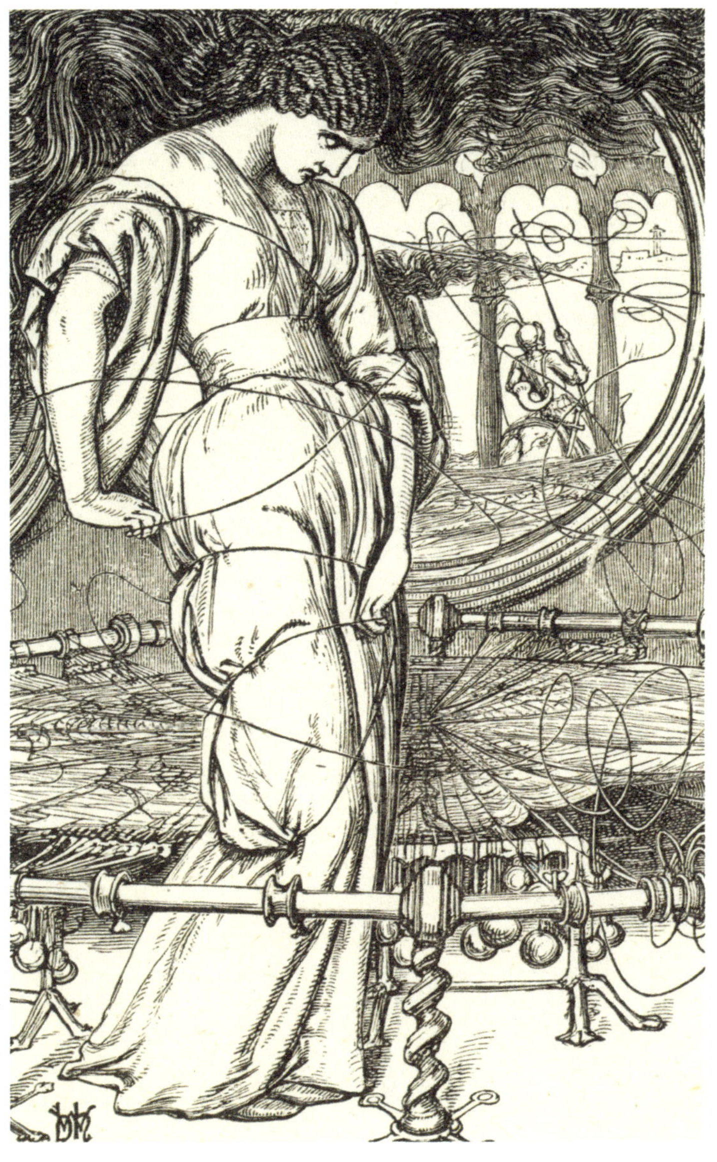

16. William Holman Hunt (1827–1910)
The Lady of Shalott, illustration for
Alfred Tennyson, *Poems*, 1857
Wood engraving
39.8 × 28.6 cm (15¾ × 11⅞ in.)
Victoria and Albert Museum, London
(V&A E.30-1910)

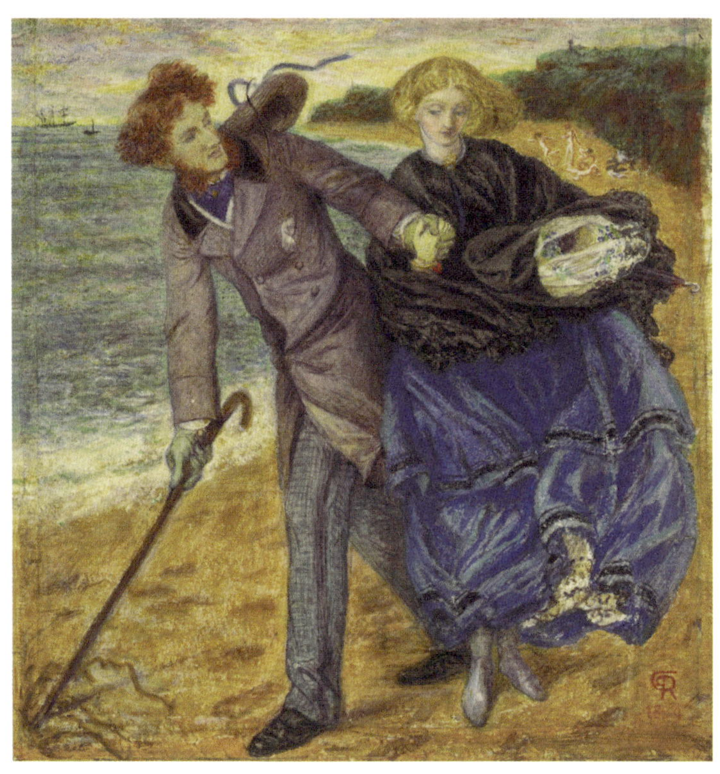

17. *Writing on the Sand*, 1858–9
Watercolour on paper
26.3 × 24.1 cm (10⅜ × 9½ in.)
Inscribed, lower right: *DGR/1859*
British Museum, London
(1886,0607.14)

A message written on the sand is impermanent. Here, a man sketches a woman's profile as his companion looks on, wondering, perhaps, if their bond will last only as long as his tribute. Fashionable dress and a recognizable seaside setting mark this watercolour as a rare departure from Rossetti's characteristic preference for historic scenes. Lizzie and Richard Rivington Holmes, who sported an impressive set of Dundreary whiskers, likely posed in the studio; Rossetti based the view of the coast at Babbacombe, near Torquay, Devon, on sketches borrowed from his friend, George Pryce Boyce.

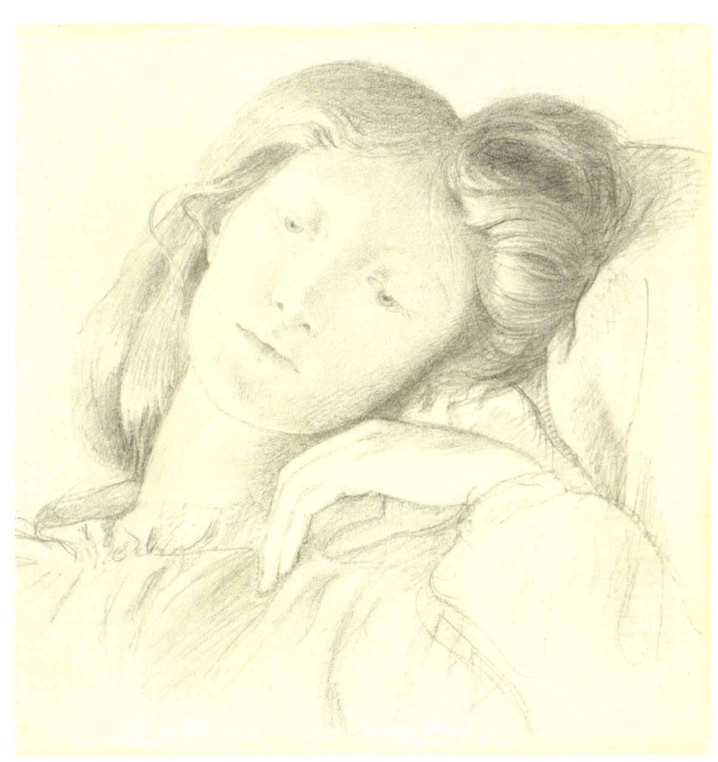

18. *Elizabeth Siddal reclining on a pillow*, 1860
Pencil on paper
26 × 25.4 cm (10¼ × 10 in.)
Fitzwilliam Museum, Cambridge (684)

After a near decade-long engagement, Rossetti and Lizzie married on 23 May 1860. They had planned to wed on the 12th – his birthday – but Lizzie's ill health forced a brief postponement. This tender likeness depicts her appearance at this time, when Rossetti feared that she 'seemed ready to die daily and more than once a day'.[40] Intimate and empathetic, it is one of his finest drawings of Lizzie, representing an actual woman, rather than an ideal.

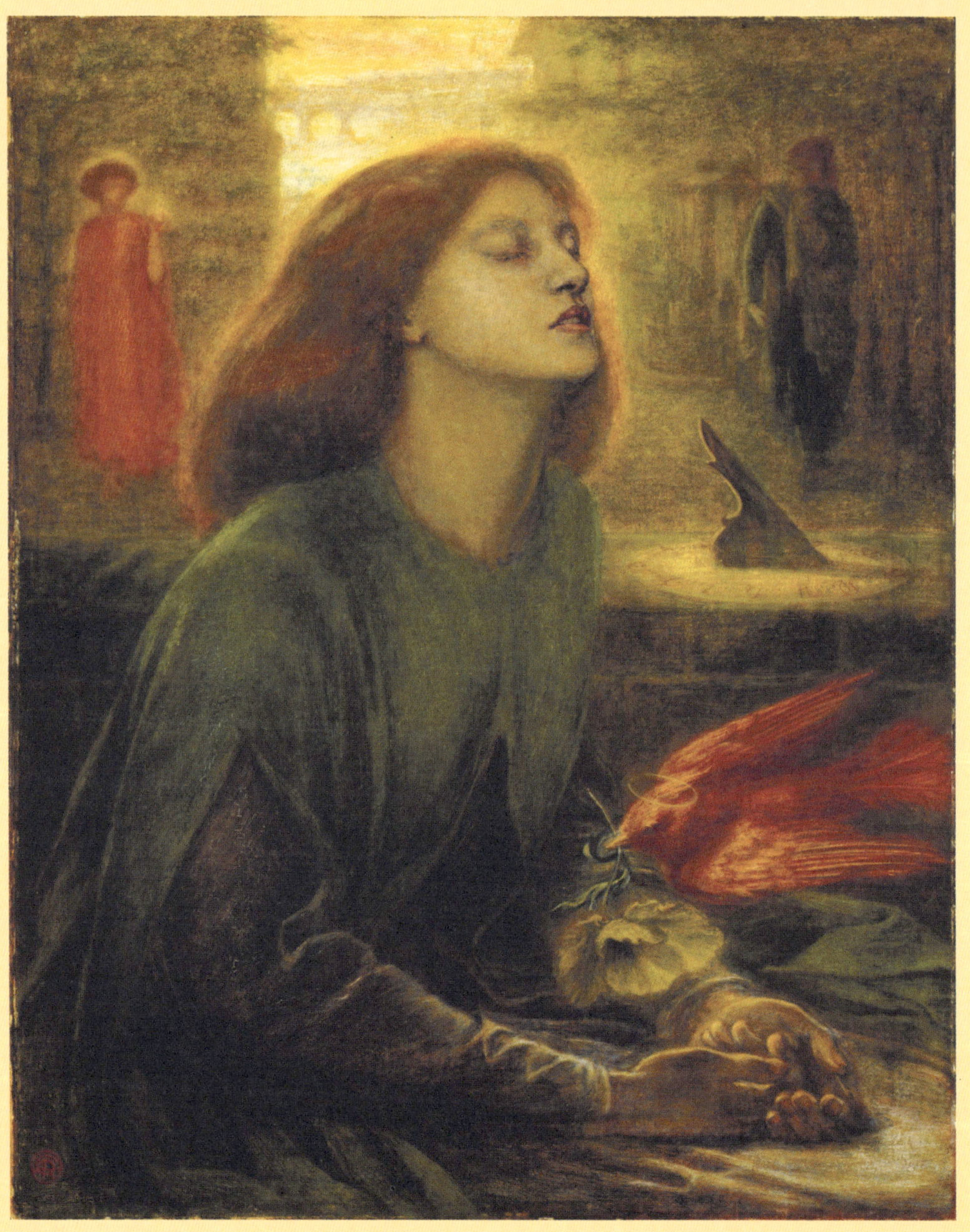

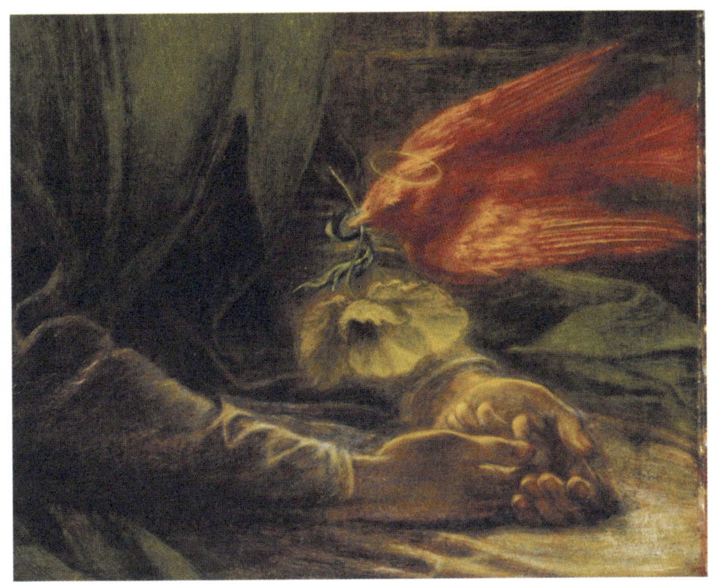

And I will say, – still sobbing as speech fails, –
That she has gone to Heaven suddenly,
And hath left Love below, to mourn with me

Dante Alighieri, *La Vita Nuova* (1294; translated by Rossetti)

19. *Beata Beatrix*, *c.* 1864–70
Oil on canvas
86.4 × 66 cm (34⅛ × 26 in.)
Inscribed, lower left, with monogram
Tate Gallery, London
(N01279)

Rossetti painted Dante's 'Blessed Beatrice' enrapt in a vision of her own death as a poignant tribute to his late wife. In a trance-like state, Beatrice accepts a white poppy from a crimson-feathered dove, while Dante and his companion Love, holding a burning heart, observe from a distance. Rossetti described it as a subject 'I have long meant to do', and he relied on sketches made during Lizzie's lifetime to ensure an excellent likeness.[41]

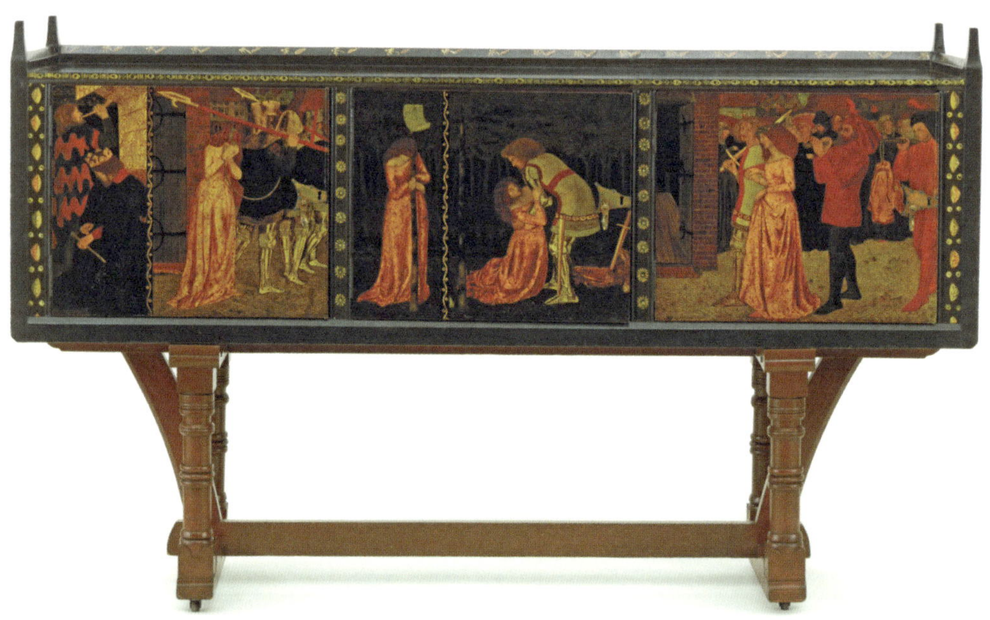

20. Philip Webb (1831–1915)
and William Morris (1834–1896)
St George Cabinet, 1861–2
Painted and gilded mahogany,
pine and oak, with copper mounts
(Morris, Marshall, Faulkner & Co.)
111 × 178 × 43 cm (43¾ × 70⅛ × 17 in.)
Victoria and Albert Museum, London
(V&A 341:1 to 8-1906)

English folklore transformed the Roman soldier who became known as St George (martyred *c.* 303) into an English knight. The version of the story preferred in Rossetti's circle can be traced back to Richard Johnson's *Most Famous History of the Seven Champions of Christendom* (1596). In it, George, who hails from Coventry, rescues the Egyptian Princess Sabra from a fearsome dragon, as seen on this cabinet exhibited at the 1862 International Exhibition. The concept and style reflect Morris and Rossetti's earliest collaboration in creating painted furniture (1856–7). Rossetti would later return to the subject in his paintings and designs for stained glass (22–5).

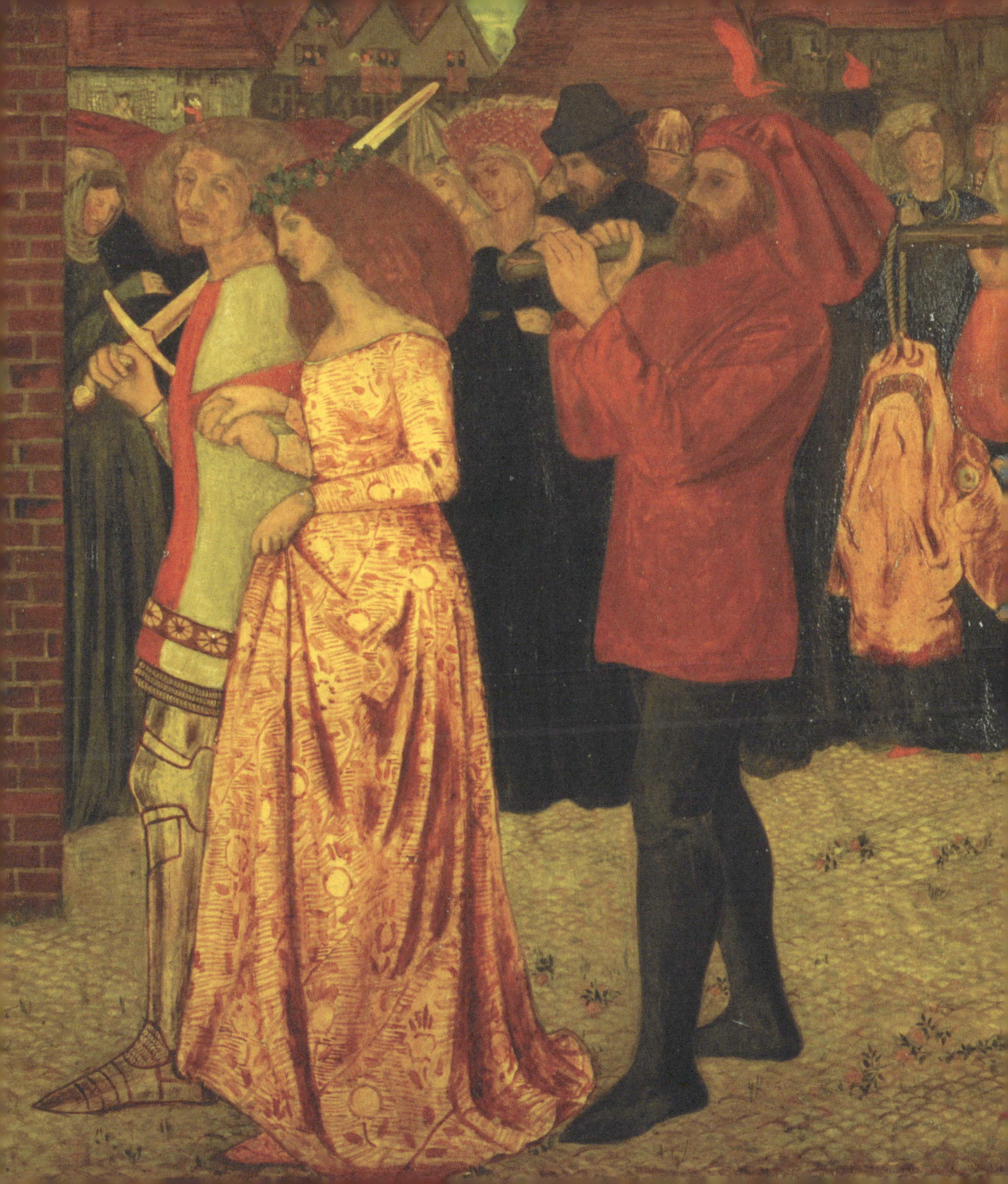

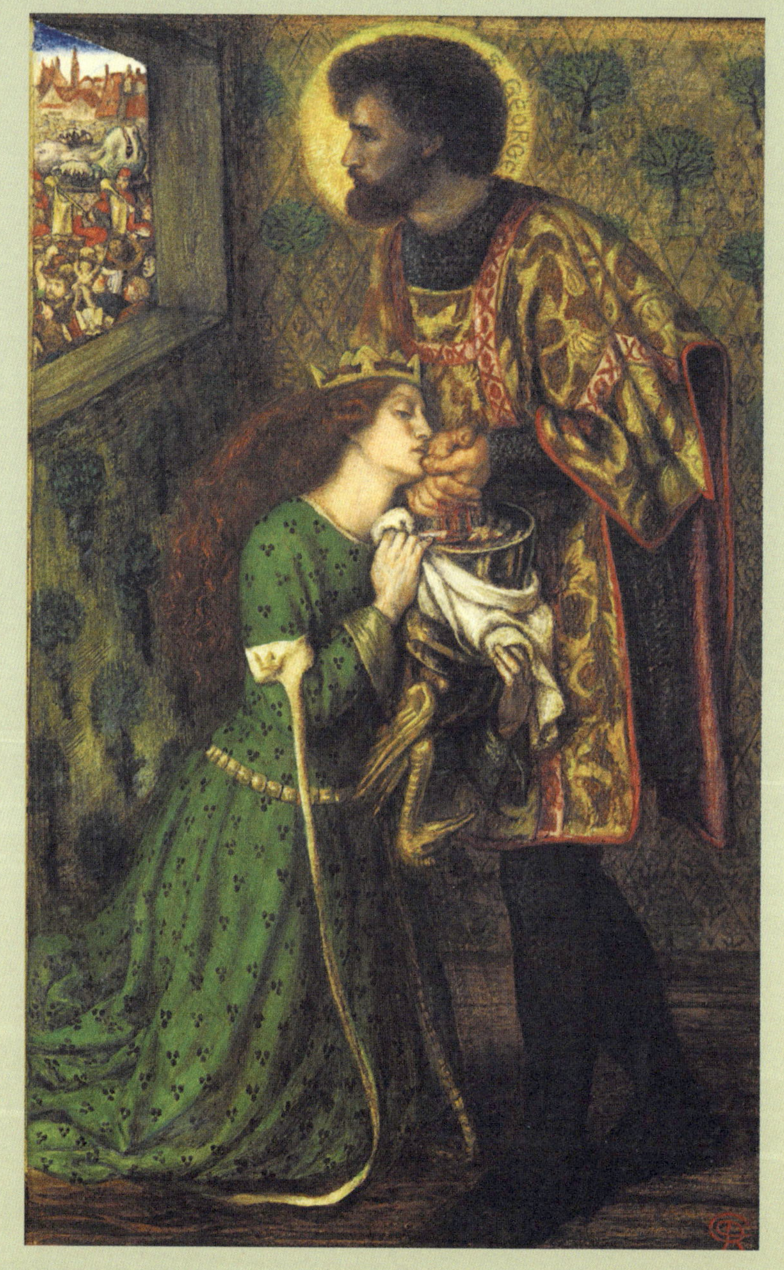
GEORGE

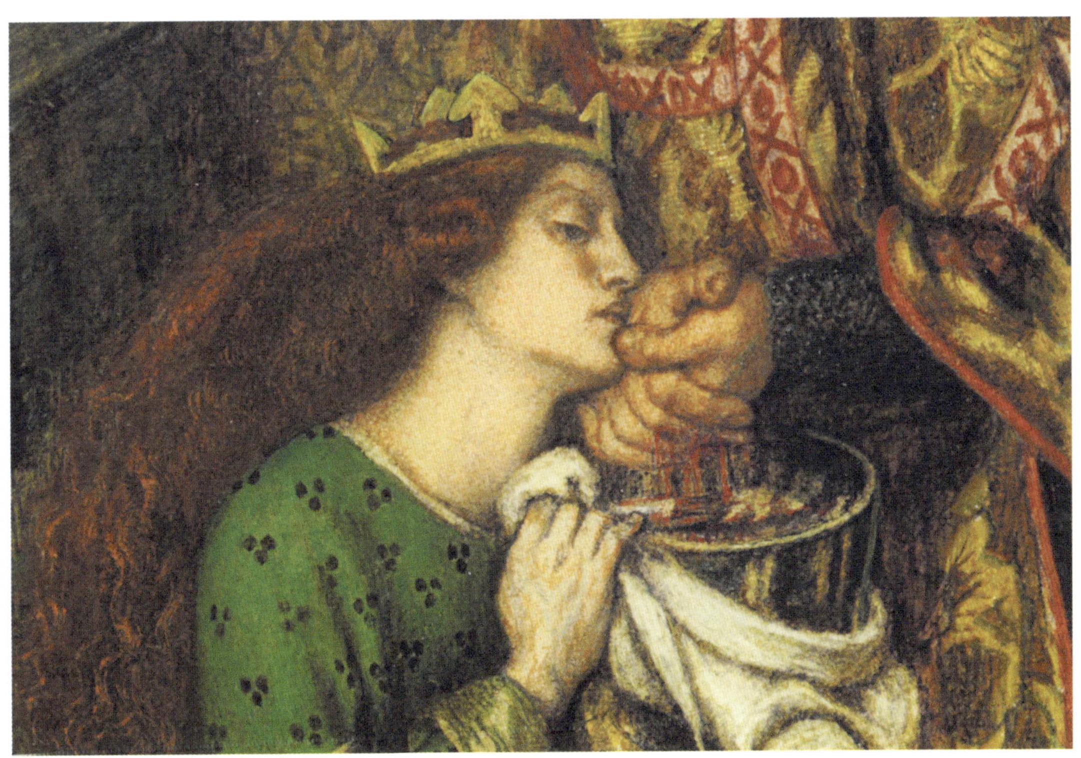

21. *St George and Princess Sabra*, 1862
Watercolour on paper
52.4 × 30.8 cm (20¾ × 12¼ in.)
Inscribed, lower right: *1862*;
on halo: *S. GEORGE*
Tate Gallery, London
(N05231)

Although Rossetti relied on the version of the St George legend as published in Thomas Percy's popular anthology, *Reliques of Ancient English Poetry* (1762), this intimate scene of George washing his bloodied hands as Sabra kneels and kisses them was his own invention. A letter to Ellen Heaton dated 24 December 1861 reveals that despite her fragile health, Lizzie posed as Sabra.[42] Rossetti reprised the position of her head and neck for his commemorative portrait, *Beata Beatrix* (**19**).

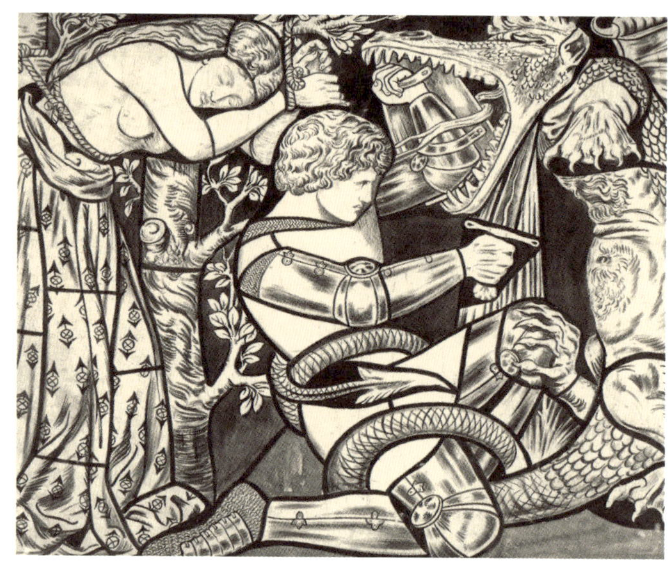

22. *St George slaying the dragon with Princess Sabra tied to a tree*, 1861–4
Brush and ink on tracing paper
49.5 × 58.4 cm (19½ × 23 in.)
Victoria and Albert Museum, London
(V&A E.1842-1946)

23. Panel, *St George and the Dragon* series, *c.* 1862
Stained and painted glass
(Morris, Marshall, Faulkner & Co.)
60.5 × 68.8 cm (23⅞ × 27⅛ in.)
Inscribed, on base of panel: *How the good Knight St George of England slew the dragon and set the Princess free*
Victoria and Albert Museum, London
(V&A C.319-1927)

Six stained-glass panels after Rossetti's designs may have been created for the textile merchant Walter Dunlop's Bradford home, Harden Grange, or for display at the 1862 International Exhibition. With bowed head and closed eyes, Sabra cannot see the deadly struggle between the fearless knight and his monstrous foe.

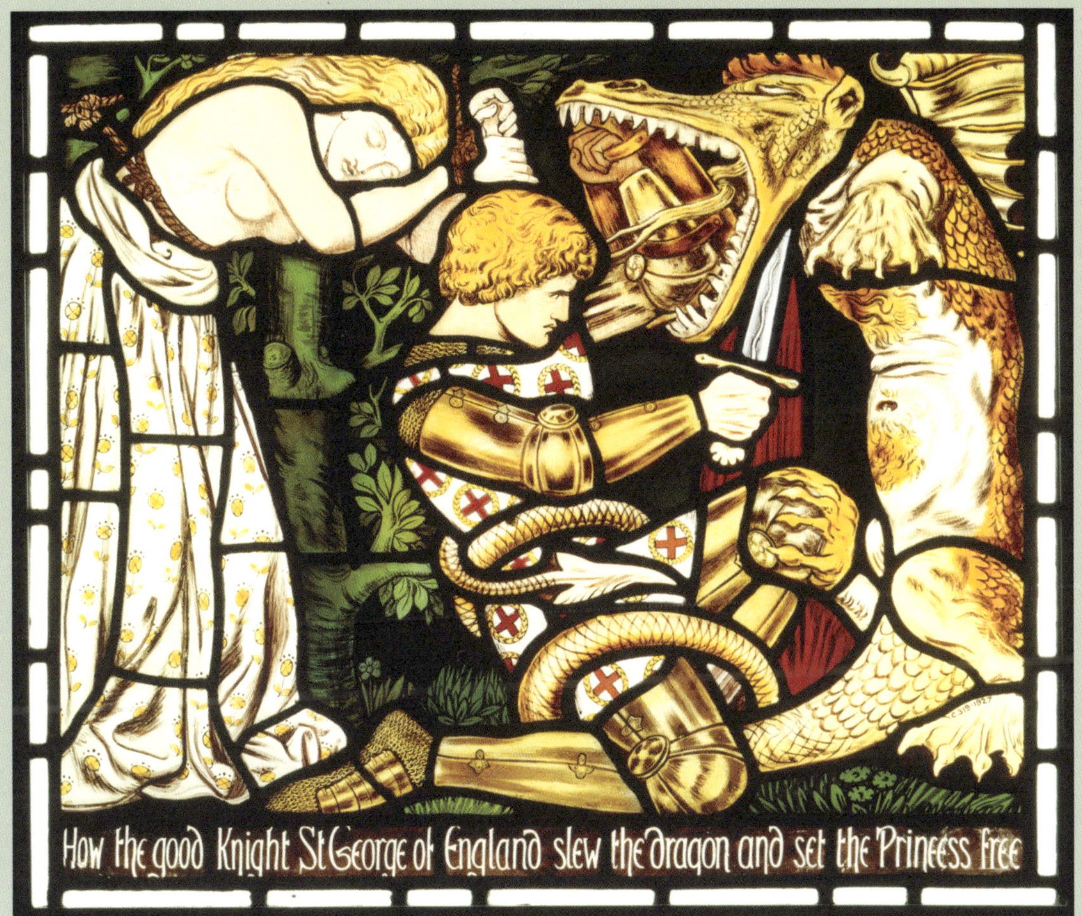
C.319-1927
How the good Knight St George of England slew the dragon and set the Princess free

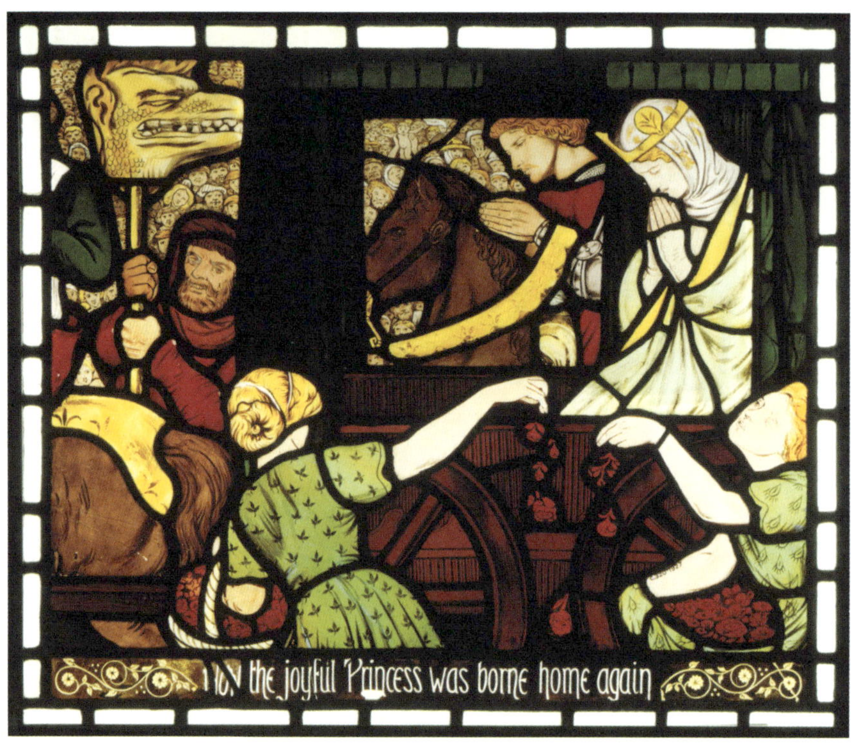

24. Panel, *St George and the Dragon* series, *c.* 1862
Stained and painted glass (Morris, Marshall, Faulkner & Co.)
60.3 × 69 cm (23¾ × 27¼ in.)
Inscribed, on base of panel: *How the joyful Princess was borne home again*
Victoria and Albert Museum, London (V&A C.320-1927)

Using vibrant, jewel-toned colours, Rossetti depicts the great rejoicing that heralded the Princess's return to her father's court. Now modestly gowned and crowned – although hardly joyful – she bends her head in worshipful thanks. Young women, dressed in grass-green gowns, toss ruby-red rose petals along the carriage path, while a rough old squire hoists the grisly trophy of the slain beast.

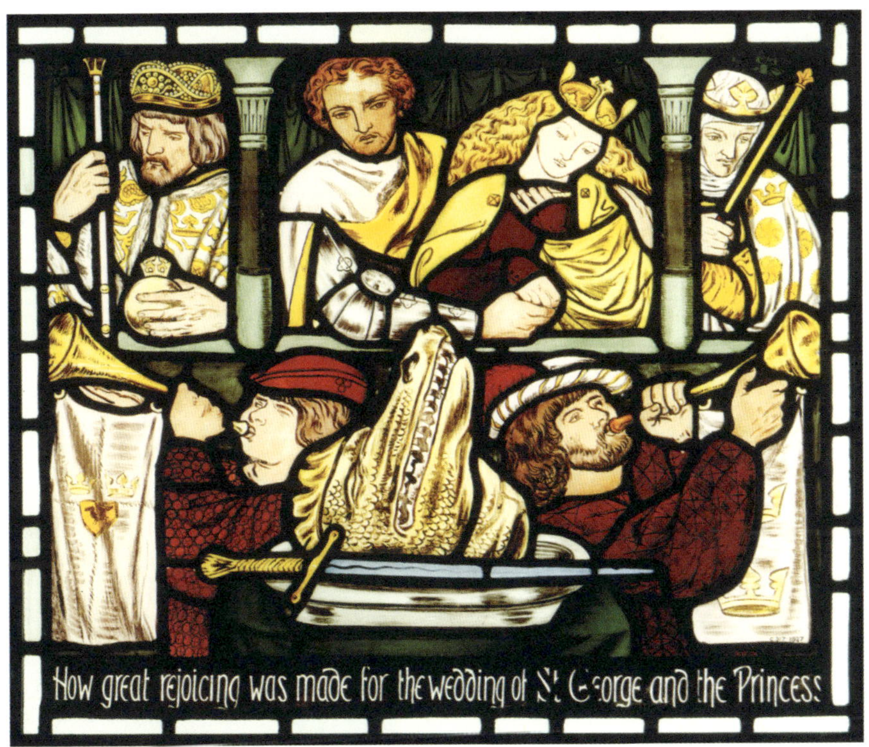

25. Panel, *St George and the Dragon* series, *c.* 1862
Stained and painted glass (Morris, Marshall, Faulkner & Co.)
60.1 × 69 cm (23¾ × 27¼ in.)
Inscribed, on base of panel:
How great rejoicing was made for the wedding of St George and the Princess
Victoria and Albert Museum, London (V&A C.317-1927)

According to the legend, before St George married his princess, he had to save her from abduction by the King of Morocco. Rossetti ends his tale after the initial rescue, as seen by the presentation of the dragon's head at the wedding celebration. The solemnity of the bride and groom stands in sharp contrast to the surrounding festivities. But the tale forecasts a happy future: 'They many years of joy did see,/ And led their lives in Coventry' (ll. 263–4).

The architect John Pollard Seddon designed this massive desk for his own use and called on his friends in the Pre-Raphaelite circle – including Rossetti, Ford Madox Brown, William Morris, Edward Burne-Jones and Val Prinsep – to decorate it. Loosely inspired by the fictionalized character of the fifteenth-century René of Anjou in Sir Walter Scott's novel *Anne of Geierstein, or the Maiden of the Mist* (1829), the panels present King René and his bride celebrating their love through the arts. *Music* (27), seen on the cabinet door at the right, and *Gardening*, the small upper-left panel, were painted by Rossetti.

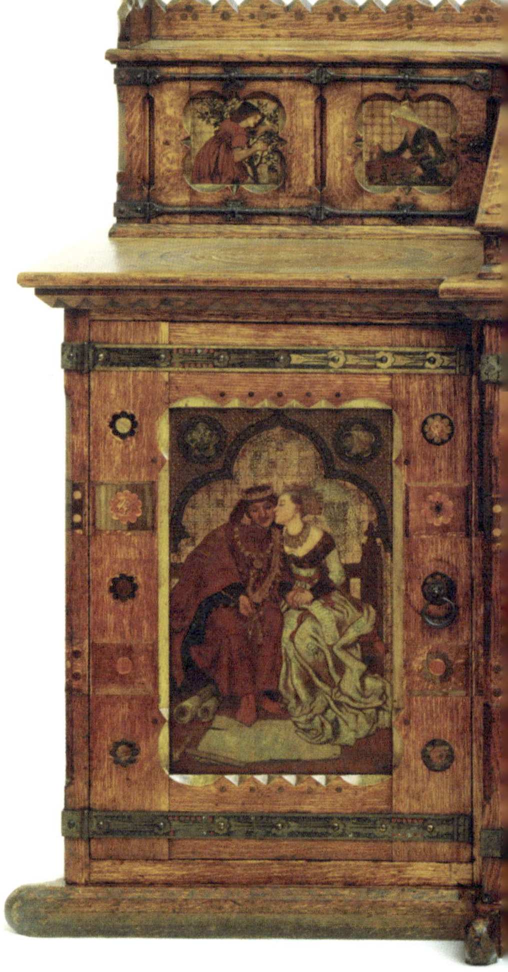

26. John Pollard Seddon (1827–1906)
King René's Honeymoon Cabinet, 1861
Oak, inlaid with various woods with painted metalwork and painted panels (Seddon & Sons)
133.4 × 252 cm (52⅝ × 99¼ in.)
Victoria and Albert Museum, London
(V&A W.10:1-28-1927)

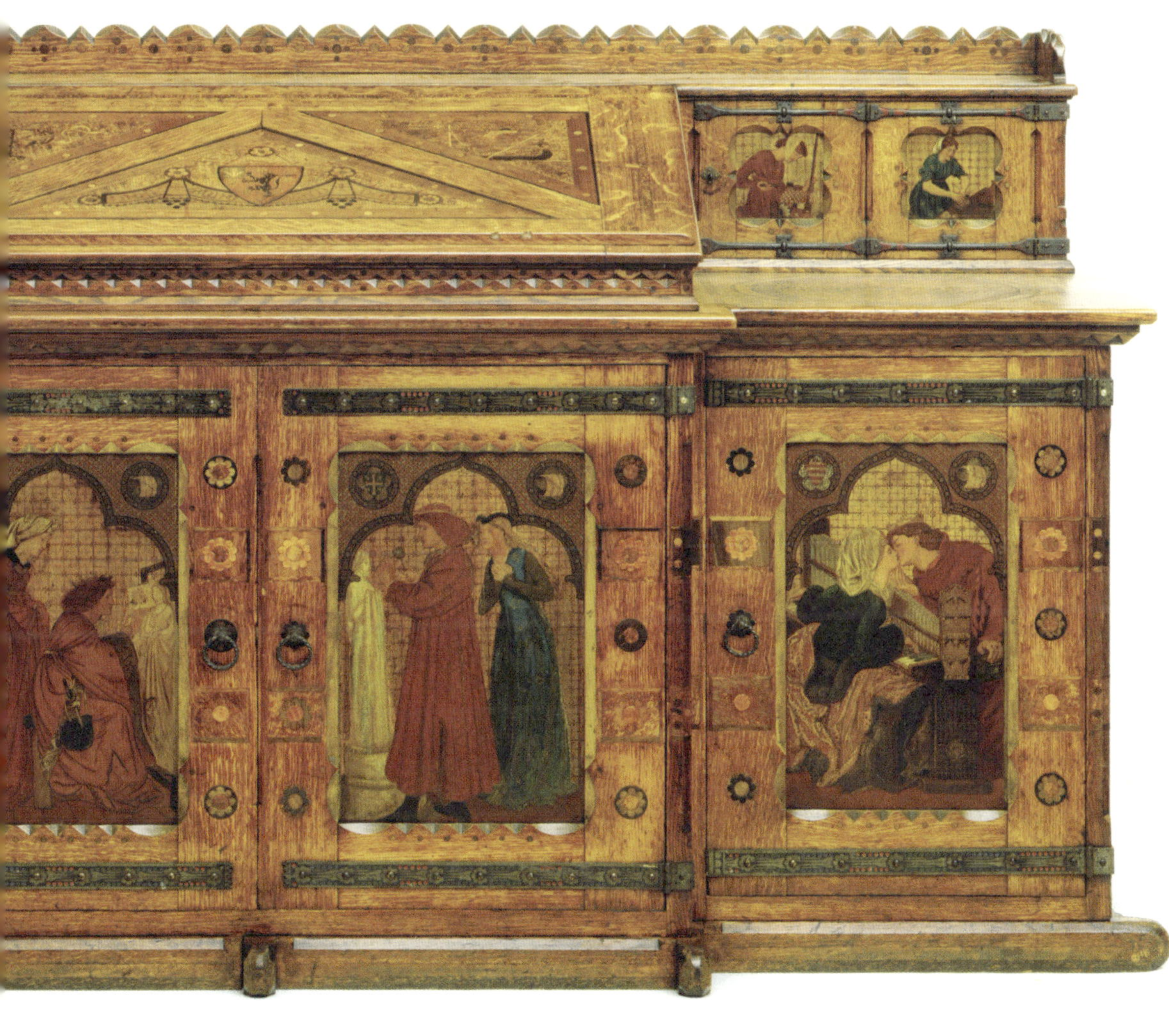

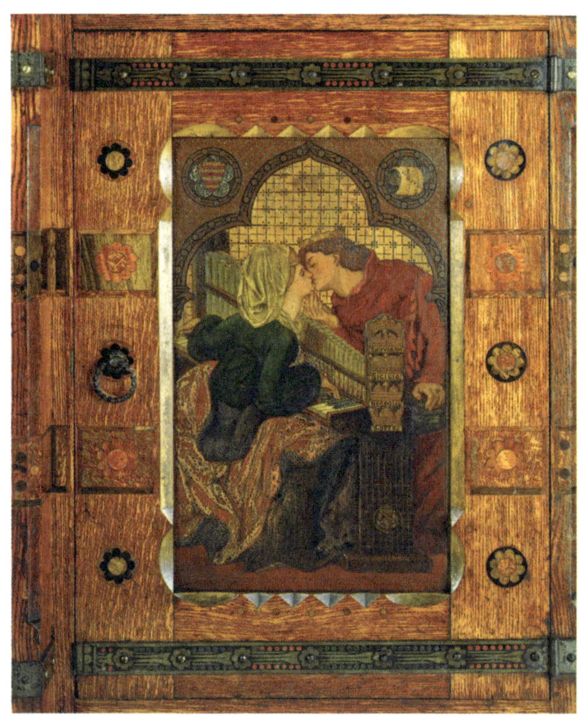

27. *Music*, from *King René's Honeymoon Cabinet*, 1861
Painted oak panel, set in chamfered and gilded frame
53 × 31.7 cm (20⅞ × 12½ in.)
Victoria and Albert Museum, London
(V&A W.10:1-28-1927)

28. *King René's Honeymoon*, *c.* 1863
Stained and painted glass (Morris, Marshall, Faulkner & Co.)
Framed: 64.2 × 54.7 cm (25⅜ × 21⅝ in.)
Victoria and Albert Museum, London
(V&A CIRC.519-1953)

The image of the young king interrupting his wife's music with a kiss recalls Rossetti's illustration for 'The Palace of Art' in the Moxon Tennyson (13). René's bride, flushed with excitement, returns his kiss with equal ardour. Rossetti used the design again as his contribution to a six-panel stained-glass suite of the subject (opposite), commissioned from Morris, Marshall, Faulkner & Co. by the artist Myles Birket Foster for his home The Hill in Surrey.

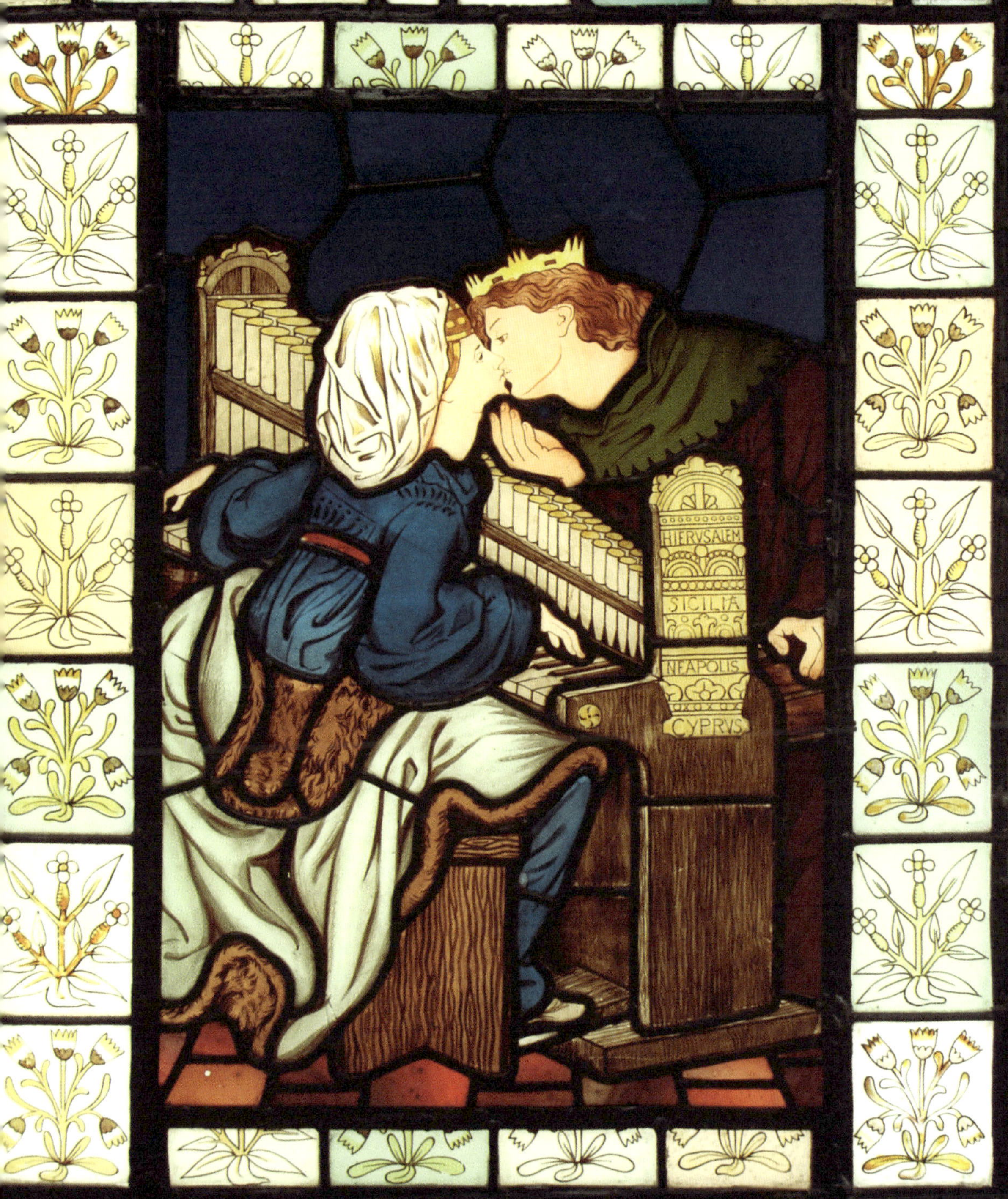
HIERVSALEM
SICILIA
NEAPOLIS
CYPRVS

29. Annie Christian Jack (1861–1942)
Embroidered picture, after
Dante Gabriel Rossetti,
The Rose Garden, c. 1890
Embroidered linen, wooden
frame covered with gilded gesso
24.1 × 18.7 cm (9½ × 7⅜ in.)
Victoria and Albert Museum, London
(V&A T.707-1972)

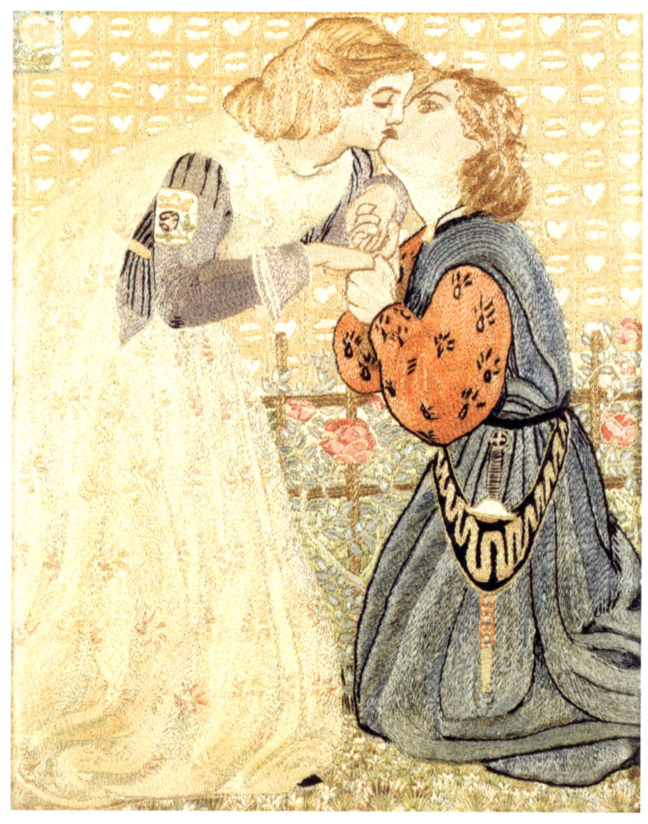

30. *The Rose Garden* (*Woman Kissing Kneeling Knight*), 1861
Etching on paper
15.9 × 11.4 cm (6¼ × 4½ in.)
Signed: *D G R*
Inscribed: *From a drawing on a zinc plate by D.G. Rossetti, intended for the title page of The Early Italian Poets, 1861*
Victoria and Albert Museum, London
(V&A E.434-1919)

Rossetti designed *The Rose Garden* (opposite) as the frontispiece for his own book of translations, but disliked the initial print, and *The Early Italian Poets from Ciullo d'Alcamo to Dante Alighieri* appeared in 1861 without it. In a variant on his long-favoured motif, the couple's fingers entwine as the woman kisses her eager suitor. Annie Christian Jack, an embroidery instructor at the South Kensington School of Design, replicated the romantic vignette with skilful stitching (above).

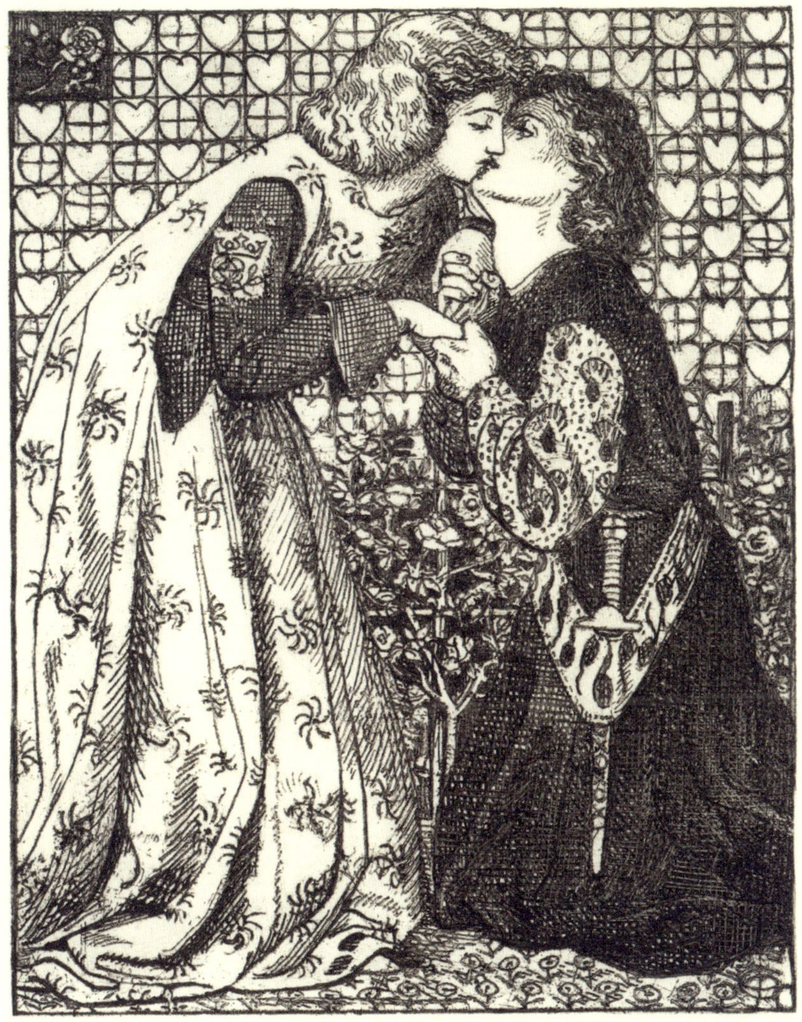

From a drawing on a zinc plate
by D. G. Rossetti, intended for the
title page of The Early Italian Poets,
1861.

The roundels on either side of this bookcase (below right) designed by Charles Forster Hayward for the military tailor John Jones, feature Rossetti's inventive personifications of natural beauty. Referring to the Latin term *flos roseus* (rose flower), 'Flos', holding a red rose, is modelled by Fanny Cornforth; 'Fructus' (opposite), holding a bunch of grapes, is modelled by Agnes Manetti, seen in this rare photograph (right). On the lower panels Rossetti painted wattle fences, reminiscent of those at Red House (fig. 7), and birds perching in treetops.

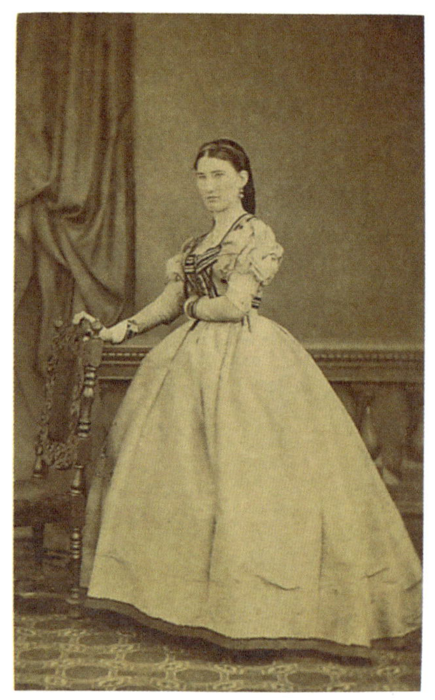

31. *Agnes Manetti*, 1863
Metropolitan Portrait Company, London
Albumen carte-de-visite
6.5 × 10 cm (2⅝ × 4 in.)
Mark Samuels Lasner Collection, University of Delaware Library, Museums and Press

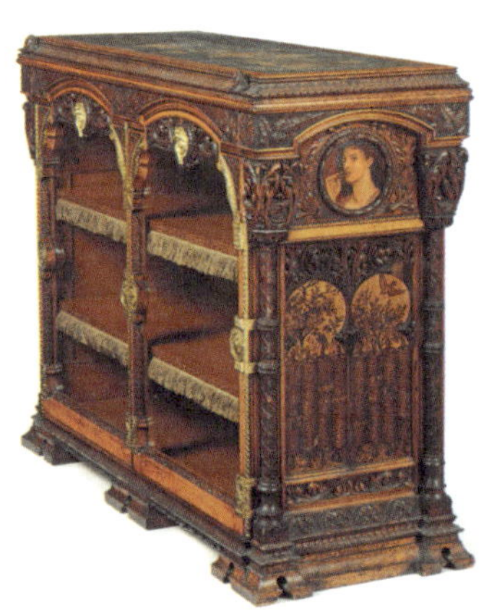

32. Charles Forster Hayward (1831–1905) and William Henry Baylis (1836–1909)
Bookcase, *c.* 1860–1
Oak, carved, painted, gilded and stained, electrogilded brass, copper alloy, enamelled slate, glass, silk (Howard & Sons)
94.3 × 116 cm (37¼ × 45¾ in.)
Victoria and Albert Museum, London
(V&A 1081:1-1882)

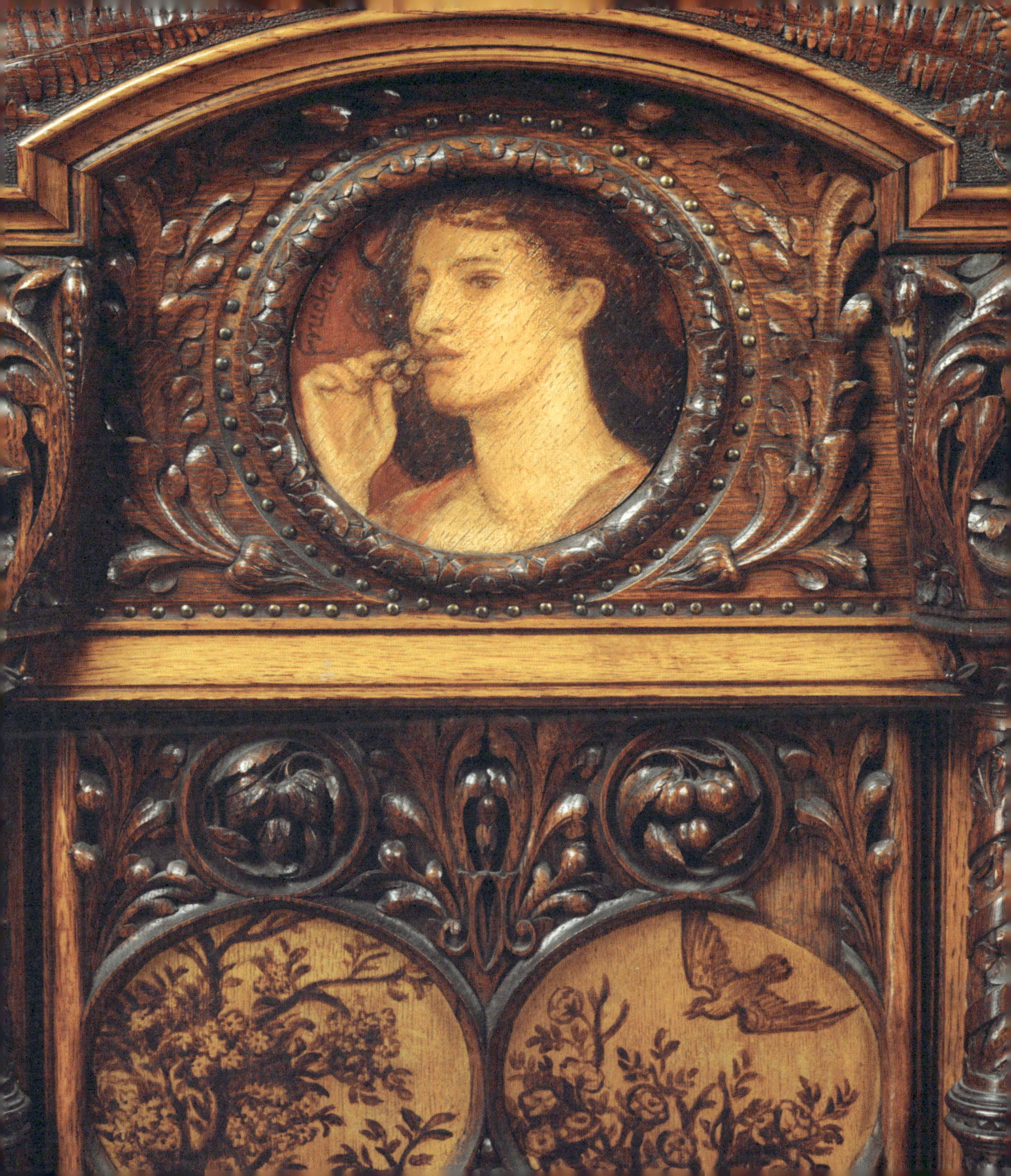

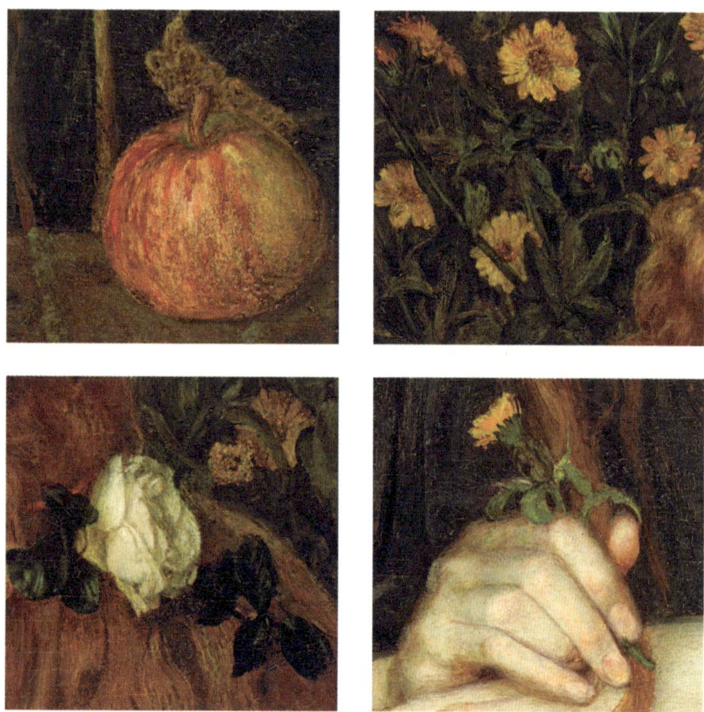

33. *Bocca Baciata* (*Lips That Have Been Kissed*), 1859
Oil on panel
32.1 × 27 cm (12⅝ × 10⅝ in.)
Signed, lower left: *G C D R*
Inscribed, reverse: *Bocca Baciata no perde venture, anzi rinnova come fa la/ Boccaccio*
Museum of Fine Arts, Boston (1980.261)

On a slip of paper attached to the painting's verso, Rossetti inscribed lines from Boccaccio's *Decameron* (*c.* 1348–50): 'The mouth that has been kissed loses not its freshness,/ Still it renews itself even as does the moon.' This sensuous bust-length portrait heralded a new direction in Rossetti's art. Using oil, rather than watercolour, for a richer, more tactile expression, he portrayed his model Fanny Cornforth as a personification of Boccaccio's paean to sensual pleasure.

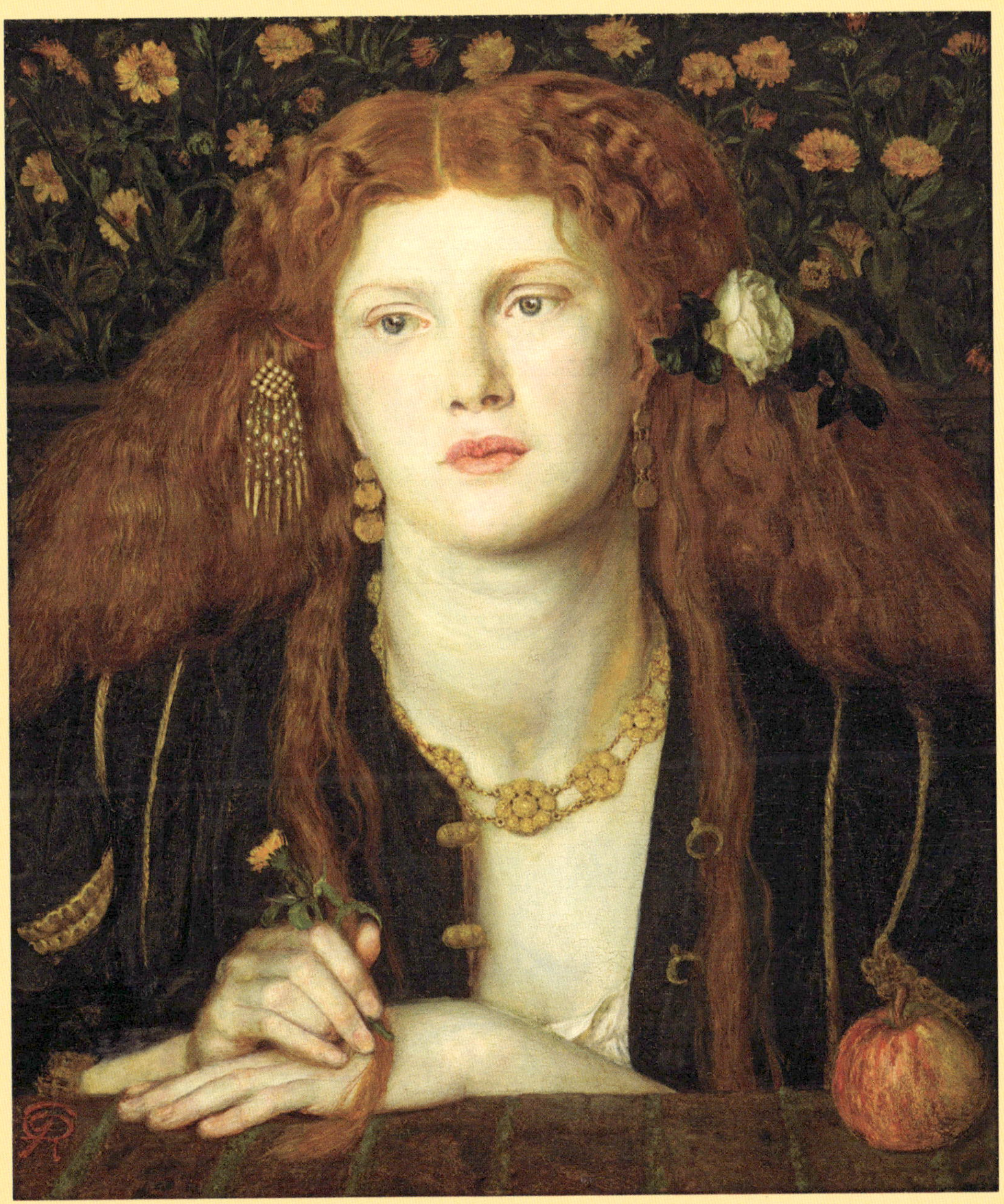

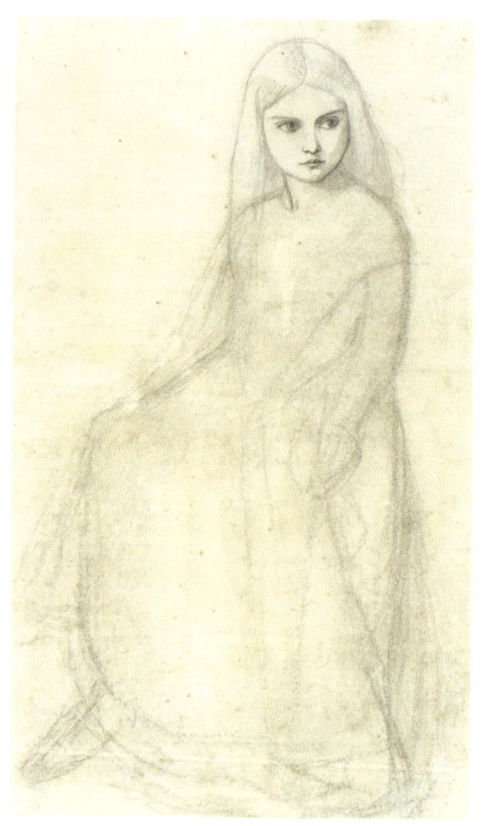

34. Drawing of a dancing girl, study for *The Borgia Family*, *c.* 1850
Graphite and black chalk
48.6 × 26.4 cm (19¼ × 10½ in.)
Inscribed, lower right, in George Boyce's hand: *Given by R. to G.P.B./ March 1st 1856;* lower left: *Borgia* (inscription faded; only word decipherable)
Victoria and Albert Museum, London
(V&A E.1159-2012)

Rossetti conceived the image of a pert yet wary girl for a group of dancing children to illustrate two lines from Shakespeare's *Richard III*: 'He capers nimbly in a lady's chamber/ To the lascivious pleasing of a lute' (Act 1, Scene 1). In his habit of reusing figures that he liked, this delicate study is associated with a watercolour of the notorious Borgia family (Tullie House Museum and Art Gallery, Carlisle), which Rossetti revised several times in the 1850s.

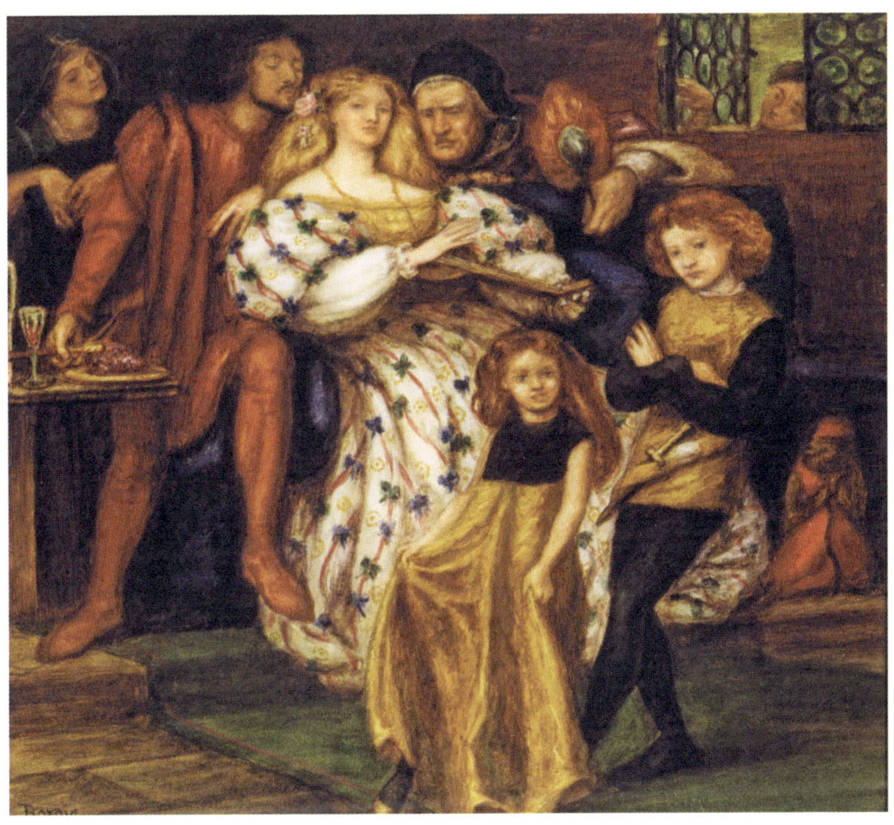

35. *The Borgia Family*, 1863
Watercolour
Framed: 52.2 × 54 cm ($20\frac{5}{8} \times 21\frac{3}{8}$ in.)
Victoria and Albert Museum, London
(V&A 72-1902)

In a later depiction of the Borgia family, Rossetti evoked a sultry atmosphere with a palette of burnished gold and blazing scarlet. With her shimmering hair and resplendent garments, Lucretia's lush beauty embodies the luxury and power associated with her family's name. Her father Pope Alexander VI and brother Cesare flank her, leaning in as if sharing conspiratorial secrets. They take no notice of the dancing girl and her partner as they enter the crowded chamber.

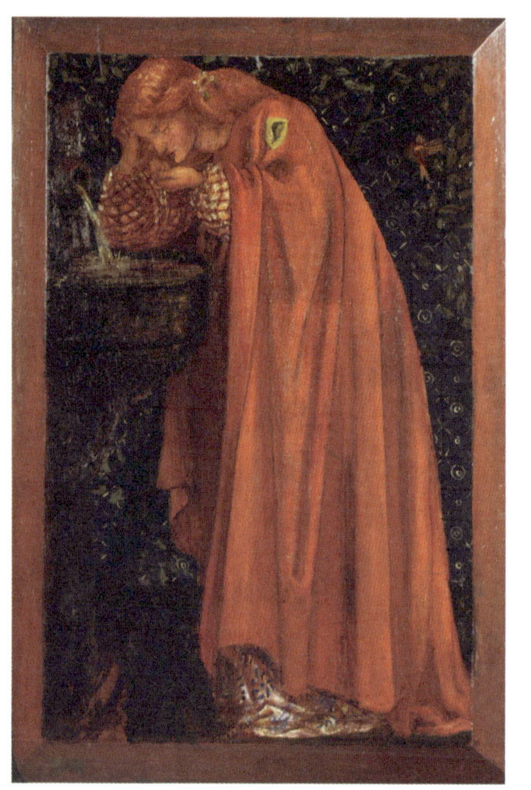

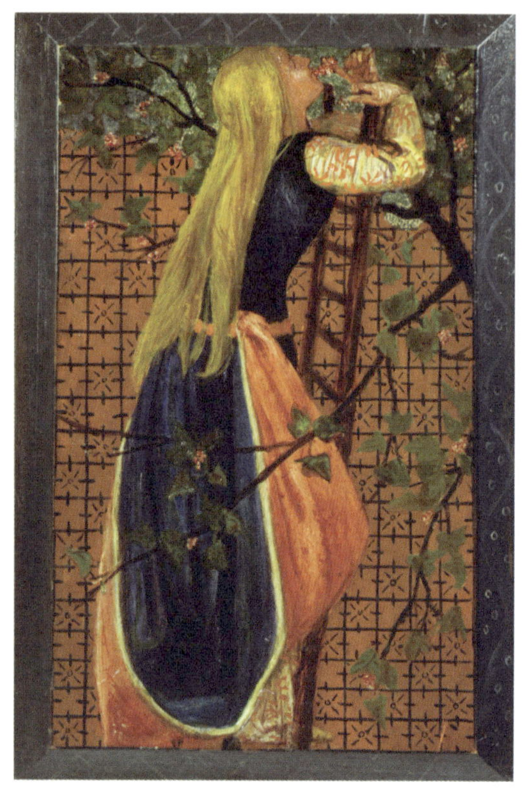

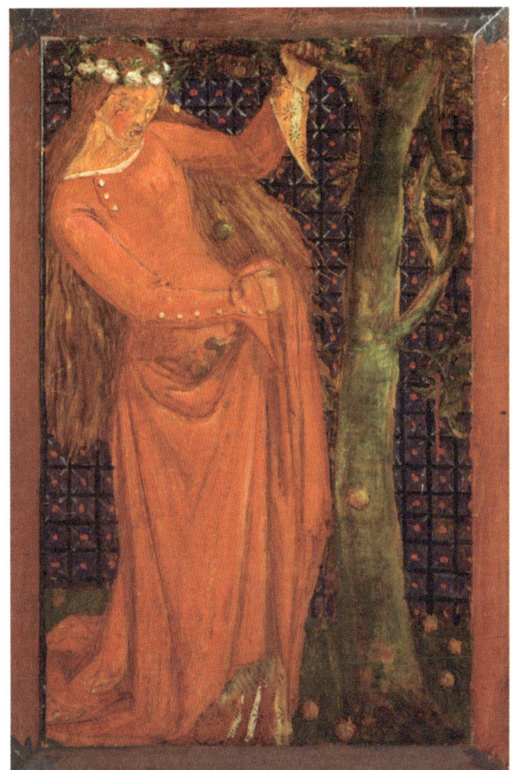

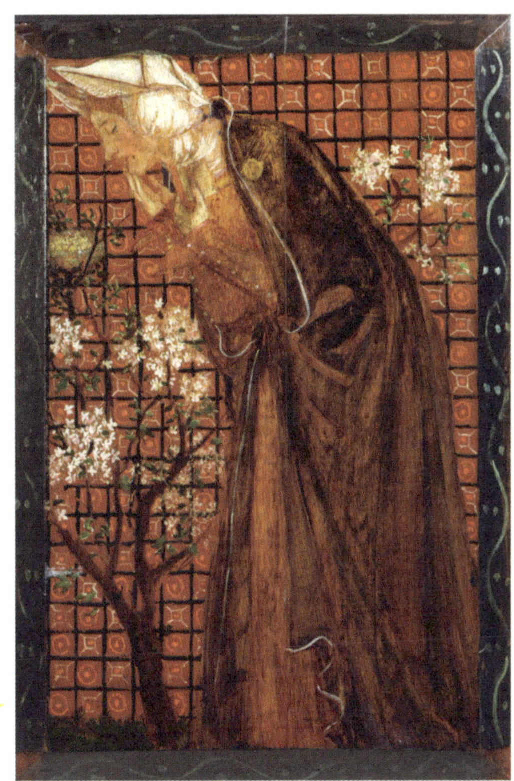

36. William Morris (1834–1896),
Edward Burne-Jones (1833–1898)
or Dante Gabriel Rossetti (1828–1882)
Four Wooden Panels, *c.* 1857–60 (?)
Oil on panel
61 × 41 cm (24$^{1}/_{8}$ × 16¼ in.) each
Victoria and Albert Museum, London
(V&A CIRC.129-1953; 311-1960; 310-1960; 128-1953)

These panels might have been painted to decorate a cabinet or bookcase of the type William Morris designed for Red House. They may depict the seasons, personified by women in medieval dress. The left-most panel is believed to have been painted by Rossetti, but none of the attributions can be verified.

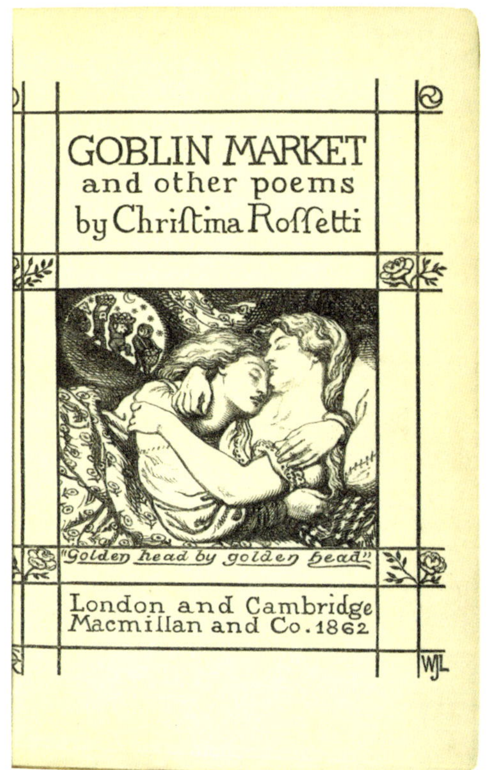

37. Title page, from Christina Rossetti, *Goblin Market and Other Poems*, 1862
Engraved by J. Linton; printed by Bradbury and Evans
Wood-engraved illustration
Book: 17.2 × 11.5 cm (6⅞ × 4⅝ in.)
Victoria and Albert Museum, London (V&A L.812-1933)

Rossetti played an active role in the publication of *Goblin Market and Other Poems*, published by Macmillan & Co., which established his sister Christina's reputation. He helped select the poems and provided designs for the binding, as well as for the title page (above) and frontispiece (opposite), which feature scenes from 'Goblin Market', a tale of supernatural seduction and the redemptive power of sisterly love. On the title page, the golden-haired sisters, Lizzie and Laura – as alike as 'two blossoms on one stem' – sleep in one another's arms.

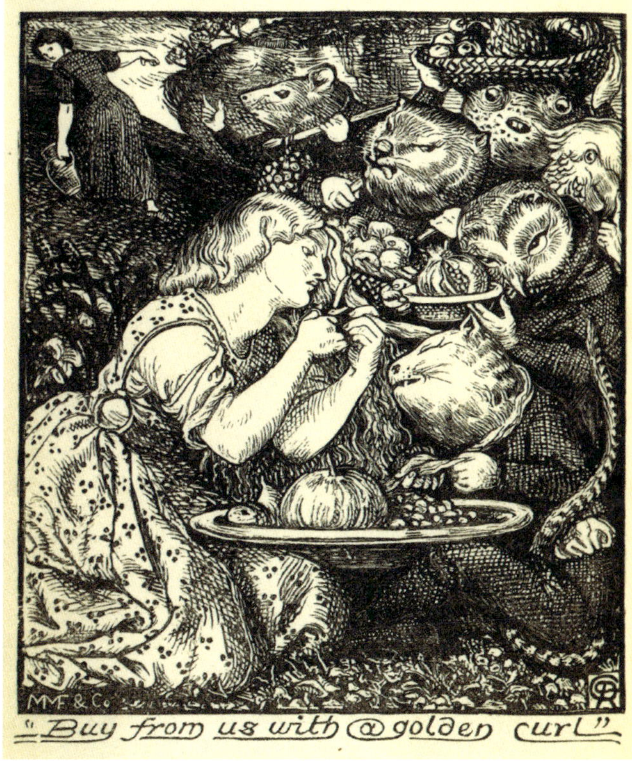

38. Frontispiece, from Christina Rossetti, *Goblin Market and Other Poems*, 1862
Engraved by J. Linton; printed by Bradbury and Evans
Wood-engraved illustration
Book: 17.2 × 11.5 cm ($6\frac{7}{8} \times 4\frac{5}{8}$ in.)
Victoria and Albert Museum, London (V&A L.812-1933)

Although Lizzie warned her to ignore them, Laura fell prey to the cries of the Goblin men who touted the irresistible sweetness of their ripe fruit. When she lamented that she could not pay them, they taunted, ‘You have much gold upon your head’, and tricked her into clipping a curl. Rossetti portrayed the goblins as hybrid horrors – animal faces on stunted human bodies – in contrast with Laura's statuesque beauty.

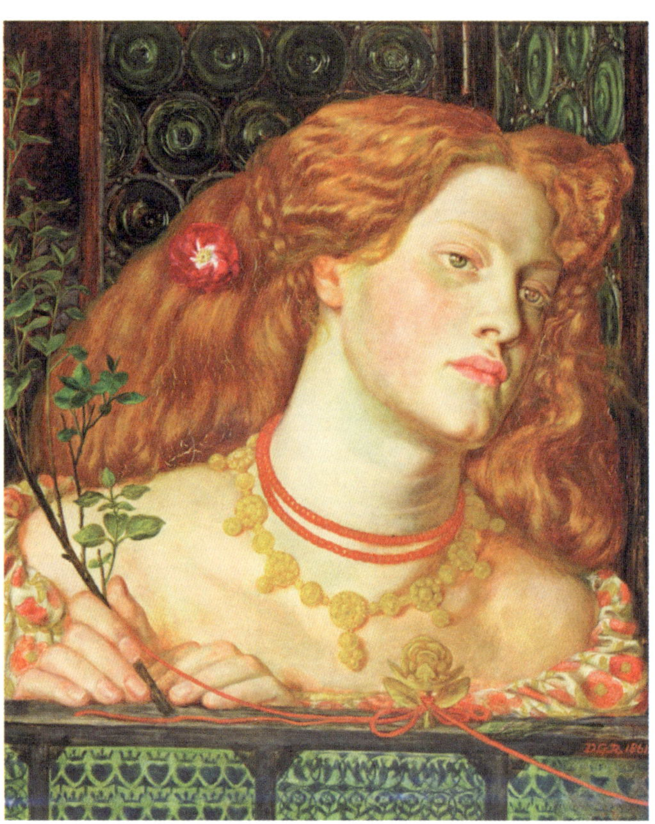

39. *Fair Rosamund*, 1861
Oil on canvas
51.9 × 41.7 cm (20½ × 16½ in.)
Inscribed, lower left, with monogram and date
National Museum of Wales, Cardiff (NMW A 169)

According to legend, King Henry II visited his mistress Rosamund at the Royal Manor at Woodstock by following a scarlet thread through a perplexing maze. His wife, Eleanor of Aquitaine, discovered the trysting place and had her rival put to death; in fact, the historic Rosamund Clifford retired to a convent. The rose motif evokes allure, from the pattern on her dress to the heated flush of her skin. Fanny Cornforth modelled for Rosamund.

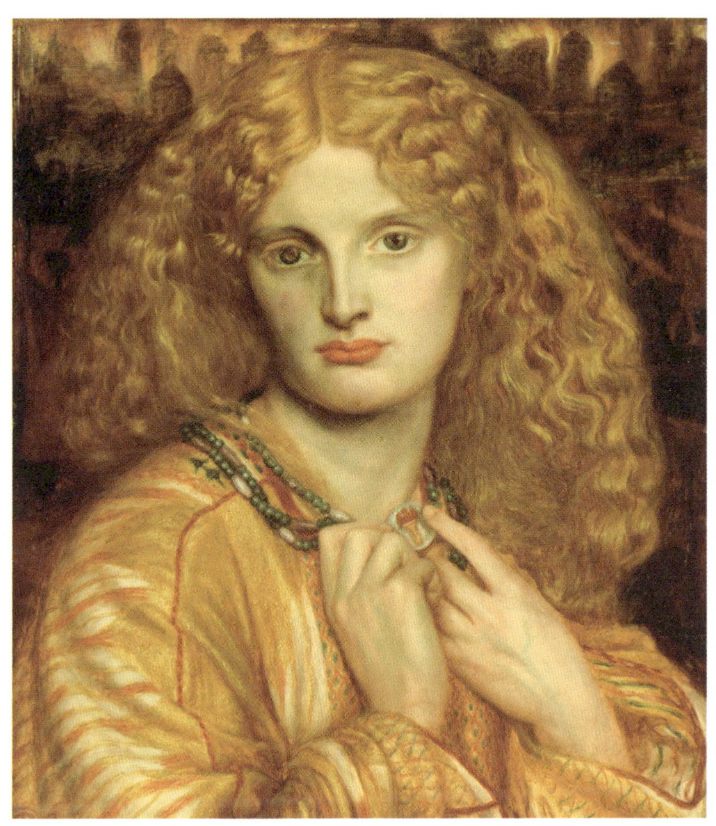

40. *Helen of Troy*, 1863
Oil on panel
32.8 × 27.7 cm (13 × 11 in.)
Inscribed, lower left, with monogram and date; reverse: *Helen of Troy* ἑλέναυς, ἕλανδρος, ἑλέπτολις *destroyer of ships, destroyer of men, destroyer of cities. Painted by G. Rossetti. 1863*
Kunsthalle, Hamburg
(2469)

To embody the new spirit in his painting, Rossetti portrayed the most seductive women in history and literature. But rather than illustrating their stories, he presented them as the epitome of female beauty. This portrait of Helen of Troy, with Annie Miller as the model, exemplifies the type: a voluptuous woman with porcelain skin, generous features and masses of shining hair, seated alone in a luxurious setting and dressed in opulent splendour.

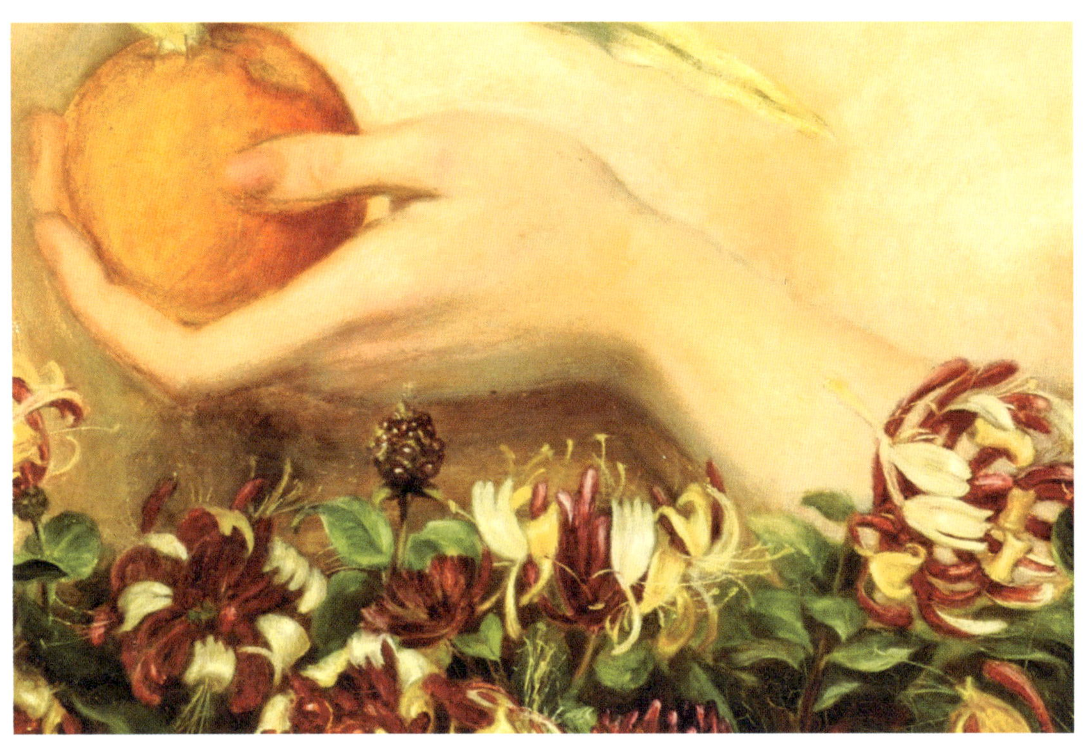

41. *Venus Verticordia*, 1863–8
Oil on canvas
81.3 × 68 cm (32⅛ × 26⅞ in.)
Inscribed, lower left: *DGR*
Russell-Cotes Art Gallery, Bournemouth
(BORGM 01897)

William Rossetti described the model for Venus as a 'striking woman, not very much less than six feet high'.[43] Rossetti himself encountered her on the street – she was a cook for a family living in Portland Place – but in 1867 covered her distinctive features with those of Alexa Wilding. The embellishments Rossetti chose – butterflies, full-blown roses and honeysuckle, the apple of discord – suggest that as a 'changer of hearts', Venus brings fickleness, carnal passion and trouble.

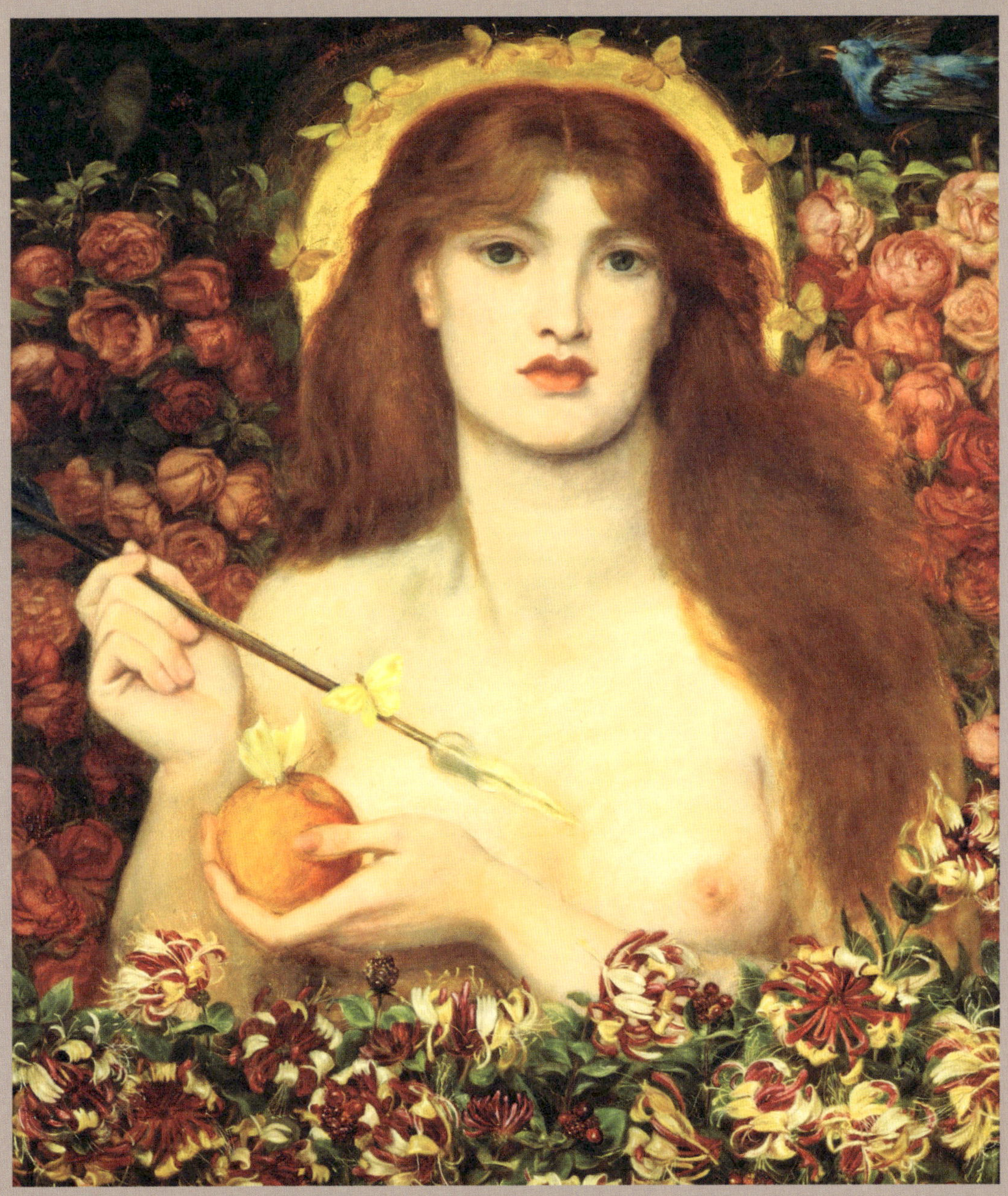

42. *The Beloved* (*'The Bride'*), 1865–6
Oil on canvas
82.5 × 76.2 cm (32½ × 30 in.)
Inscribed, lower left, with monogram and date
Tate Gallery, London
(N03053)

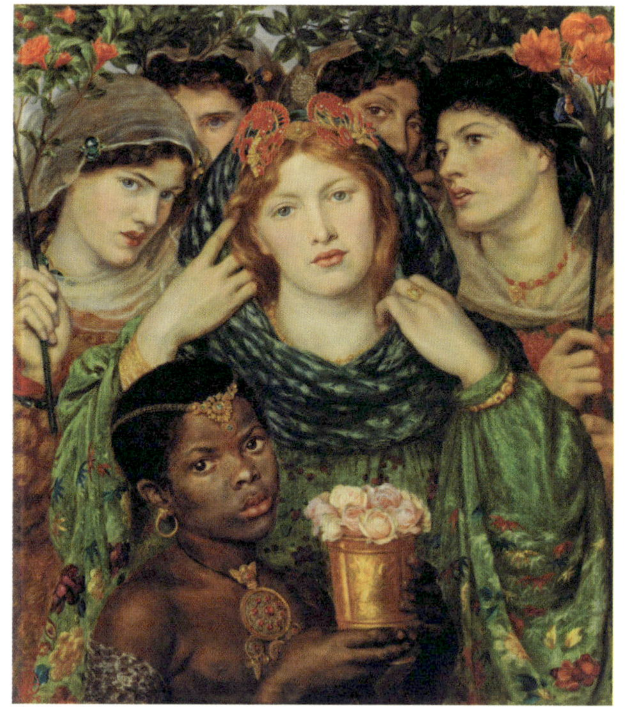

The Beloved (above) began as a portrait of Dante's Beatrice, but Rossetti judged professional model Marie Ford's complexion to be too bright and changed the subject to the arrival of the bride in the *Song of Solomon*. Although the bride declares, 'I am very dark, but comely' (1:5), Rossetti emphasized Marie's creamy, peach-flushed skin and russet hair by surrounding her with darker-skinned brunette models, including Keomi Gray, a woman believed to be of Romany descent, who was introduced into the Pre-Raphaelite circle by Frederick Sandys. Little is known about her, but Rossetti's drawing (opposite) brings her to life.

43. *Study of a Head*, 1865
Pencil on paper
36.8 × 33.7 cm (14½ × 13⅜ in.)
Inscribed, lower left, with monogram and date
Victoria and Albert Museum, London
(V&A E.2914-1927)

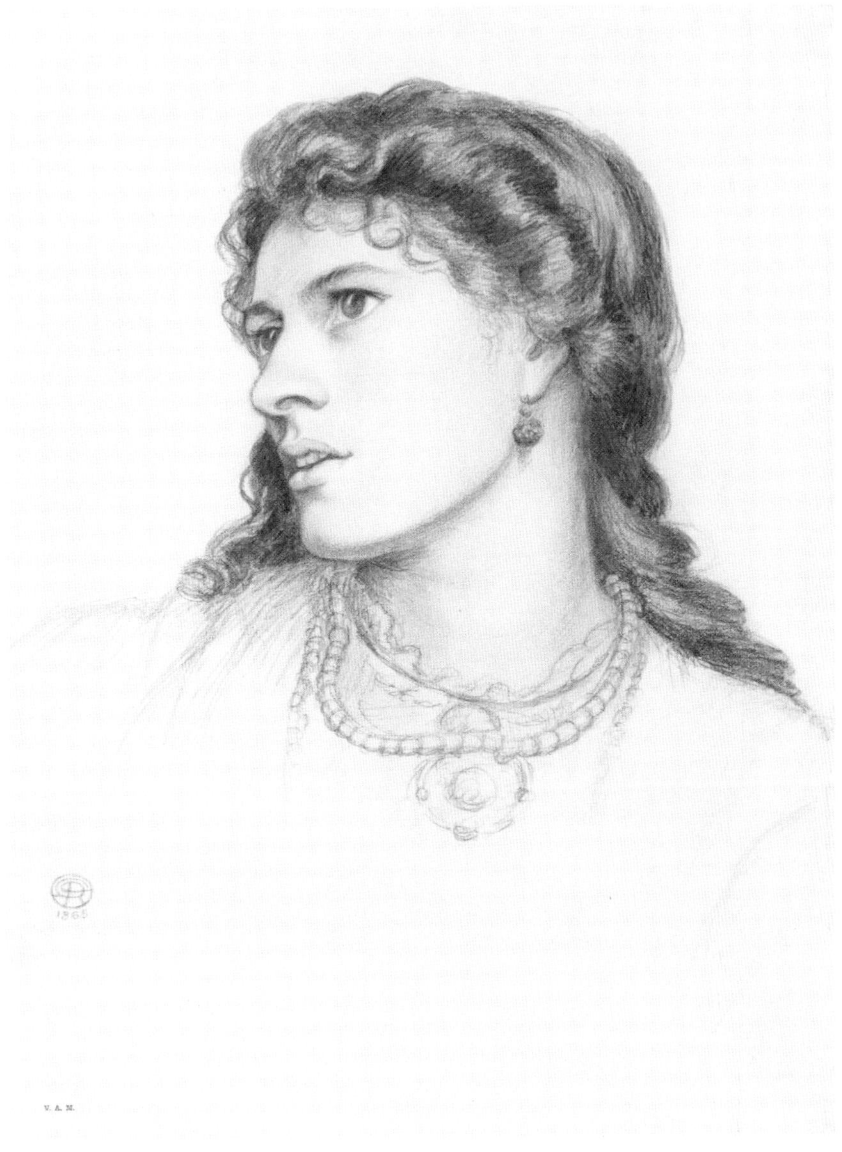

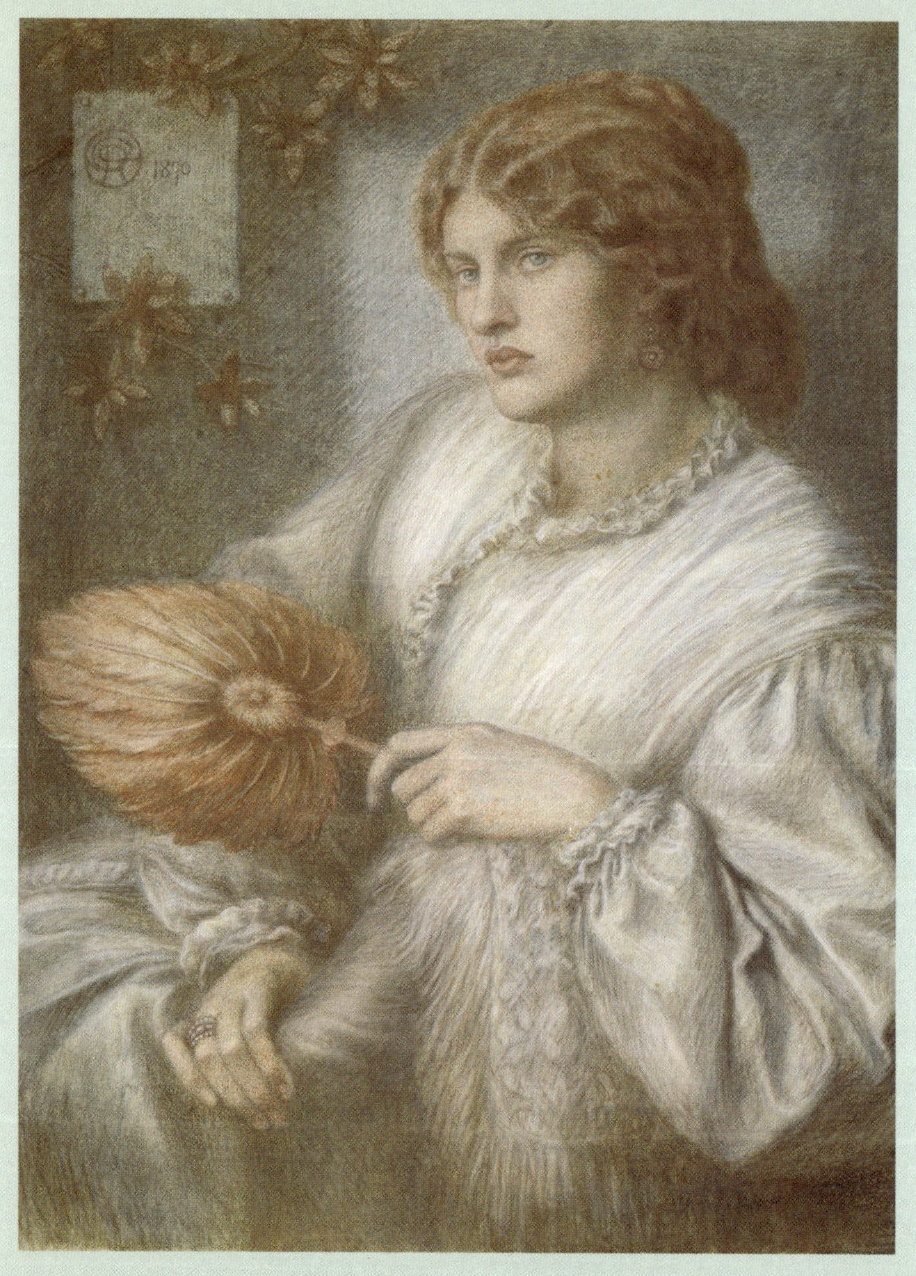
1870

44. *Woman with a Fan (Fanny Cornforth)*, 1870
Coloured chalks on paper
95.8 × 71.1 cm (37¾ × 28 in.)
Inscribed, upper left: *DGR 1870*
Birmingham Museums and Art Gallery (1904P414)

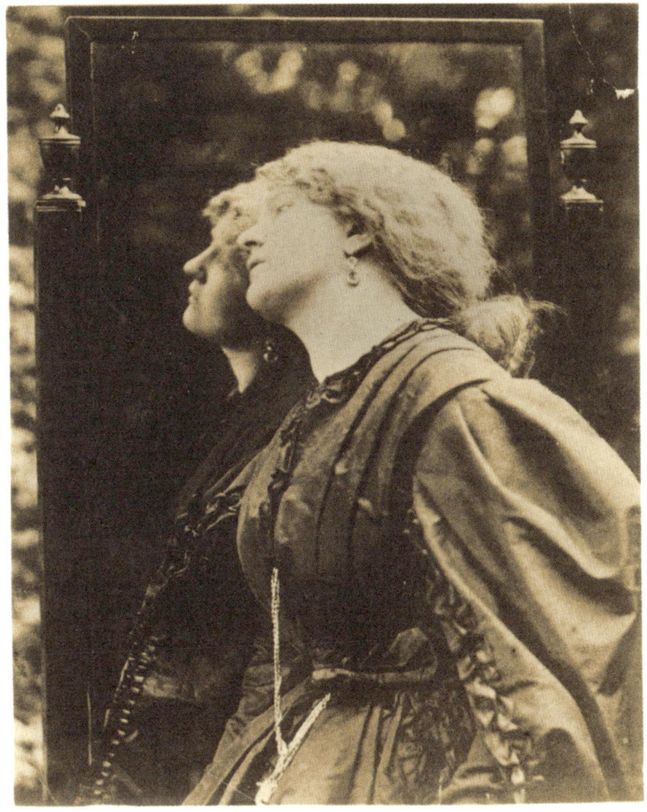

45. William Downey (1829–1915)
Fanny (Cornforth) Schott, *c.* 1863
Photograph
15.3 × 13.3 cm (6⅛ × 5¼ in.)
Delaware Art Museum, Wilmington

The white dress and languorous pose in *Woman with a Fan* (opposite) recall Fanny Cornforth's appearance in the original composition of *Lady Lilith* (49); here, Rossetti portrays Fanny as he knew her after more than a decade of amicable companionship. The photograph (above) confirms the painting's excellence as a likeness. A letter to Fanny dated 1872 mentions the possibility of selling 'the large drawing I did of you', suggesting that it was in her possession.[44]

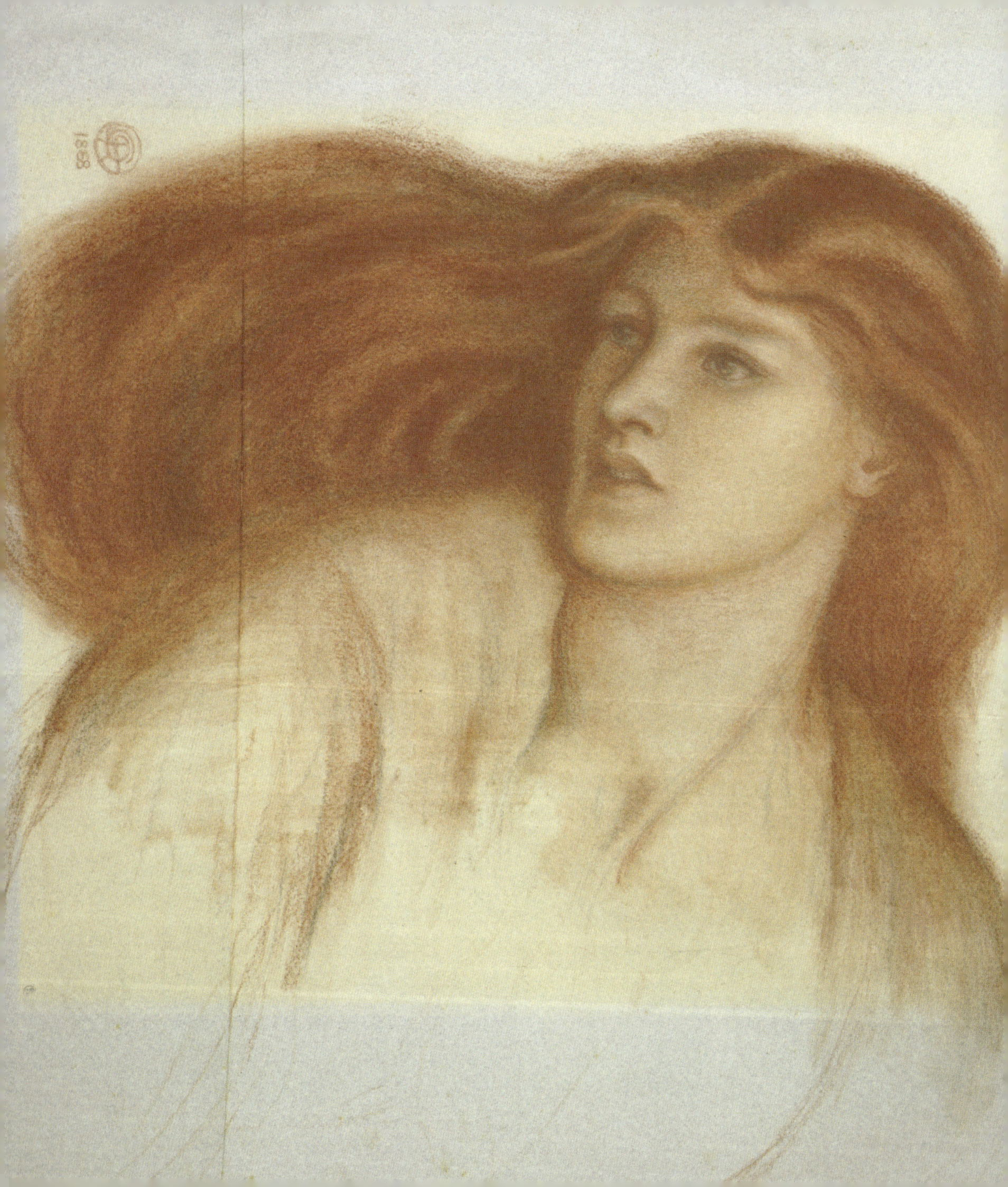
1868

46. *Head of Andromeda*, 1868
Chalk on grey paper
53.1 × 45.7 cm (21 × 18 in.)
Inscribed, lower left,
with monogram and date
Victoria and Albert Museum, London
(V&A CAI.6)

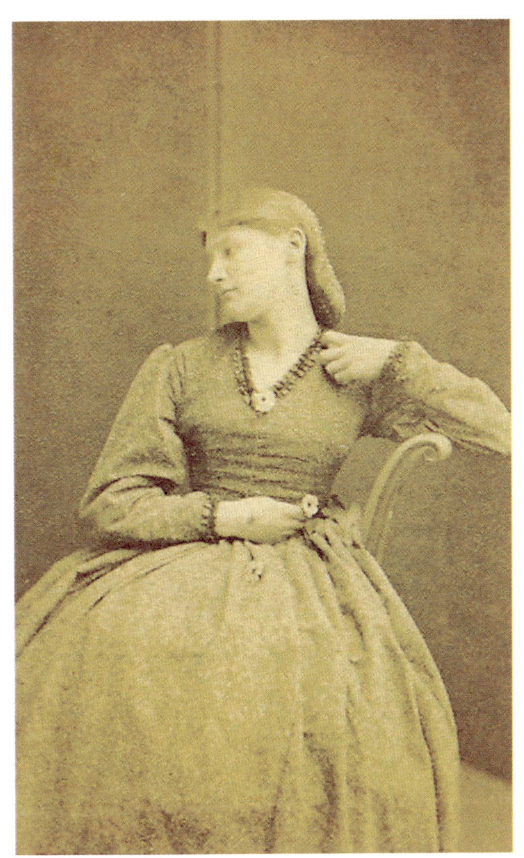

47. John Robert Parsons (*c.* 1826–1909)
Photograph of Alexa Wilding, *c.* 1870
Albumen carte-de-visite
5.7 × 10.5 cm (2¼ × 4¼ in.)
Mark Samuels Lasner Collection, University of Delaware Library, Museums and Press

The first time Rossetti asked Alexa Wilding to come to his studio, she ignored the invitation. By sheer chance he saw her again and convinced her to sit for a figure of Andromeda, looking at the reflection of Medusa's severed head in a pool of water. Rossetti never realized the painting, but paid Alexa a weekly retainer for exclusive sittings. Her serene, regular features gave him a blank canvas for almost any character.

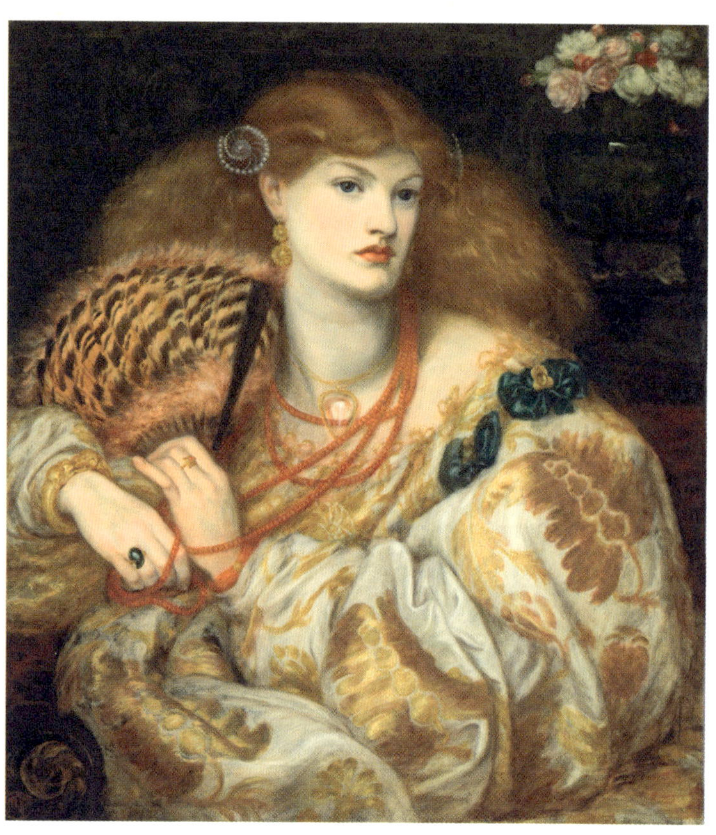

48. *Monna Vanna*, 1866
Oil on canvas
88.9 × 86.4 (35 × 34⅛ in.)
Tate Gallery, London
(N03054)

Rossetti first titled this portrait *Venus Veneta* in his belief that it represented 'the Venetian ideal of female beauty'.[45] Inspired by the passage in *La Vita Nuova* in which Dante sees his friend's mistress Giovanna (Vanna) with Beatrice and thinks of spring, he altered the name. Although Rossetti chose a third title – *Belacolore* ('fair colour') – in 1873, *Monna Vanna* (loosely translated as 'vain woman') has endured, perhaps in the assumption that her luxurious attire is a reference to vanity.

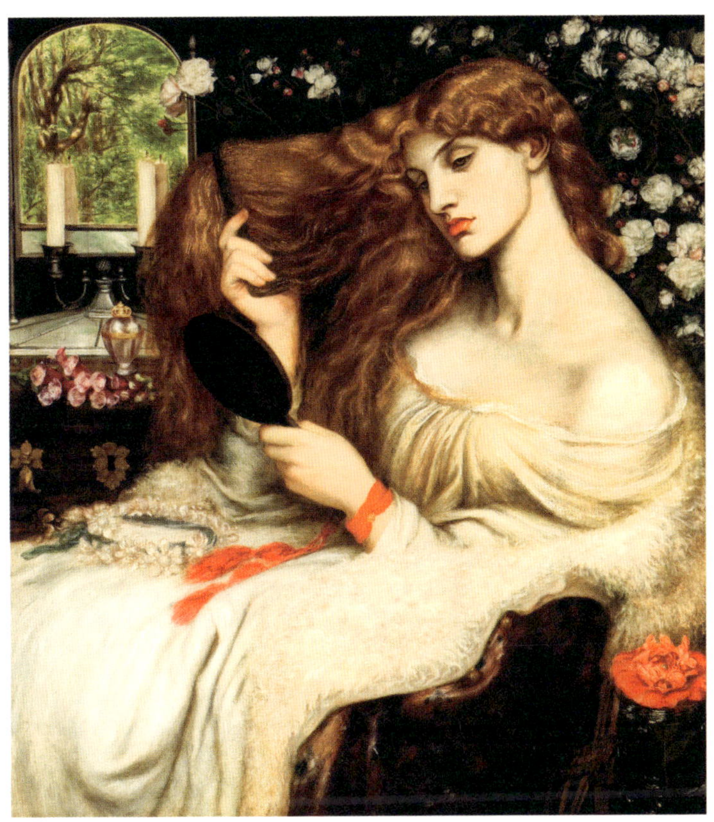

49. *Lady Lilith*, 1864–8, altered 1872–3
Oil on canvas
99.1 × 86.4 cm (39 × 34 in.)
Inscribed, left (on table):
D G Rossetti 1868
Delaware Art Museum, Wilmington
(1935-29)

In the sonnet written for this painting, Rossetti describes Lilith as 'the witch' Adam 'loved before the gift of Eve'. Lilith is not mentioned in the Book of Genesis; the tradition that she was Adam's first wife, rejected for her refusal to submit to his will, seems to have first emerged in the early medieval period. Although Fanny Cornforth posed for the original composition, Rossetti repainted the work with Alexa Wilding's likeness at the request of his patron, Frederick Richards Leyland.

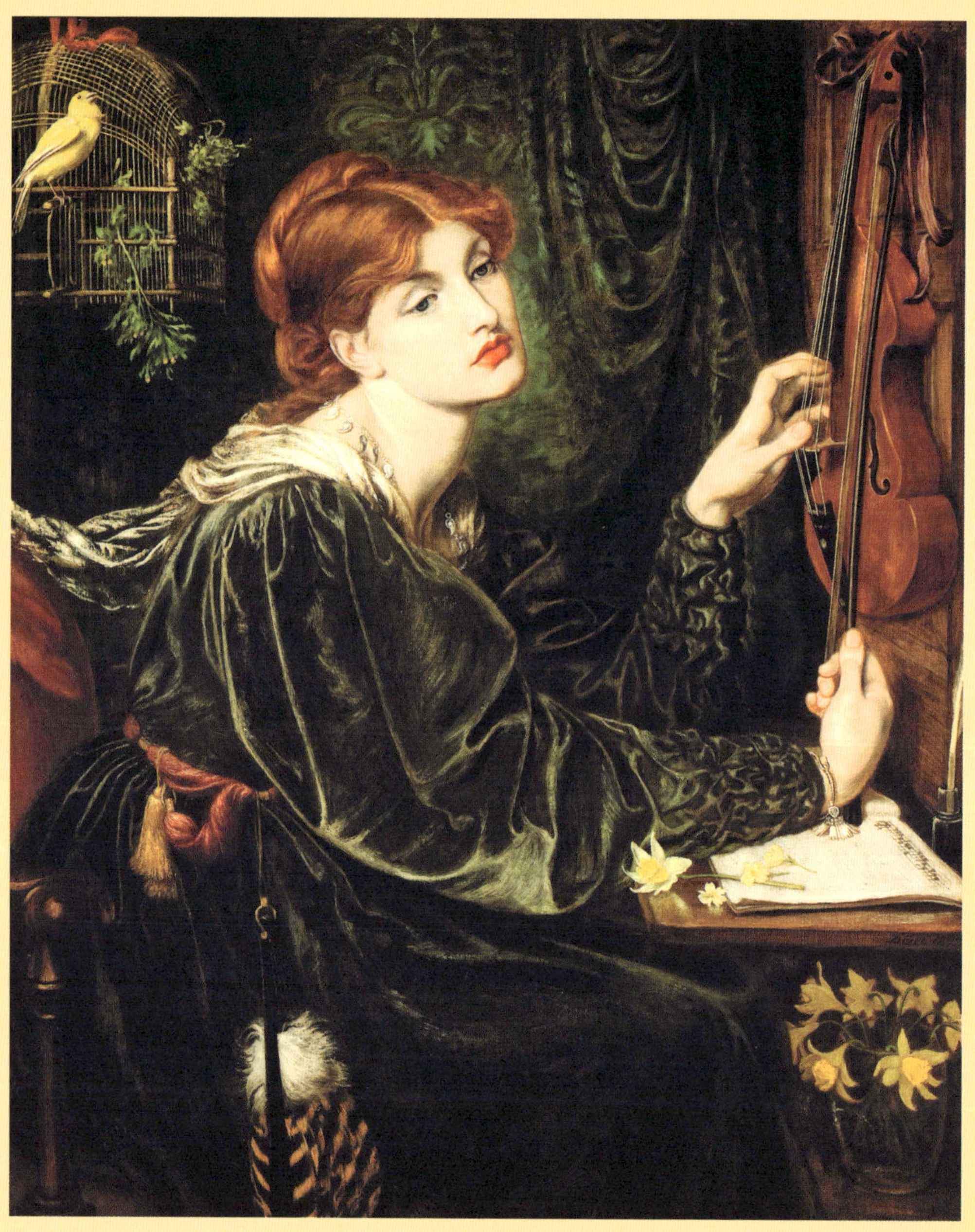

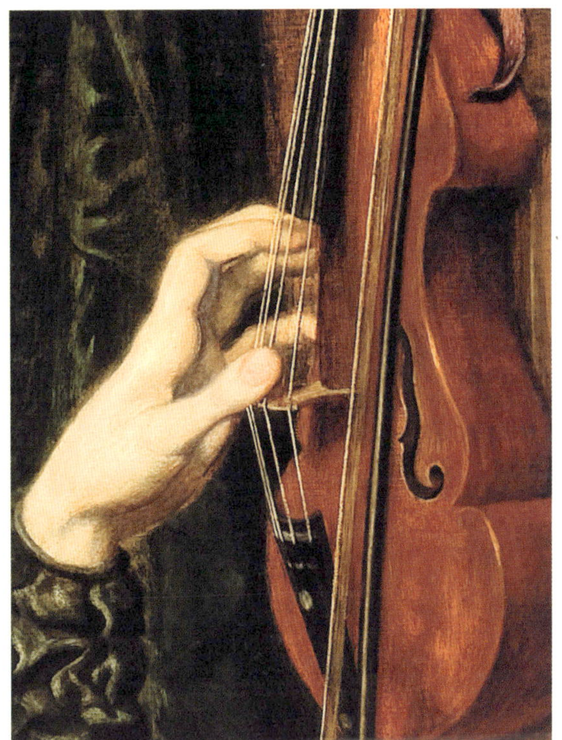

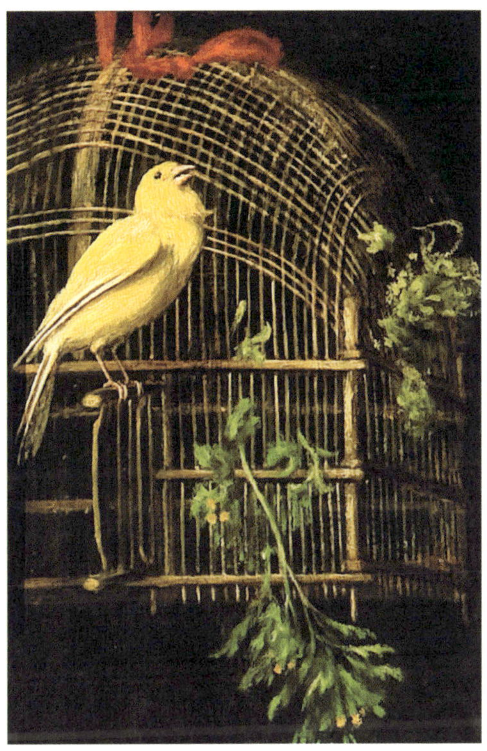

50. *Veronica Veronese*, 1872
Oil on canvas
109.2 × 88.9 cm (43 × 35 in.)
Inscribed, lower right: *D G R 1872*
Delaware Art Museum, Wilmington
(1935-28)

Although non-narrative in the conventional sense, Rossetti's Venetian portraits always have a subject in terms of mood, aesthetic and motif. He described this painting as a woman whose thoughts wander from her music into a 'passionate reverie'.[46] The rich green velvets and brocades, as well as the foliage, present a sumptuous contrast to Alexa Wilding's ivory skin and auburn hair, and her indeterminable expression strikes the right note of enigmatic self-absorption.

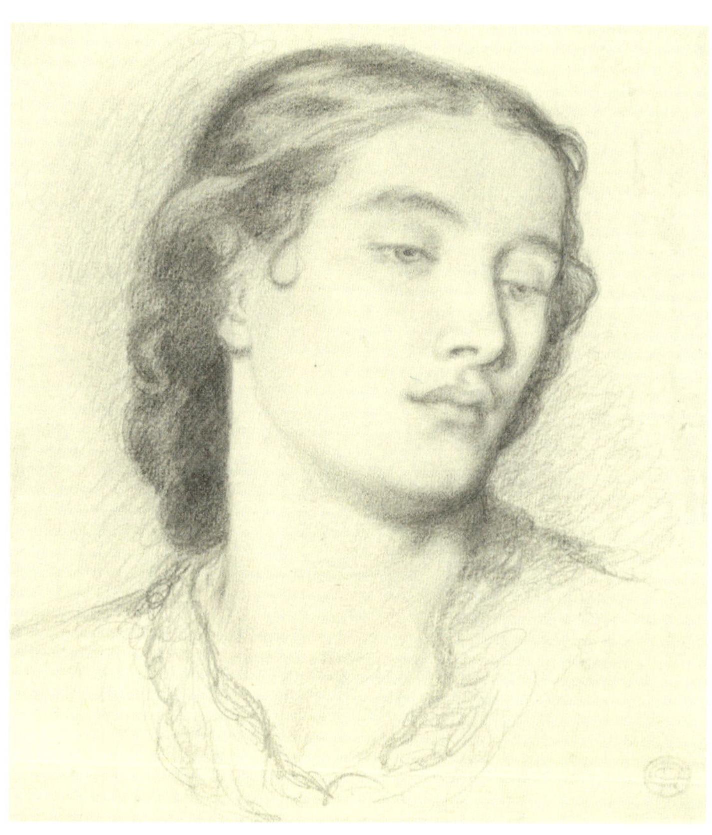

51. *Study of the head of a woman*, n.d.
Pencil on paper
24.1 × 20.3 cm (9½ × 8 in.)
Victoria and Albert Museum, London
(V&A CAI.7)

Although some of the facial features of this sitter reflect Rossetti's ideal – wide forehead, lifted upper lip, curved jawline and columnar neck – the set of her eyes, soft yet full eyebrows and fine tendrils of her hair evoke a distinct individual. Neither her identity nor the date of this sketch is known, but her expression of plaintive interiority is unmistakable.

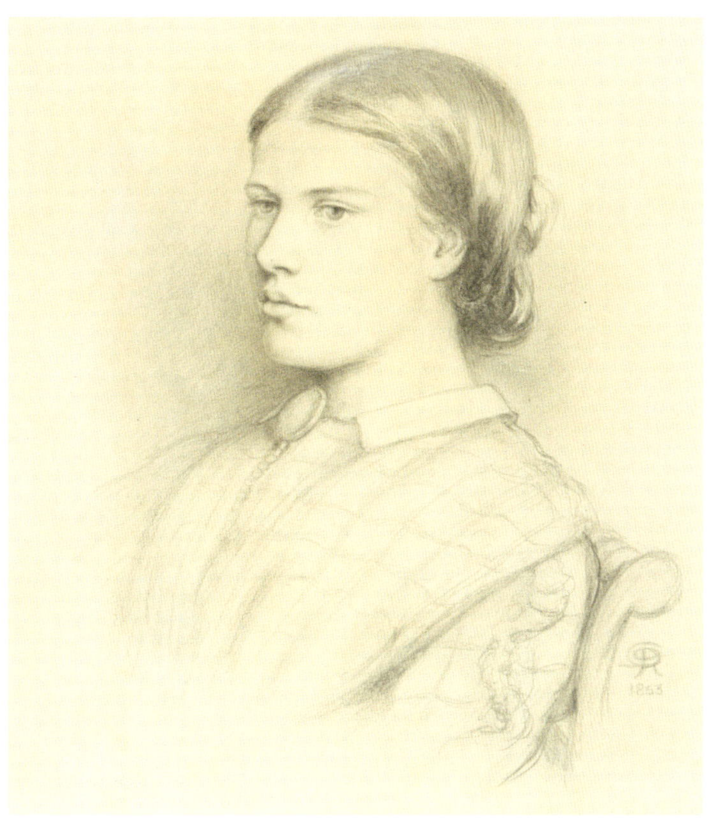

52. *Henrietta Polydore as a young woman*, 1863
Pencil on paper
29.8 × 24.4 cm (11¾ × 9⅝ in.)
Inscribed, with monogram and date
Victoria and Albert Museum, London
(V&A E.147-1928)

Henrietta Polydore, daughter of the Rossetti siblings' maternal uncle Henry, was their sole cousin. Henry Polydore, a lawyer, had anglicized the family name of Polidori, perhaps to play down his Italian heritage. The circumstances surrounding this portrait are not known, but Christina Rossetti recorded several visits with Henrietta in 1864. Rossetti's detailed depiction – from her narrowed eyes and firm chin, to her neatly coiffed hair and the cameo on her modest dress – suggest a studied likeness.

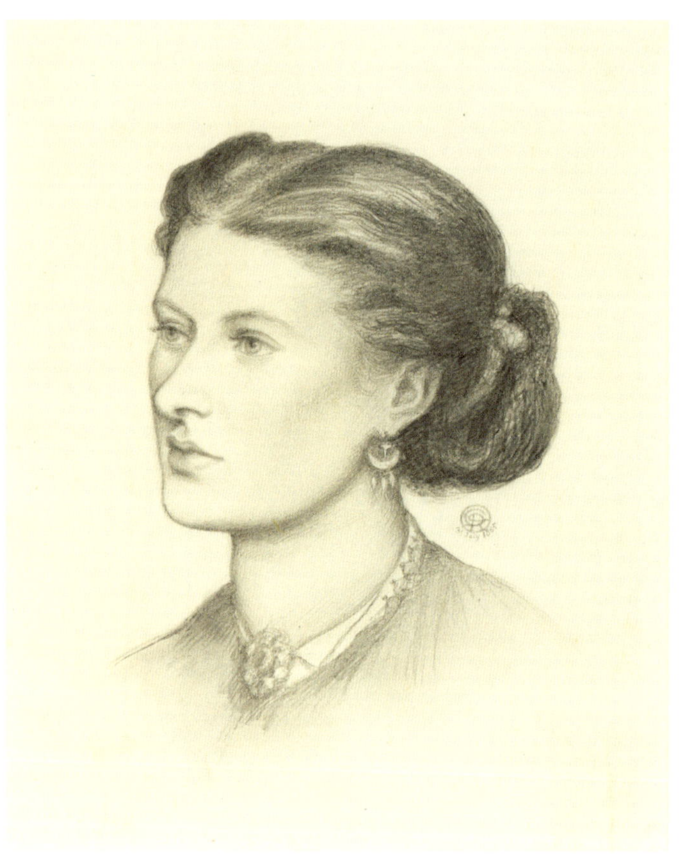

53. *Portrait of Mrs C.A. Howell*,
31 July 1865
Pencil on paper
25.4 × 17.8 cm (10 × 7 in.)
Victoria and Albert Museum, London
(V&A E.2915-1927)

Francis Catherine Howell, known as Kitty, married her cousin Charles Augustus Howell in September 1867. Little is known about her, but her husband had been friends with Rossetti from the time they met in 1857. In the year that Rossetti made this sharply observed portrait sketch of Kitty, John Ruskin engaged Charles Augustus Howell as his private secretary; he later worked for both Rossetti brothers as a picture dealer and business agent.

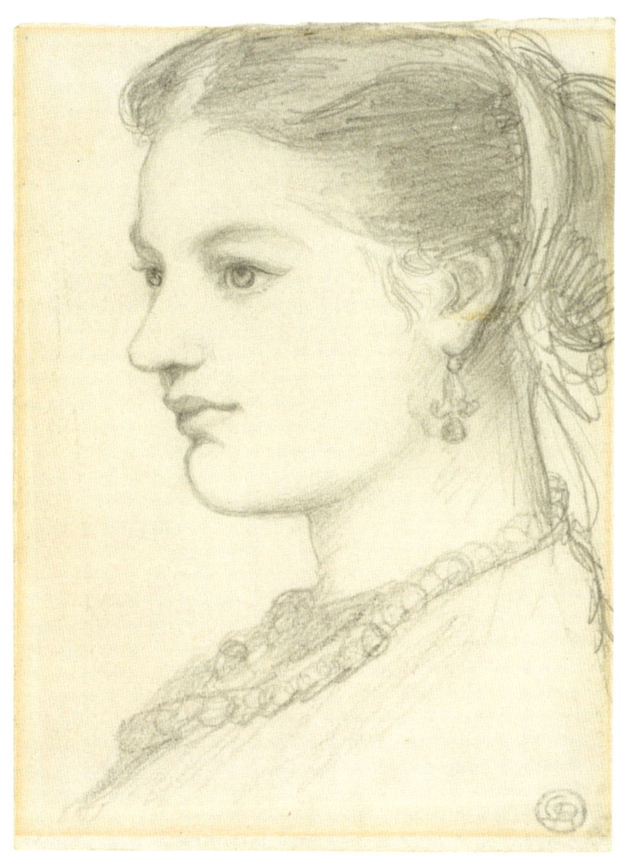

54. *Study of the head of a girl*, n.d.
Pencil on paper
17.8 × 12.7 cm (7 × 5 in.)
Victoria and Albert Museum, London
(V&A E.13-1925)

Throughout the 1860s and early 1870s, Rossetti deftly sketched female portraits in pencil. Whether a recognizable acquaintance or, as here, an unknown sitter, he paid keen attention to details of hairdressing and jewellery. The shape of the sitter's drop earring and the manner in which her chignon is fastened with a ribbon are as carefully rendered as the slope of her nose and the heavy curve of her jaw and chin.

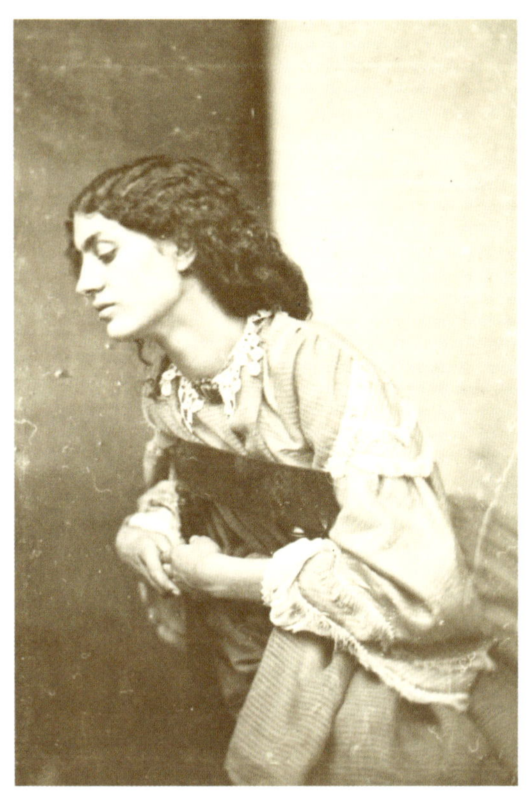

55. *Jane Morris*, by an unknown photographer, *c.* 1858
Albumen print
14.6 × 9.4 cm (5¾ × 3¾ in.)
Victoria and Albert Museum, London (V&A 1752-1939)

When Rossetti approached Jane Burden on an Oxford street in 1857 and asked if she would be his model, she was no doubt surprised; her family regarded her as plain. Her dark, rippled hair, chiselled features and attenuated proportions did not conform to contemporary standards of beauty, but Rossetti found the difference compelling. He convinced Jane to pose as Guenevere (Rossetti and Morris preferred this traditional spelling over 'Guinevere', as popularized by Tennyson) and transformed the daughter of a stablehand into a queen.

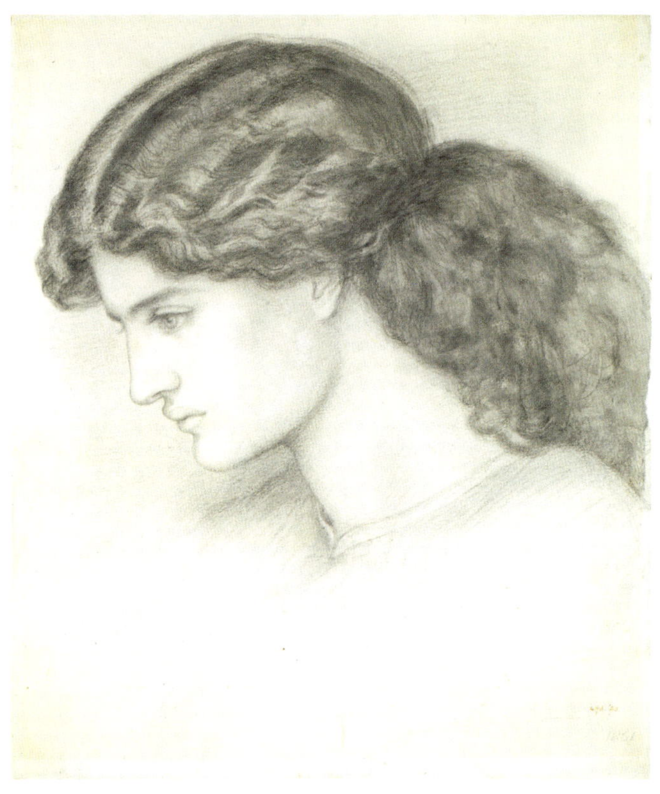

56. *Profile of a lady* (*Jane Morris*), 1861
Pencil and Indian ink
34.6 × 28.9 cm (13⅝ × 11½ in.)
Victoria and Albert Museum, London
(V&A 493-1883)

This sketch of Jane relates to her portrayal as the Virgin in the central panel of *The Seed of David* (1858–64), a tripartite altarpiece Rossetti was painting for Llandaff Cathedral in Cardiff at the time. The actress Ruth Herbert had sat for initial sketches in 1858, but Rossetti set aside the project. When he resumed work, he used his friends from the Red House circle as models; Algernon Charles Swinburne, Edward Burne-Jones and William Morris all appear in the final version of the altarpiece.

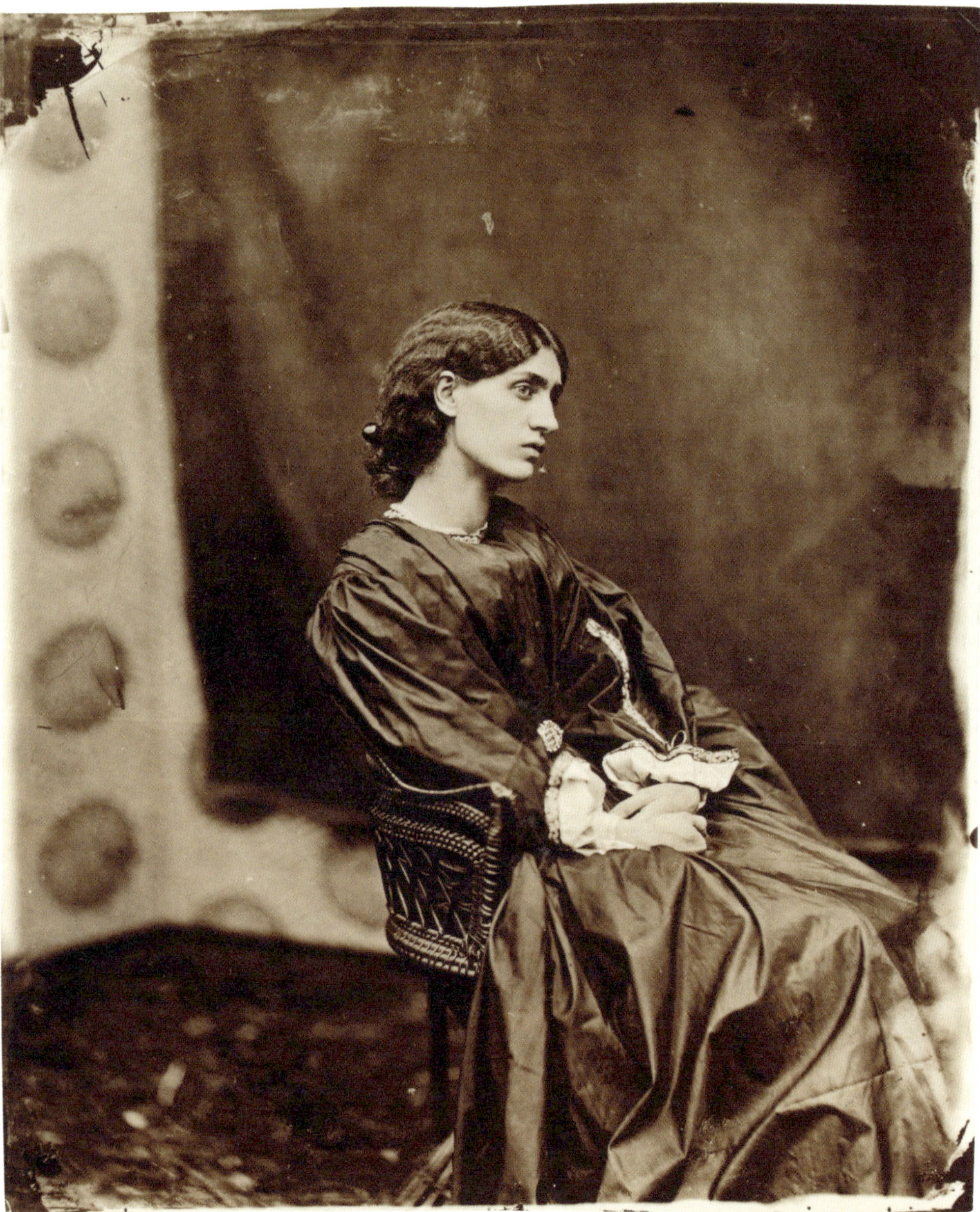

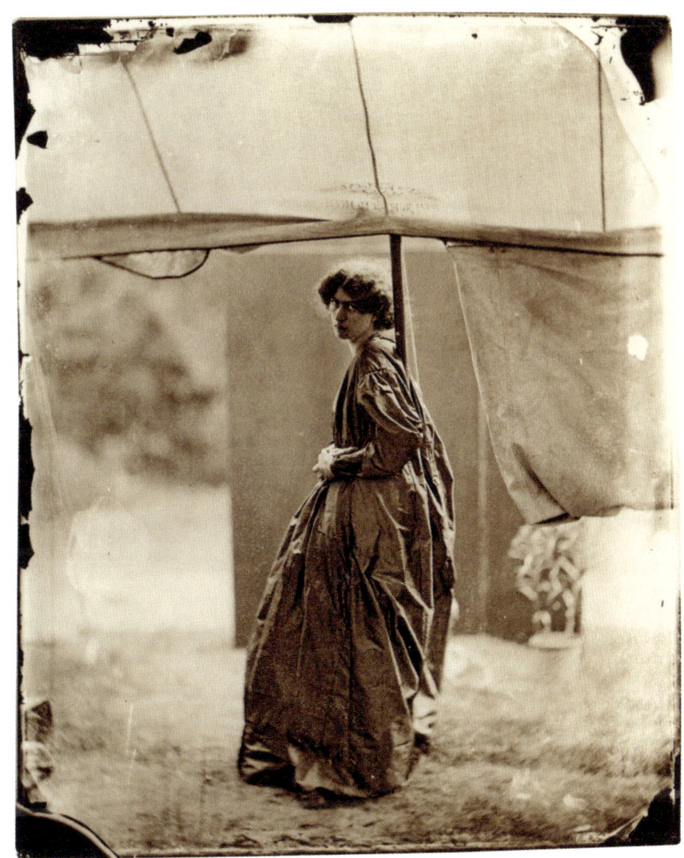

57. John Robert Parsons (*c.* 1826–1909)
Jane Morris, posed by Rossetti, 1865
Modern gelatin silver print
25.3 × 20 cm (10 × 7⅞ in.)
Victoria and Albert Museum, London
(V&A 819-1942)

58. John Robert Parsons (*c.* 1826–1909)
Jane Morris, posed by Rossetti, 1865
Modern gelatin silver print
25.6 × 20.3 cm (10⅛ × 8 in.)
Victoria and Albert Museum, London
(V&A 823-1942)

Early in July 1865, Rossetti invited Jane to Tudor House to be photographed by John Robert Parsons. Although Parsons was a well-respected professional, Rossetti controlled every aspect of the session. He hired a marquee for the garden, arranged chairs and textiles, and set every one of the poses. Intended to serve as *aide-mémoires* when Jane could not come to the studio, the photographs established her as Rossetti's reigning muse.

59. John Robert Parsons (*c.* 1826–1909)
Jane Morris, posed by Rossetti, 1865
Albumen print
17.1 × 13.3 cm (6¾ × 5¼ in.)
Victoria and Albert Museum, London
(V&A 1746-1939)

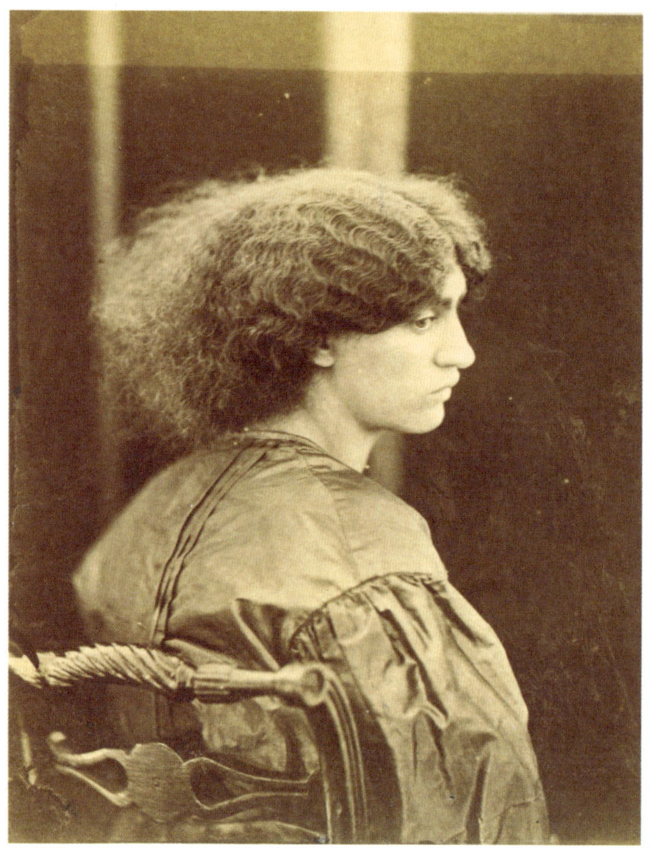

60. John Robert Parsons (*c.* 1826–1909)
Jane Morris, posed by Rossetti, 1865
Albumen print
18.8 × 14.6 cm (7½ × 5¾ in.)
Victoria and Albert Museum, London
(V&A 1747-1939)

William Morris's poem 'In Praise of My Lady' (1858) describes his fiancée's striking physical features: ivory-pale skin, wide-set eyes, pensive lips and cheeks, 'hollow'd a little mournfully'. He likened her long, pliant neck to a knight's pennon, and her thick, dark waves of hair to a 'strange metal', divinely forged, 'thread by thread'. By the time Parsons photographed her, Jane's unconventional beauty had redefined Rossetti's art.

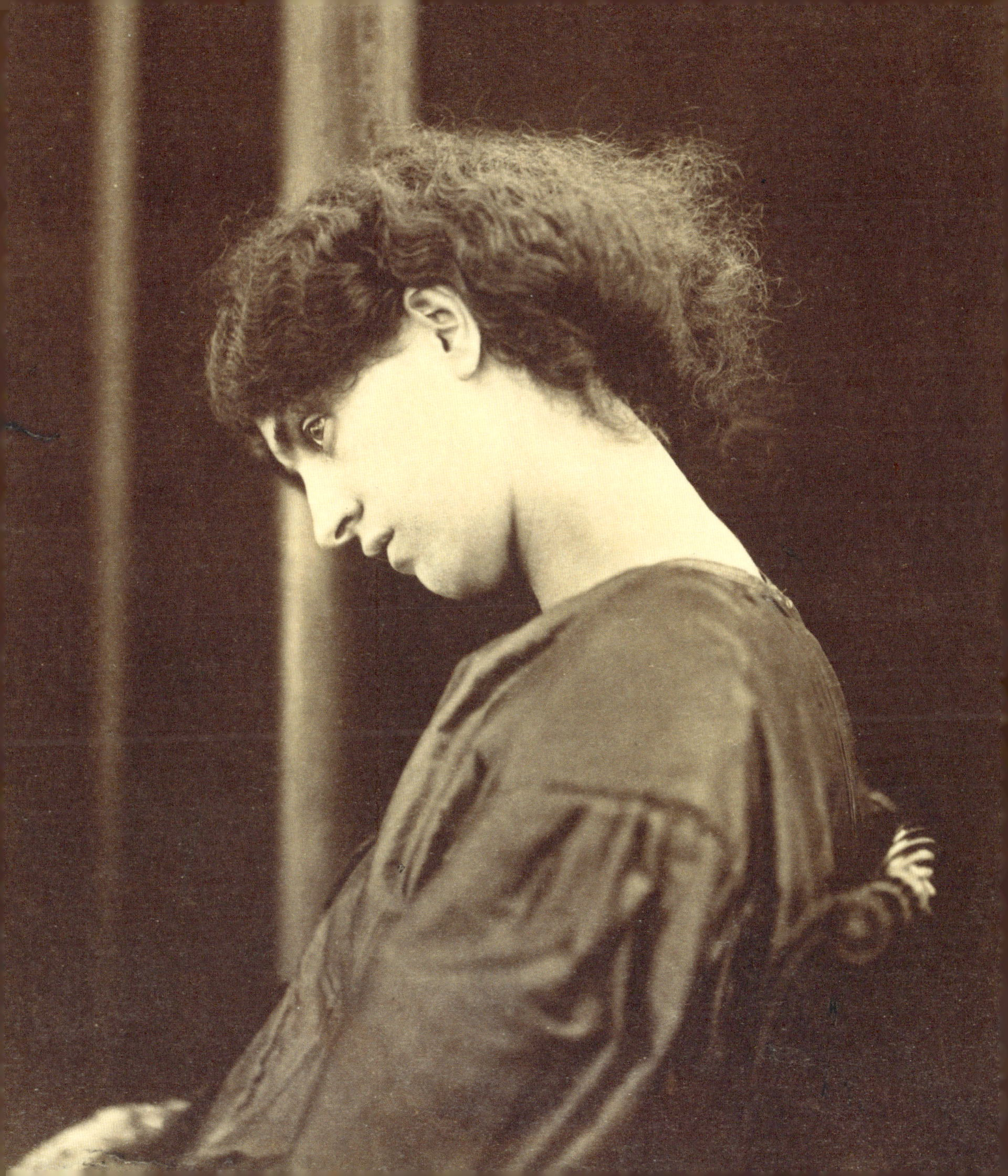

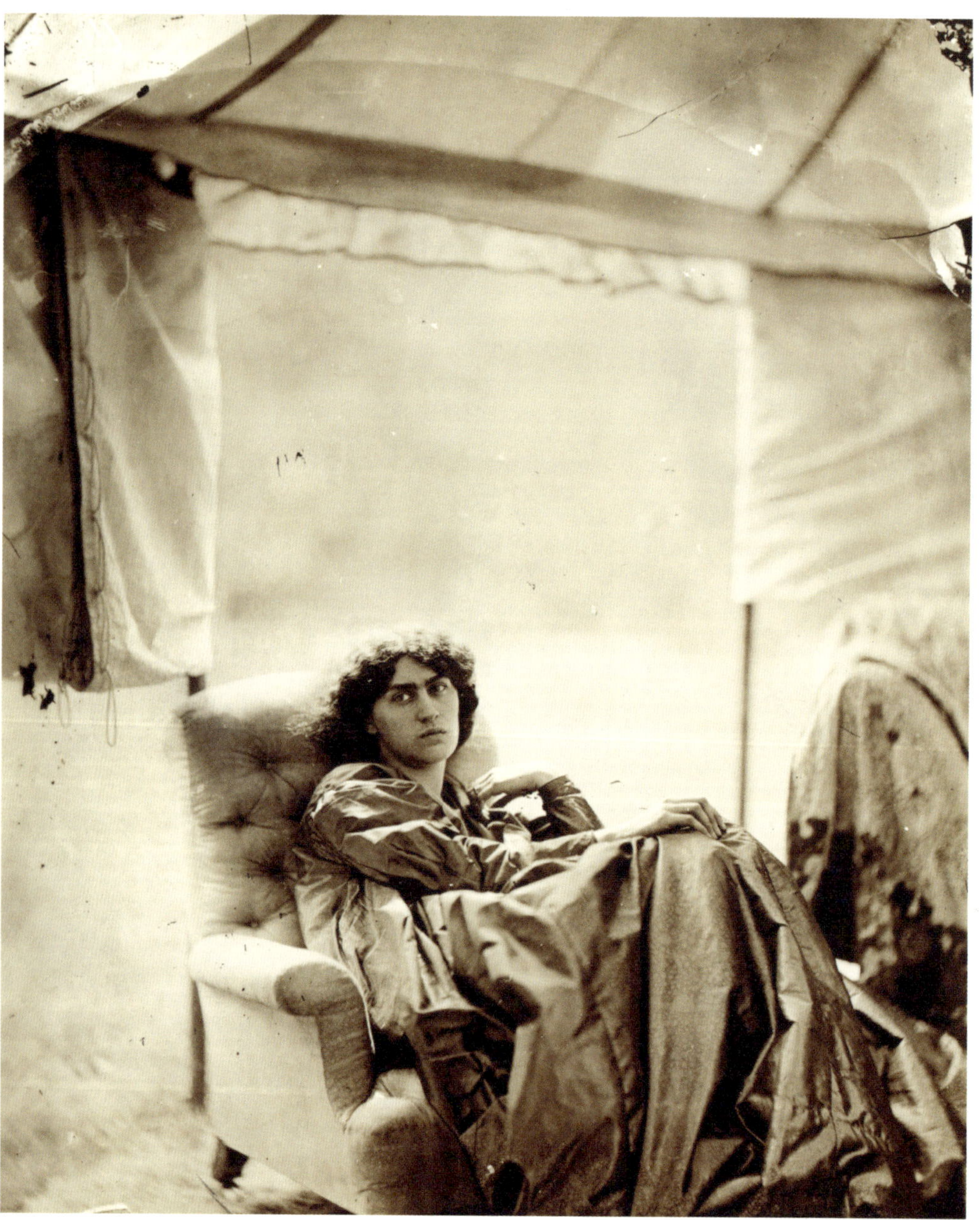

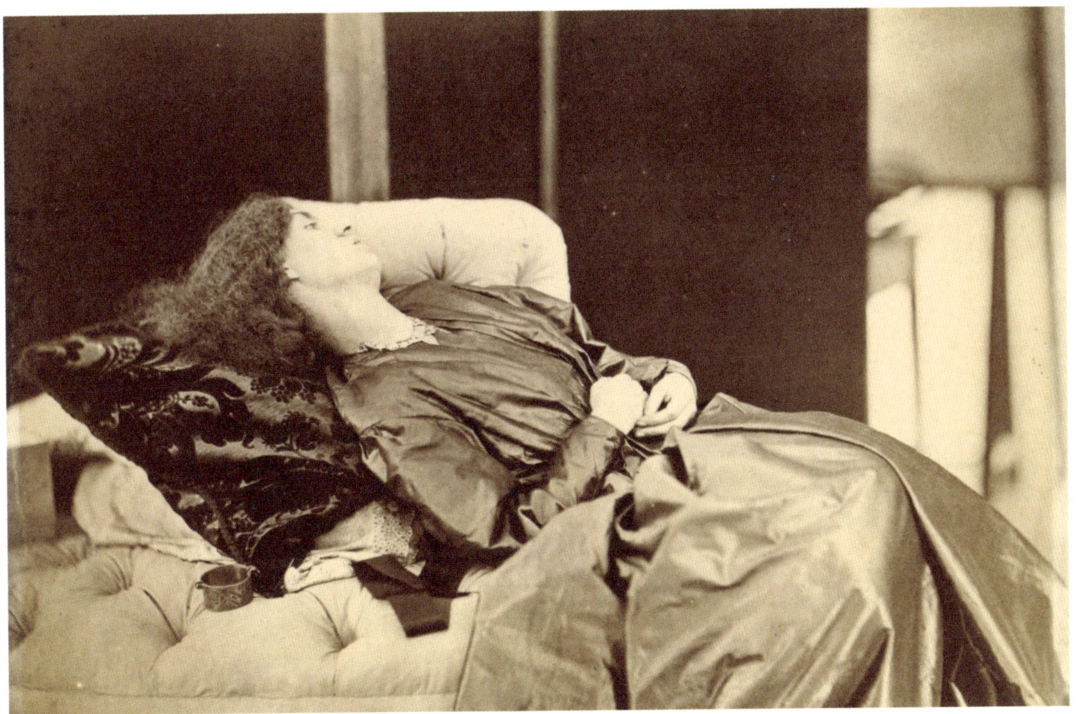

61. John Robert Parsons (*c.* 1826–1909)
Jane Morris, posed by Rossetti, 1865
Albumen print
16.5 × 19.7 cm (6½ × 7⅞ in.)
Victoria and Albert Museum, London
(V&A 1744-1939)

62. John Robert Parsons (*c.* 1826–1909)
Jane Morris, posed by Rossetti, 1865
Modern gelatin silver print
25.2 × 20.5 cm (10 × 8⅛ in.)
Victoria and Albert Museum, London
(V&A 825-1942)

As studio aides, the photographs document a range of poses, from standing or seated to supine, which would be useful in future paintings. But they also emphasize Jane's natural grace, her brooding intensity and long-fingered, expressive hands. They are as much a testament to Rossetti's growing infatuation with Jane as a practical substitute for her presence in his studio, and they allow us to see her through his eyes.

63. John Robert Parsons (*c.* 1826–1909)
Jane Morris, posed by Rossetti, 1865
Albumen print
16.2 × 14.7 cm (6½ × 5⅞ in.)
Victoria and Albert Museum, London
(V&A 1748-1939)

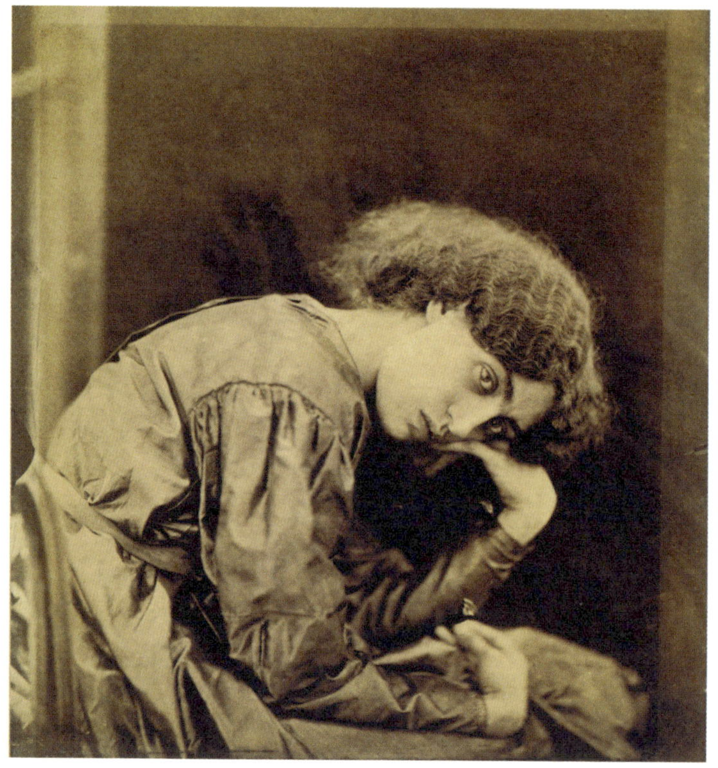

64. *Reverie*, 1868
Coloured chalk on paper
86 × 72 cm (33⅞ × 28⅜ in.)
Inscribed, upper left (on scroll), with monogram and date
Ashmolean Museum, Oxford
(WA1939.9)

Rather than as templates for his paintings, Rossetti used Parsons's photographs as a departure point for his imaginative idealization. In *Reverie* (opposite), he relaxed Jane's coiled posture, clawed fingers and woeful expression into a gentle evocation of wistful reflection. Rossetti hung it over the mantelpiece in Tudor House; the drawing was one of his favourite depictions of her. Although the photographs served as reference material, as well as a tribute to Jane, Rossetti always preferred to have her sit for him.

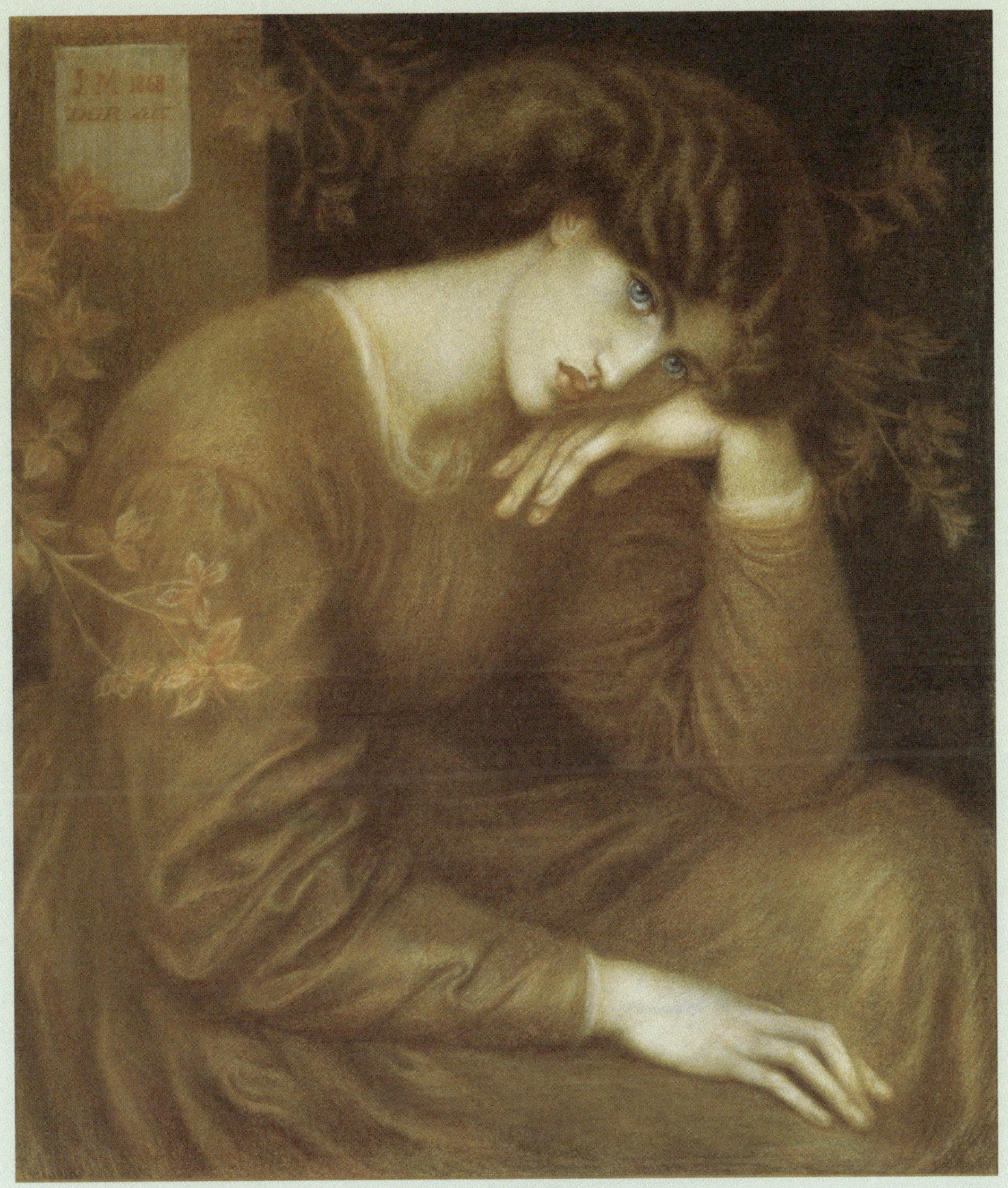

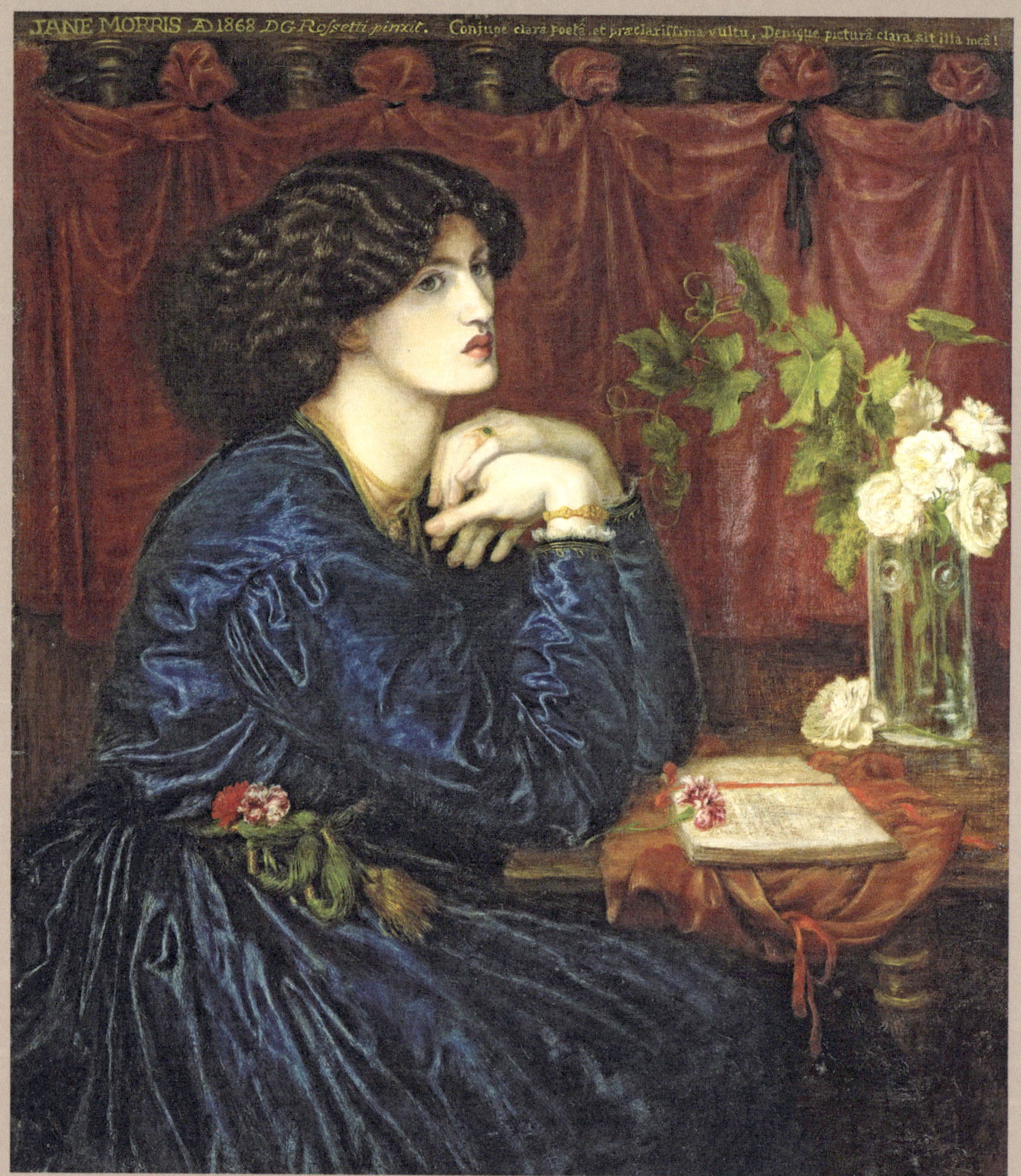
JANE MORRIS AD 1868 DG Rossetti pinxit. Conjuge clara poetâ, et præclarissima vultu, Denique picturâ clara sit illa meâ!

65. *Mrs William Morris, The Blue Silk Dress*, 1868
Oil on canvas
110.5 × 88.9 cm ($43^{5}/_{8}$ × 35 in.)
Inscribed, at top of canvas: *Jane Morris AD 1868 D G Rossetti, pinxit. Conjuge clara poetâ et praeclasrissima, vultu, Denique picturâ clara sit illa meâ*
Kelmscott Manor, Oxfordshire

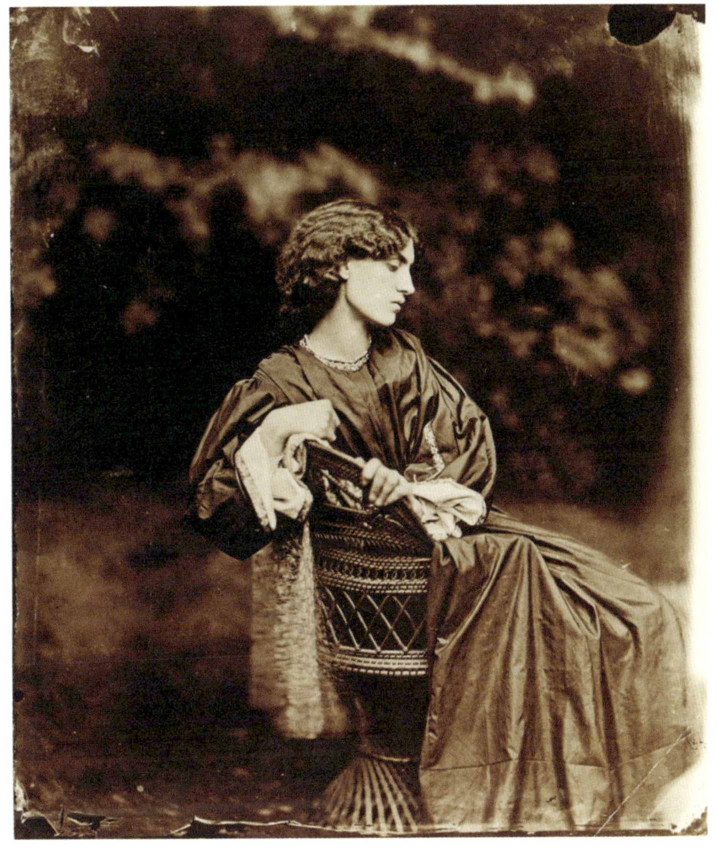

66. John Robert Parsons (*c.* 1826–1909)
Jane Morris, posed by Rossetti, 1865
Albumen print from wet collodion-on-glass negative
21.3 × 16.6 cm ($8^{1}/_{2}$ × $6^{5}/_{8}$ in.)
Victoria and Albert Museum, London (V&A 1738-1939)

Jane made this brilliant blue dress from a pattern she had used before; Rossetti asked her to wear it prior to the sittings to soften the silk. Morris commissioned the portrait, and the position of his wife's hands gives prominence to her wedding ring. But in the Latin inscription at the top, Rossetti asserts his prerogative as the painter: *Famous for her poet-husband, and famous for her face, may my picture add to her fame!*

The 'gold chain' that gives this exquisite unfinished chalk portrait (opposite) its title was Jane's own. She wore the long, flexible chain – crafted from small, mesh links – doubled or tripled, often with her wedding ring dangling among other charms (right). Here, in an intimate yet enigmatic likeness, the ring is nowhere to be seen; her bare hands rest on a low wall near clinging tendrils of ivy, a symbol of marital fidelity.

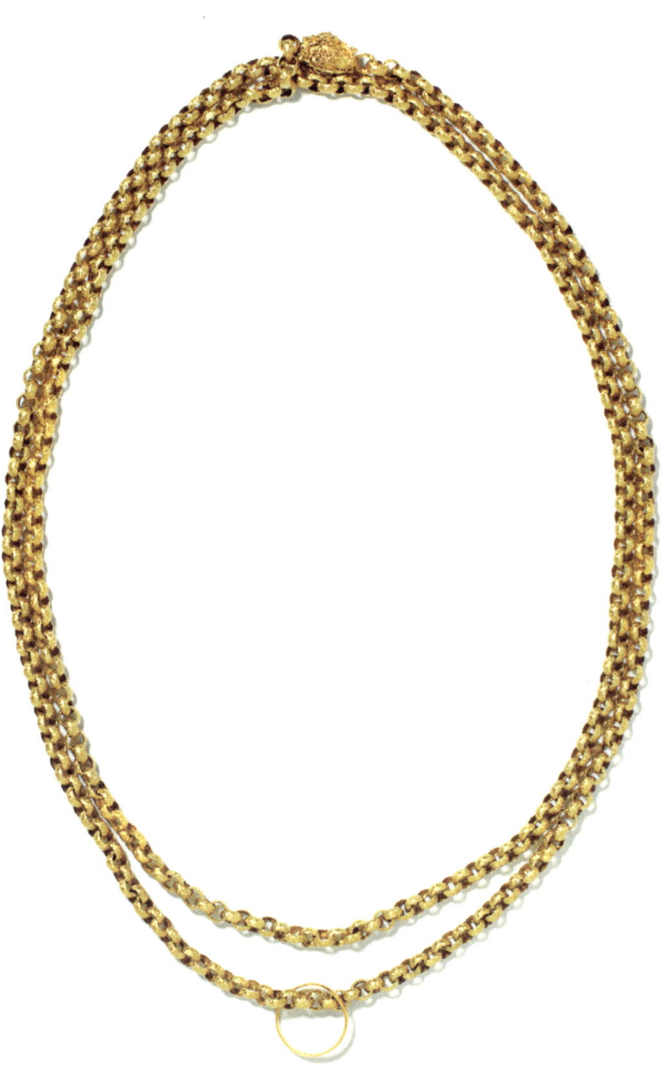

67. Jane Morris's wedding ring and gold chain, 1858, by an unknown maker
22 carat gold
Chain: Diameter 1.2 cm (½ in.); length 64 cm (25¼ in.)
Ring: Diameter 1.9 cm (¾ in.); depth 3 mm (⅛ in.)
On ring: London hallmark for 1858; maker's mark 'JO'
Victoria and Albert Museum, London (V&A M.37-1939, M.37A-1939)

68. *Aurea Catena* (*Portrait of Mrs Morris*), 1868
Graphite and coloured chalk on blue wove paper, faded to greenish grey
76.8 × 62.6 cm (30¼ × 24⅝ in.)
Fogg Museum, Boston (1943.744)

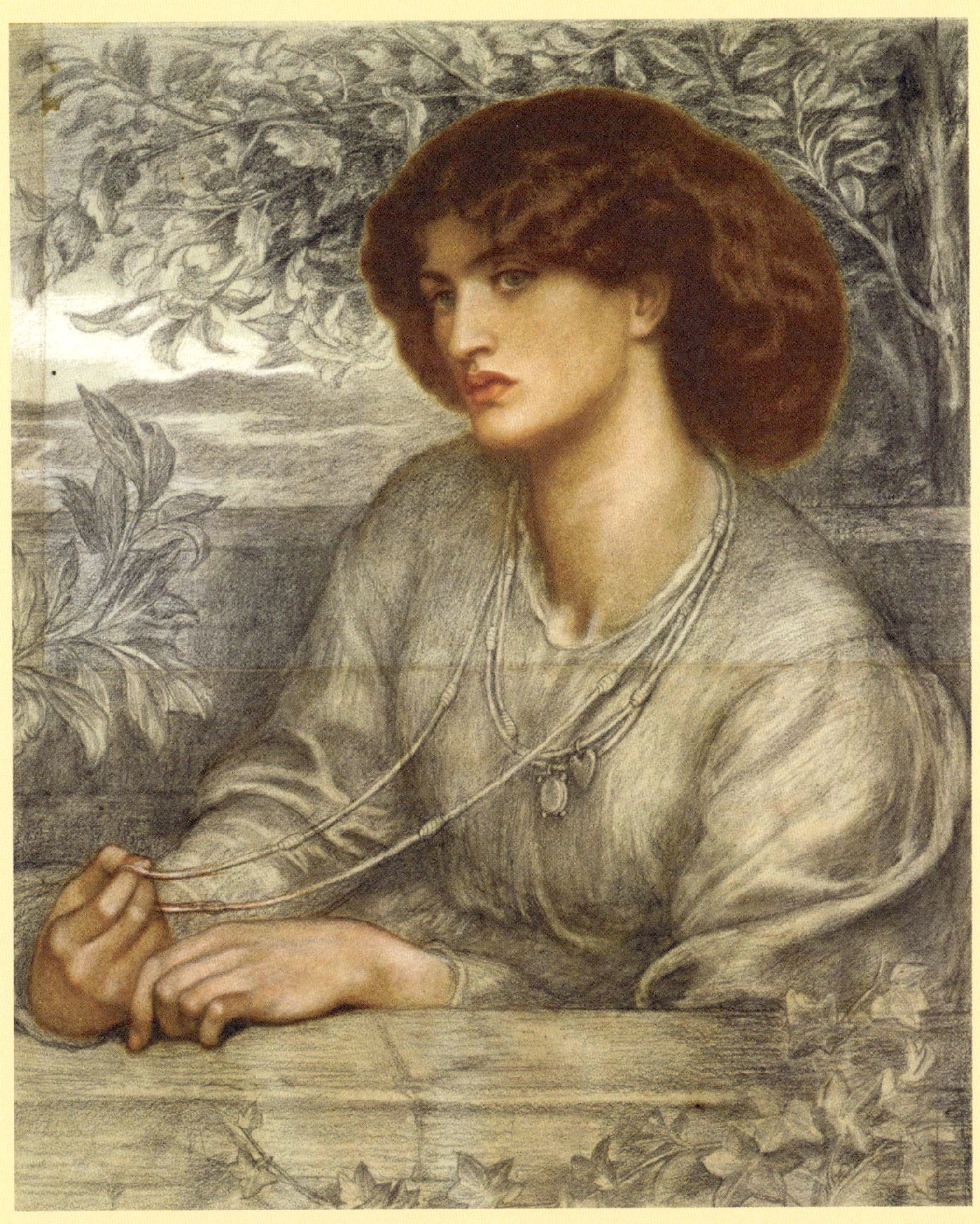

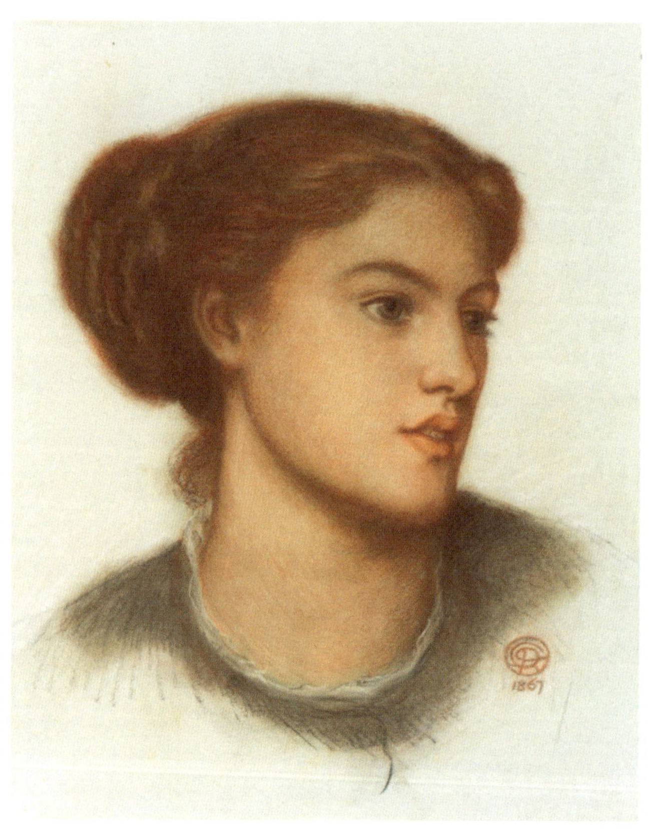

69. *Portrait of a Lady*, 1867
Red and black chalk on blue-grey paper
46.4 × 36.8 cm (18⅜ × 14½ in.)
Victoria and Albert Museum, London
(V&A CAI.5)

Rossetti blurred the line between idealized beauty and naturalistic portraiture in his deft depictions of women in coloured chalks on lightly tinted paper. This unnamed sitter may be Ellen Smith, a laundress whom he had been drawing since 1863. But the arched eyebrows and bowed upper lip recall Alexa Wilding's features; according to a photograph from this time (47), Alexa dressed her hair in a similar fashion.

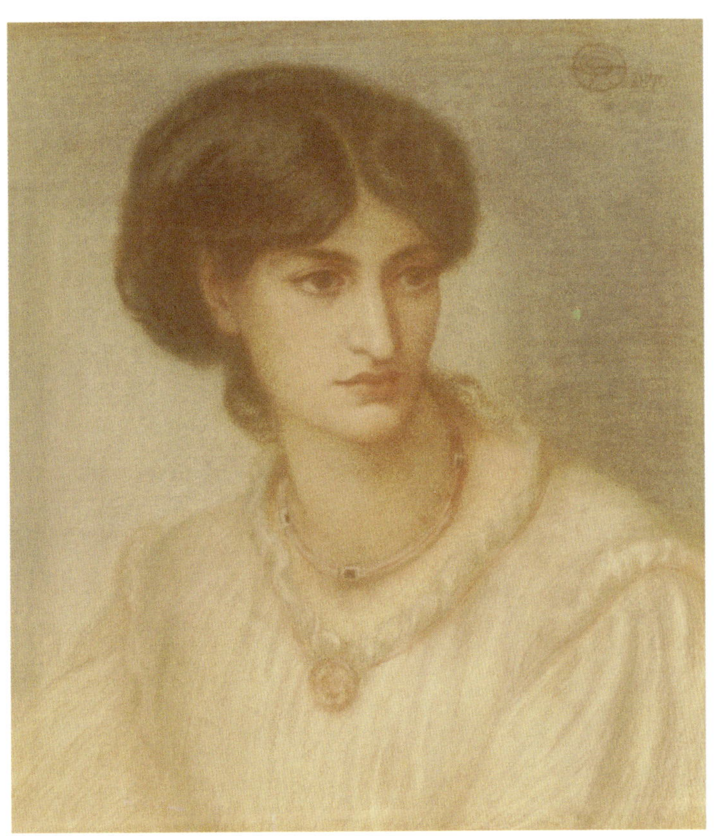

70. *Aglaia Ionides*, 1870
Pastel
54 × 45.7 cm (21¼ × 18 in.)
Inscribed, upper right,
with monogram and date
Victoria and Albert Museum, London
(V&A CAI.1150)

As a daughter of the Council-General for Greece, Aglaia Ionides led a cultured life in London. Her parents were art patrons and regularly entertained at their Holland Park home, where she met George du Maurier, George Frederic Watts and James McNeill Whistler, as well as Rossetti. Known as one of the 'Three Graces', along with her cousins Marie Spartali and Maria Zambaco (74), Aglaia married Theodore John Coronio in 1855.

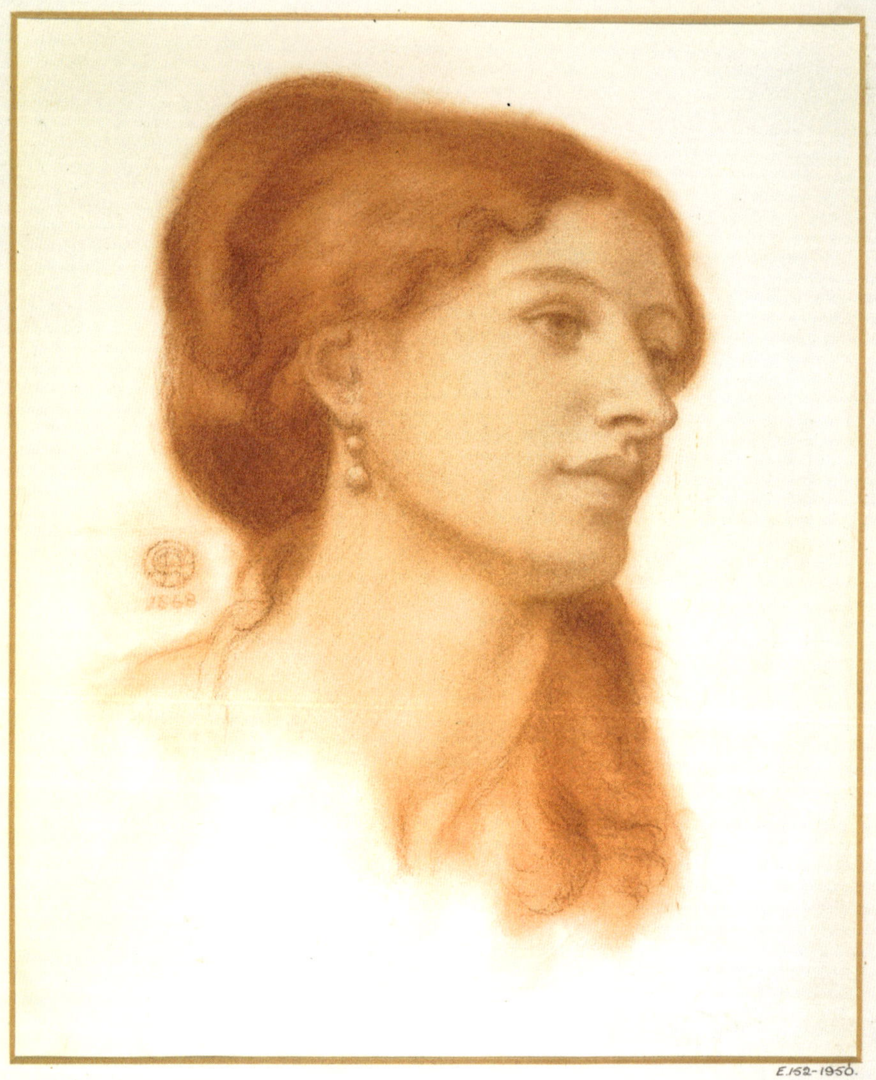

GABRIEL CHARLES DANTE ROSSETTI

1828-1882

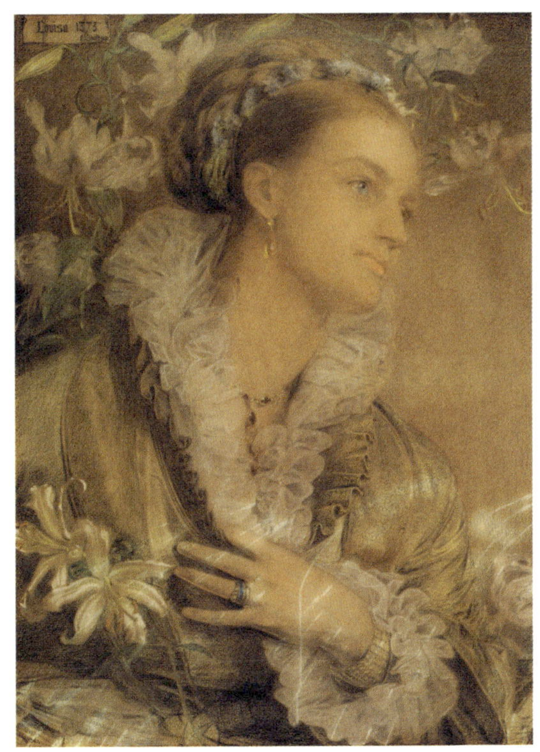

71. *Louisa, wife of Murray Marks*, 1868
Red chalk on paper
35.6 × 24.8 cm (14 × 9¾ in.)
Inscribed, left, with monogram and date
Victoria and Albert Museum, London
(V&A E.152-1950)

72. Frederick Sandys (1829–1904)
Louisa, 1873
Coloured chalks
76.8 × 54.6 cm (30¼ × 21½ in.)
Victoria and Albert Museum, London
(V&A P.41-1939)

This tender chalk study (opposite) depicts Louisa Marks, the wife of one of Rossetti's most supportive friends. Murray Marks dealt in art and antiques; as well as selling the artist's works, he helped Rossetti build his collection. Made for Marks, the drawing stayed in the family for two generations. Another portrait of Louisa Marks in the same pose (above), made by Frederick Sandys five years later, echoes Rossetti's decision to emphasize her long neck and abundant hair.

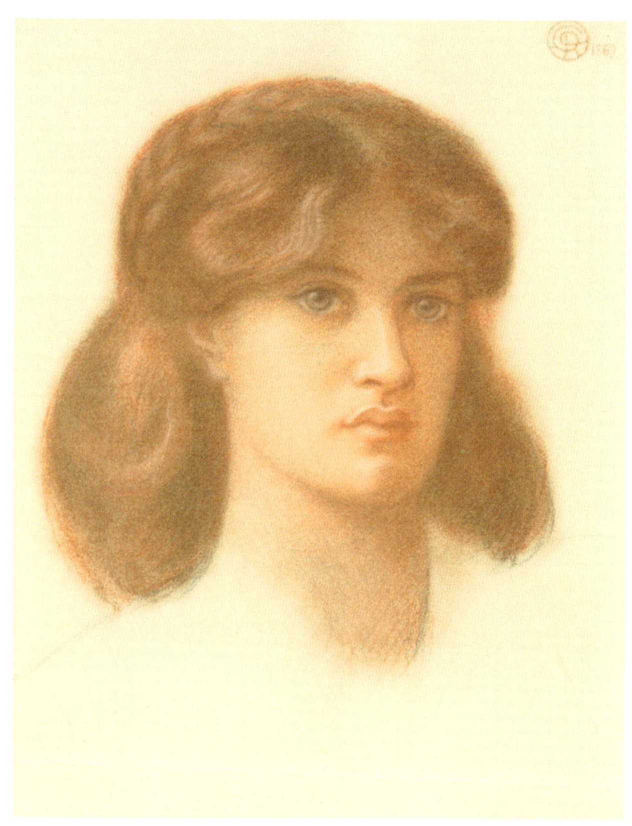

73. *Portrait of a woman, with head facing to front, and long braided hair,* 1869
Red chalk and pencil on slightly tinted paper
49 × 36.7 cm (19⅜ × 14½ in.)
Inscribed, upper right, with monogram and date
Victoria and Albert Museum, London (V&A E.327-1990)

William H. Hardinge likened a visit to Rossetti's studio in 1878 to encountering people 'whom I knew by repute and recognized at once'. The images of women were of the 'well-known Rossetti type', a designation so familiar that it required no explanation when Hardinge published his article in 1890.[47] This red-chalk study of an unidentified sitter – likely an amalgam of Rossetti's favourite models – illustrates the type: melancholic gaze, full lips, columnar neck and abundant hair.

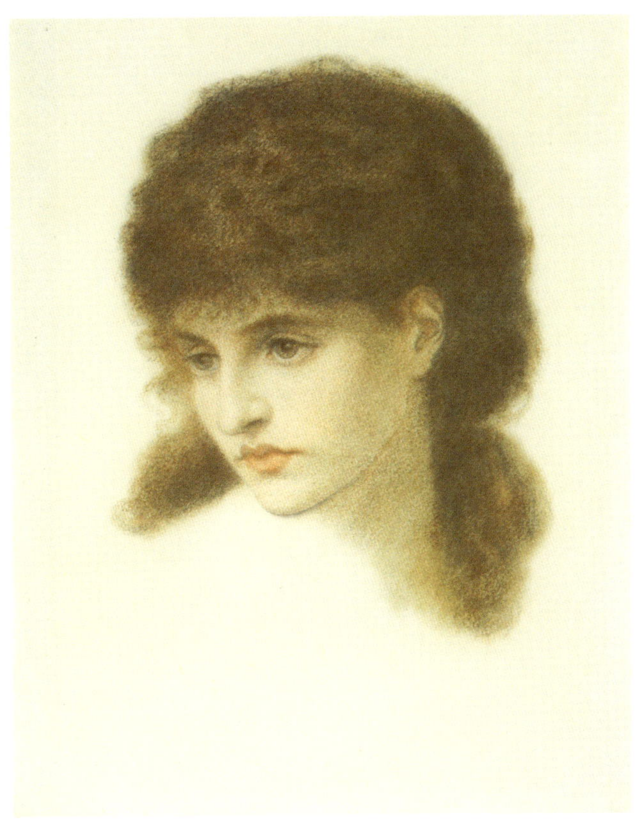

74. *Maria Zambaco*, *c.* 1869
Coloured chalks on pale-green paper
51.6 × 38.9 cm (20⅜ × 15⅜ in.)
Victoria and Albert Museum, London
(V&A CAI.1149)

An artist in her own right, Maria Zambaco was a constant presence in Edward Burne-Jones's studio during the late 1860s. His infatuation with her led to a tempestuous – and ultimately humiliating – affair. Rossetti drew Maria several times in 1869 and 1870 and came to admire her during the sittings. In a letter to Jane, Rossetti described her as 'extremely beautiful' and, viewing her circumstances through a romantic lens, claimed that Maria's beauty was enhanced by all her 'love and trouble'.[48]

In *La Vita Nuova*, an ailing Dante dreams of Beatrice's death. Rossetti first painted the theme in watercolour in 1856. This oil version similarly features Beatrice on her death bier with two attendants. Dante watches in sorrow as Love bestows a farewell kiss. Rossetti painted Jane Morris as Beatrice, giving her golden-red hair. Perhaps he wanted to illuminate Jane's face under the canopy's shadow, or he may have desired to fuse her image with that of his first model for Beatrice, Elizabeth Siddal.

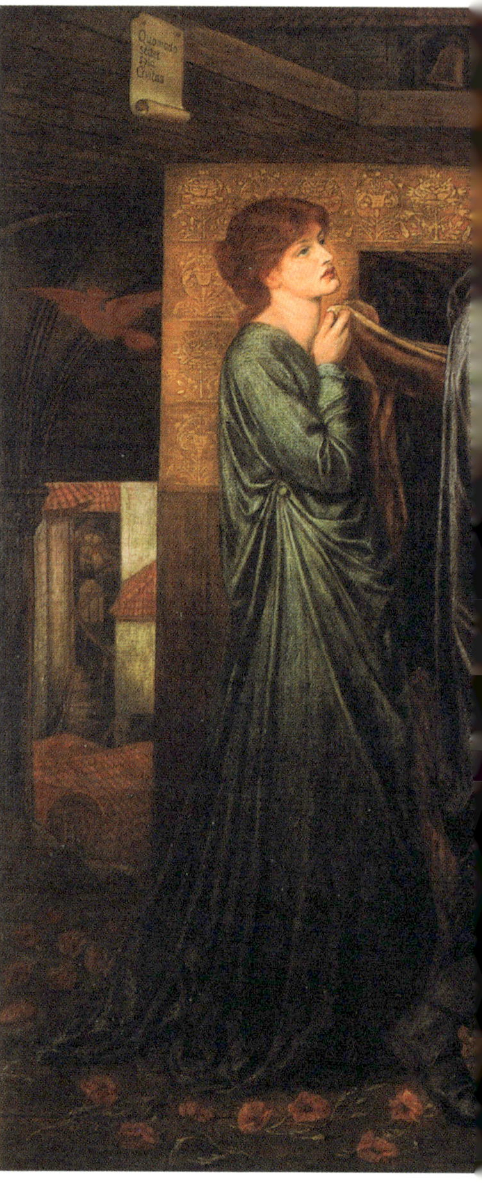

75. *Dante's Dream at the Time of the Death of Beatrice*, 1871
Oil on canvas
216 × 312.4 cm (85⅛ × 123 in.)
Walker Art Gallery, Liverpool
(WAG 3091)

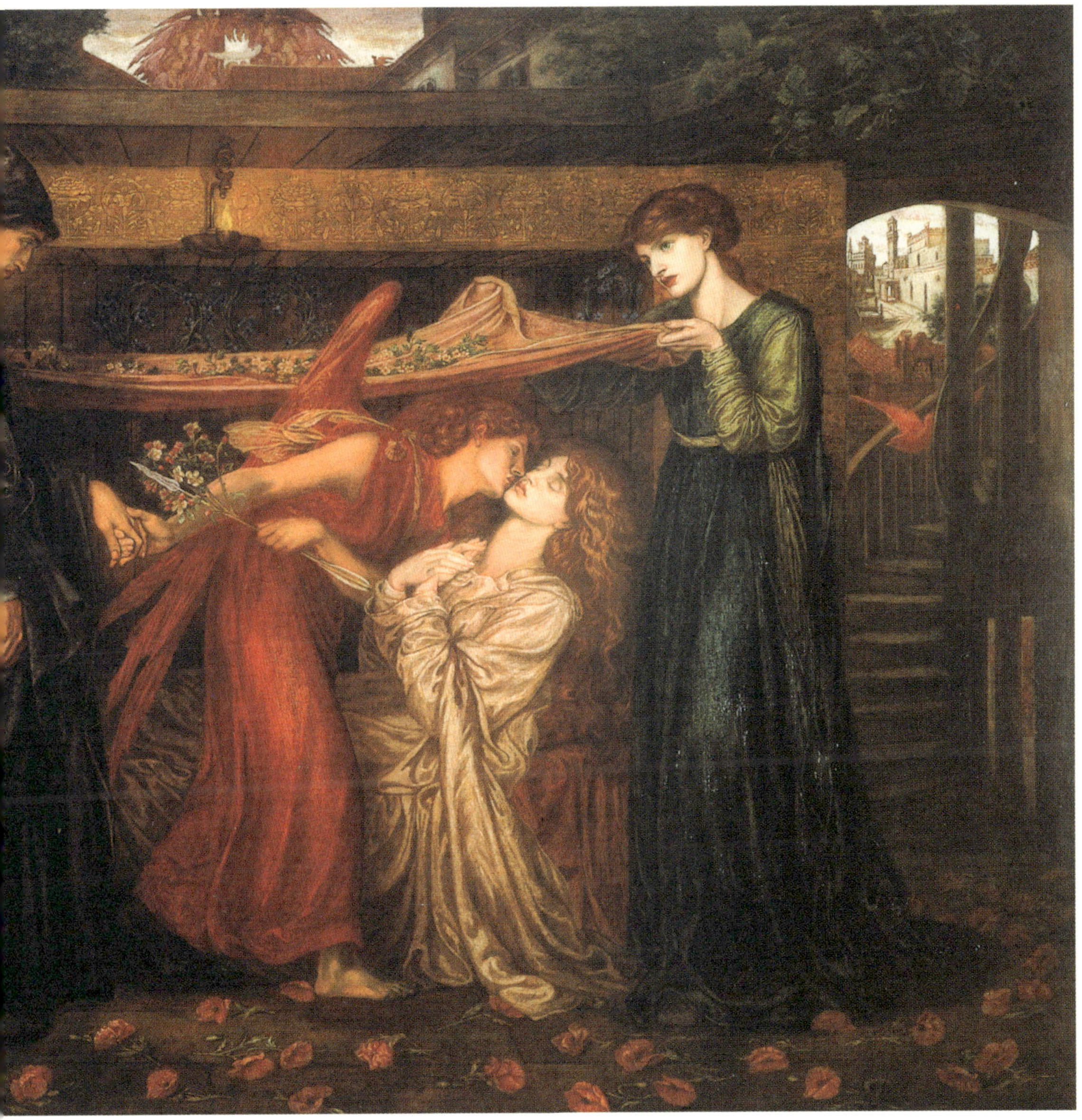

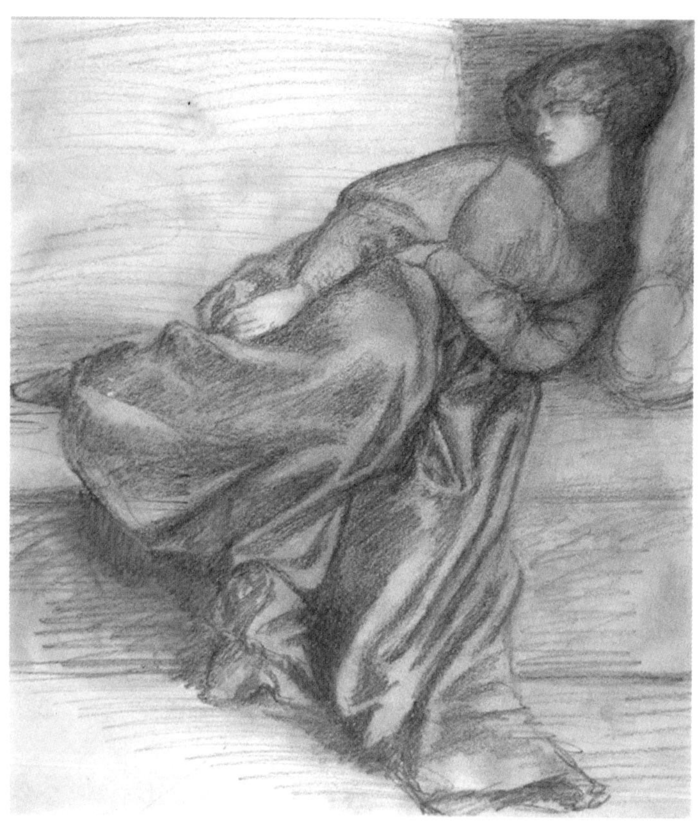

76. *Jane Morris*, 1870
Pencil on paper
36.8 × 30.5 cm (14½ × 12⅛ in.)
Mark Samuels Lasner Collection, University of Delaware Library, Museums and Press

Rossetti sketched Jane reclining at least a dozen times. Perhaps he believed that a state of repose best displayed her languorous grace and self-contained dignity, but Jane, suffering from back pain and other chronic complaints, found the position more comfortable than sitting. During a visit to the Morrises' home in 1869, Henry James recalled that she rested on a sofa in the corner: a 'dark silent medieval woman with her medieval toothache'.[49]

'*Je n'en reviens-pas* – she haunts me still. A figure cut out of a missal – out of one of Rossetti's or Hunt's pictures – to say this gives but a faint idea of her, because when such an image puts on flesh and blood, it is an apparition of fearful and wonderful intensity. It's hard to say [whether] she's a grand synthesis of all the pre-Raphaelite pictures ever made – or they a "keen analysis" of her – whether she's an original or a copy. In either case she is a wonder. Imagine a tall lean woman in a long dress of some dead purple stuff, guiltless of hoops (or of anything else, I should say) with a mass of crisp black hair heaped into great wavy projections on each of her temples, a thin pale face. A pair of strange, sad, deep, dark Swinburne eyes, with great thick black oblique brows, joined in the middle and tucking themselves under her hair, a mouth like "Oriana" in our illustrated Tennyson, a long neck, without any collar, and in lieu thereof of some dozen strings of outlandish beads – in fine Complete. On the wall was a large nearly full-length portrait of her by Rossetti, so strange and unreal that if you hadn't seen her, you'd pronounce it a distempered vision, but in fact an extremely good likeness.'

Henry James, letter to Alice James (12 March 1869)

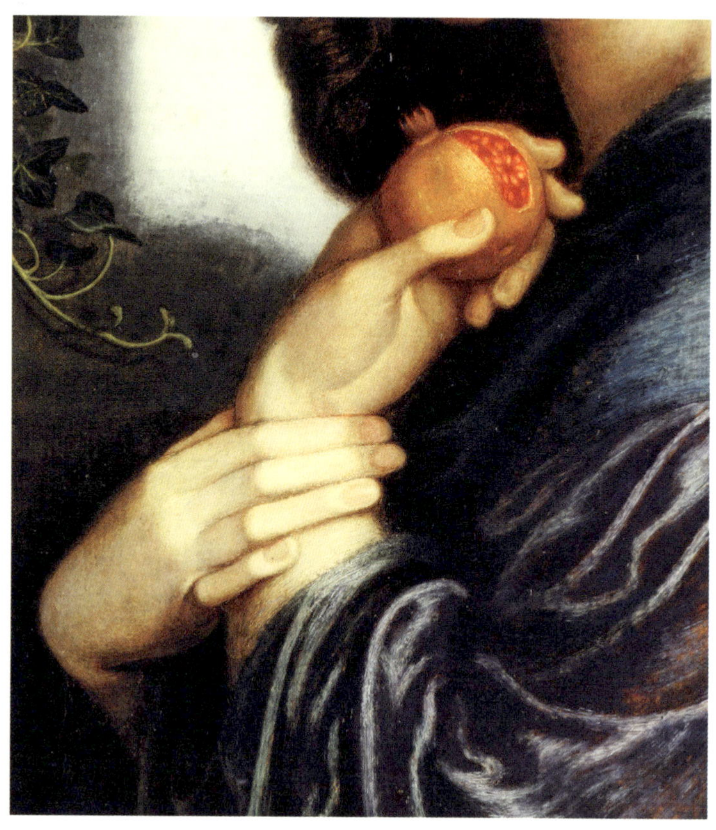

77. *Proserpine*, 1874
Oil on canvas
125.1 × 61 cm (49³/₈ × 24¹/₈ in.)
Inscribed, lower left, on scroll: *DANTE GABRIELE ROSSETTI RITRASSE NEL CAPODANNO DEL 1874*
Tate Gallery, London
(N05064)

On Morris's suggestion, Rossetti painted Proserpine, Hades' unfortunate bride, who was forced to reside in the underworld for six months of every year. Of eight versions (this is the seventh), all featuring Jane, three survive in a complete state. With long, nervous fingers, Proserpine clutches a pomegranate; eating its seeds sealed her fate. The curling ivy represents a persistent memory, and although the smoking lamp sheds no light, the radiance behind her recalls the world she knew.

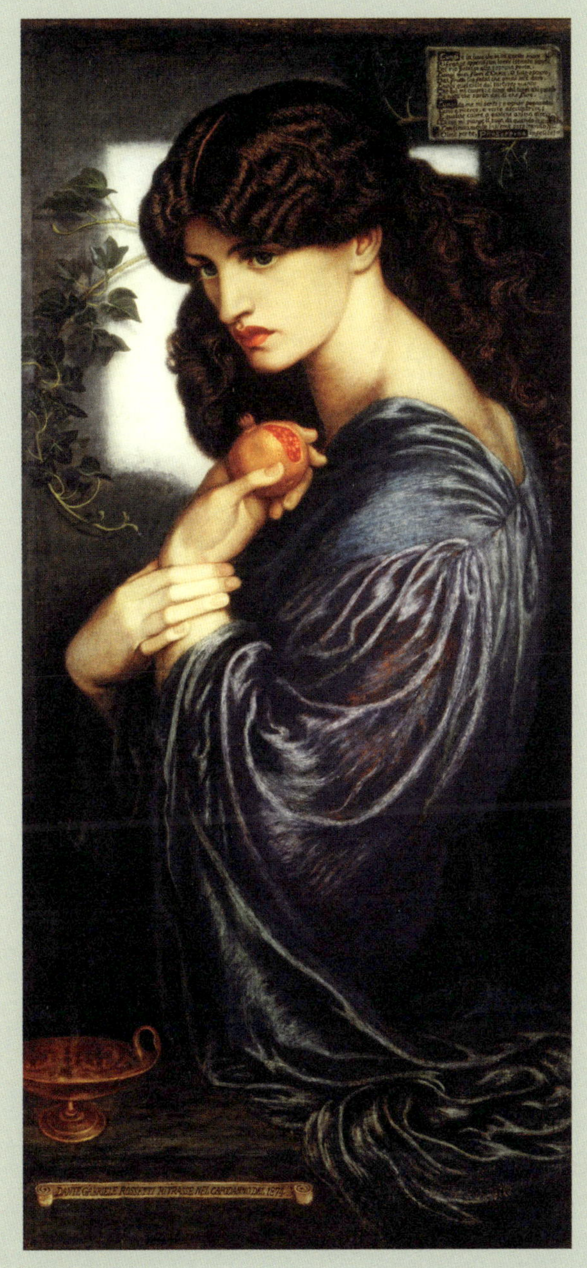

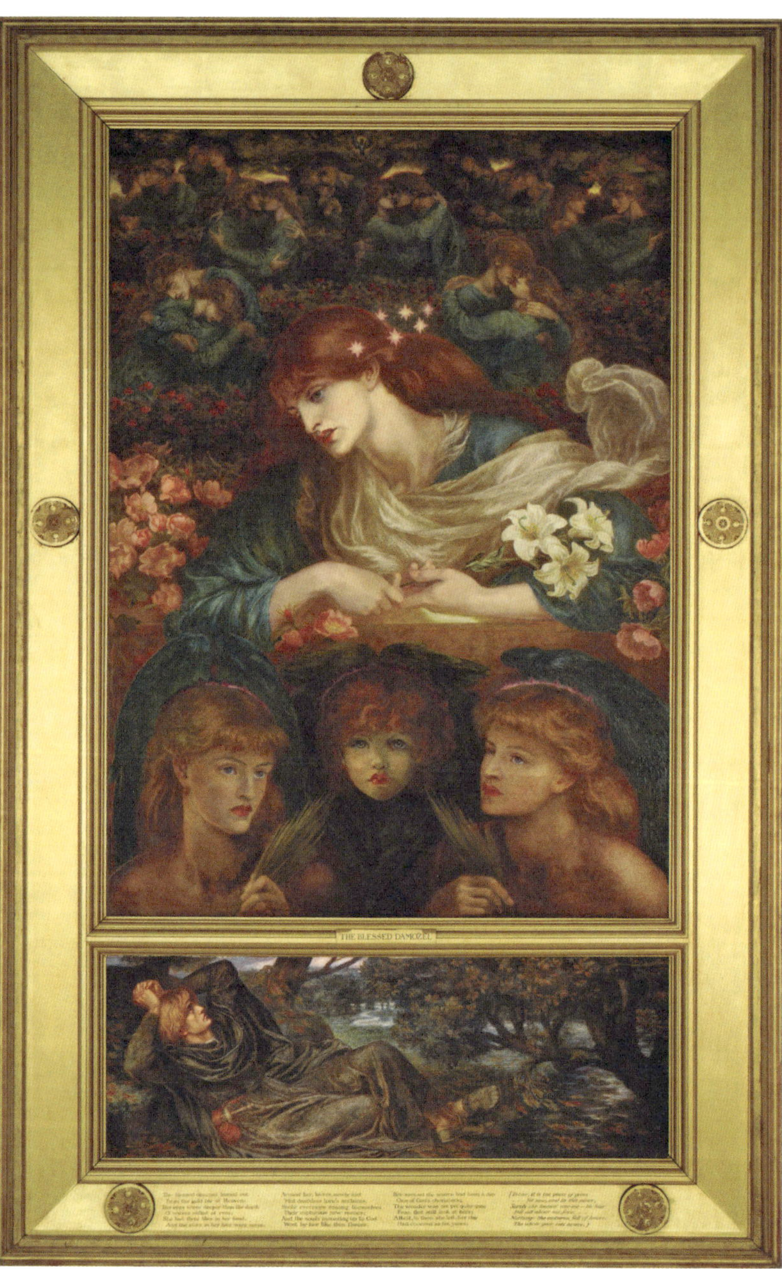
THE BLESSED DAMOZEL

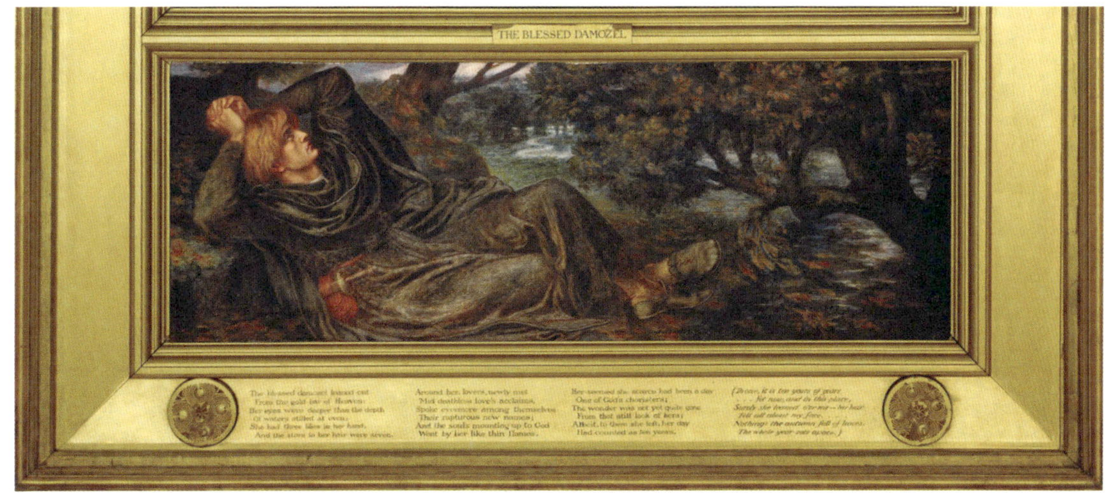

And still she bow'd herself and stoop'd
   Out of the circling charm;
Until her bosom must have made
   The bar she lean'd on warm,
And the lilies lay as if asleep
   Along her bended arm

'The Blessed Damozel' (1850), ll. 43–8

78. *The Blessed Damozel*, 1875–8
Oil on canvas
Upper portion: 136.8 × 96.5 cm (53⅞ × 38 in.)
Predella: 35.2 × 96.2 cm (13⅞ × 37⅞ in.)
Framed: 212.1 × 133 cm (83½ × 52⅜ in.)
Fogg Museum, Boston
(1943.202)

Although Rossetti wrote the first version of 'The Blessed Damozel' in 1847, he did not explore its pictorial potential until his late career. The visual details of the painting – three lilies, seven stars, hair 'like ripe corn' – follow closely the descriptive language of the poem. Of all his dual works of art, here Rossetti comes closest to an illustration, as the Damozel leans over 'the gold bar of Heaven' to exchange a glance with her earthbound lover.

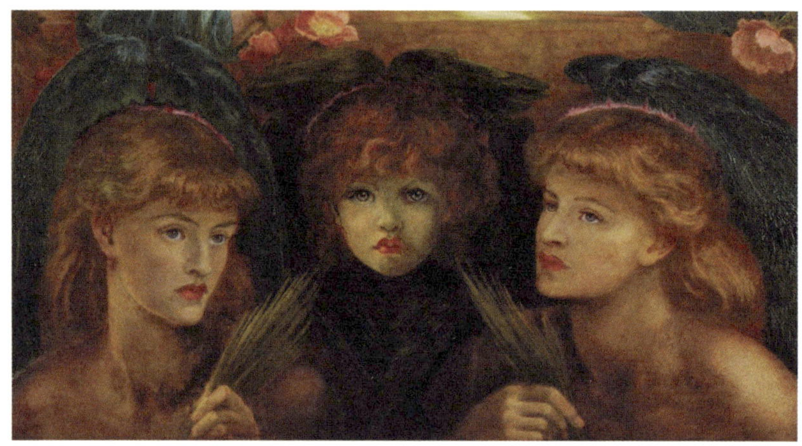

79. *The Blessed Damozel*, 1875
Black and red chalk on
pale-green paper
78.7 × 71.1 cm (31 × 28 in.)
Victoria and Albert Museum, London
(V&A E.262-1946)

This exquisite chalk study for a subsidiary figure in *The Blessed Damozel* reveals how Rossetti used preparatory sketching to establish mood and aesthetic, rather than to build his composition. Neither this exact posture nor the close likeness to Alexa Wilding appears in the finished painting. In fact, as a portrait, the sketch is far more lyrical and less mannered than the final depiction. Alexa also sat for the face and figure of the Damozel.

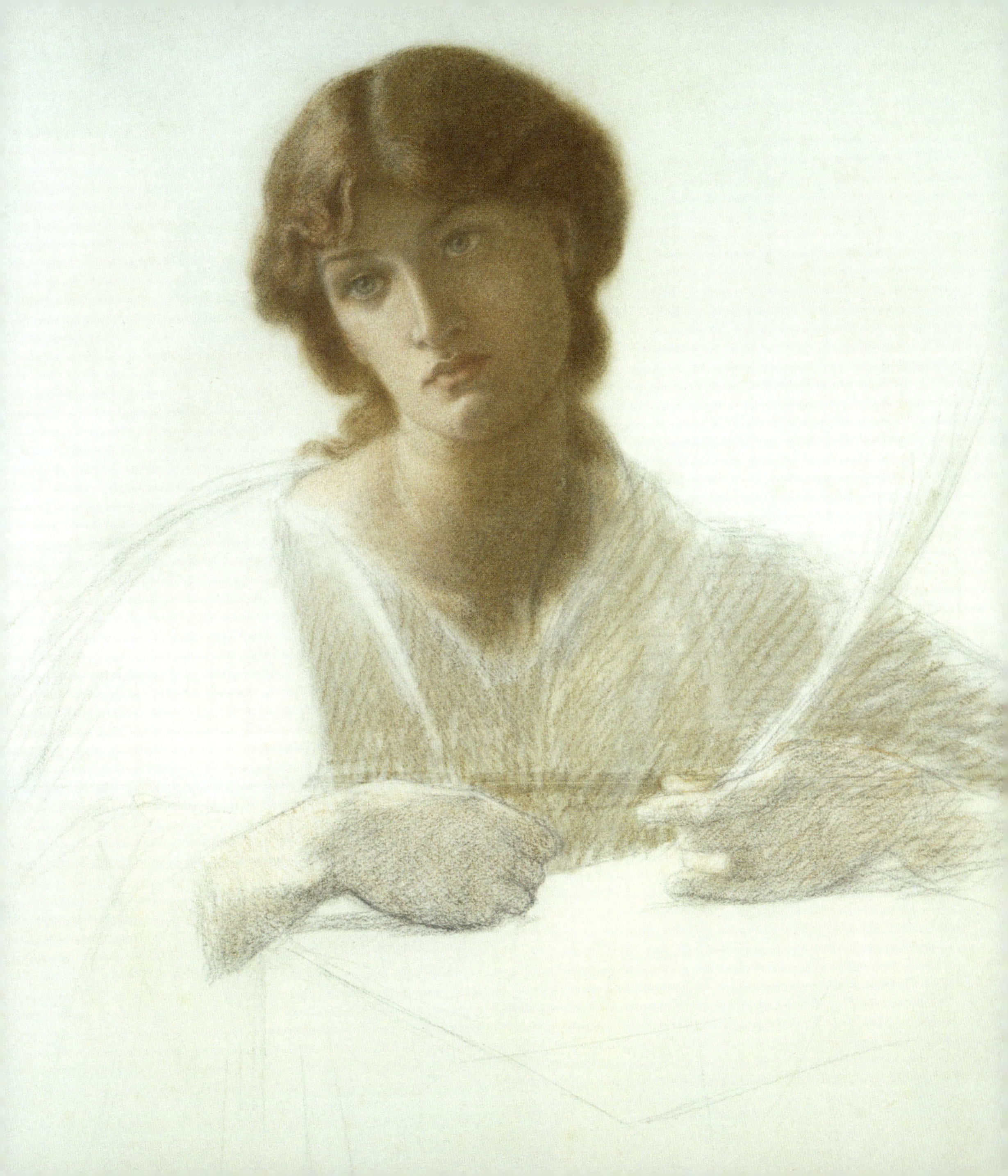

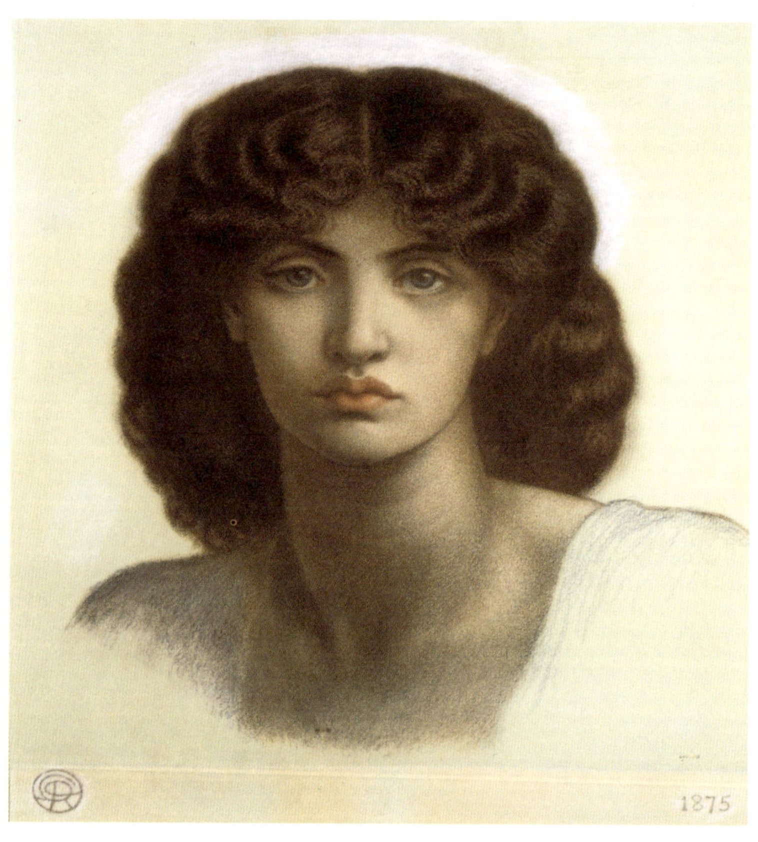

80. *Study of Jane Morris for Astarte Syriaca*, 1875
Coloured chalks
54.6 × 44.7 cm (21½ × 17⅝ in.)
Inscribed, lower right, with monogram and date
Victoria and Albert Museum, London
(V&A 490-1883)

This chalk portrait of Jane was intended as a study for *Astarte Syriaca* (opposite), Rossetti's monumental painting of the Mesopotamian goddess, Astarte. He exaggerated her natural features – the distinct arc of her brows, the sculpted mould of her lips, her aureole of rippled hair – to create his own icon of beauty. The sitting took place in November 1875, when Jane visited Aldwick Lodge in Bognor Regis, Sussex, where Rossetti planned to spend the winter.

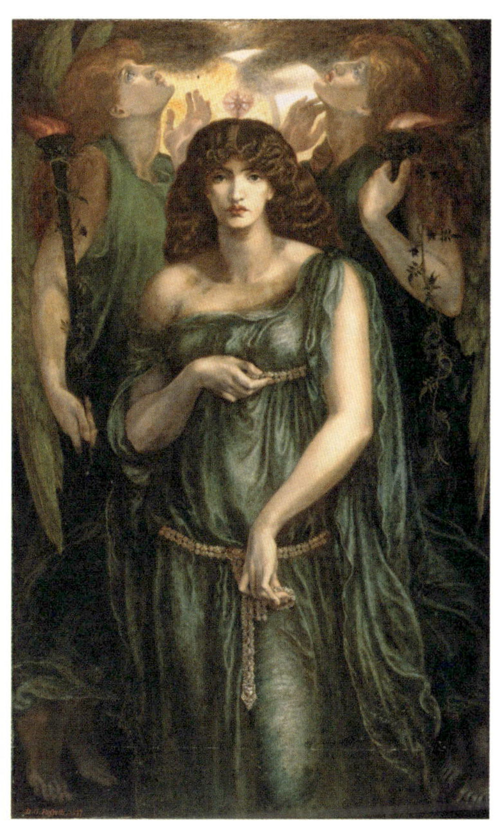

81. *Astarte Syriaca*, 1876–7
Oil on canvas
185 × 109 cm (72⅞ × 43 in.)
Manchester Art Gallery
(1891.5)

Jane brought her younger daughter May with her when she returned to Bognor Regis in March 1876 for her final sittings. As the picture progressed, Rossetti further stylized her likeness into the 'Amulet, talisman and oracle' of 'Love's all-penetrative spell', which he described in the sonnet he wrote for the painting. May posed for the torch-bearing attendant on the left, and Rossetti probably used a professional model, rather than Jane, for the robust body of the goddess.

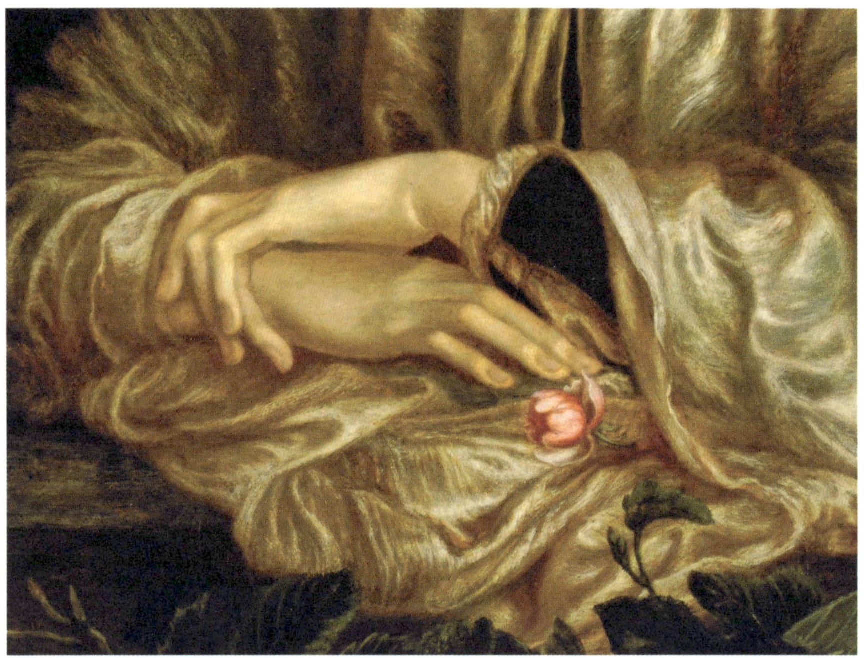

82. *La Donna della Finestra*, 1879
Oil on canvas
100.7 × 74 cm (39⁵⁄₈ × 29¹⁄₈ in.)
Fogg Museum, Boston
(1943.200)

Rossetti derived his belief in the consoling power of beauty from a passage in *La Vita Nuova*. After Beatrice's death, Dante wanders the streets until he catches a glimpse of a young woman at a window, gazing kindly back at him. Basing his depiction on studies made earlier in the decade, Rossetti portrayed his own ideal of comeliness and compassion through the likeness of Jane Morris. Her position at a window ledge recalls that of Smeralda Bandinelli in the Botticelli portrait that Rossetti owned from 1867 to 1880 (fig. 10).

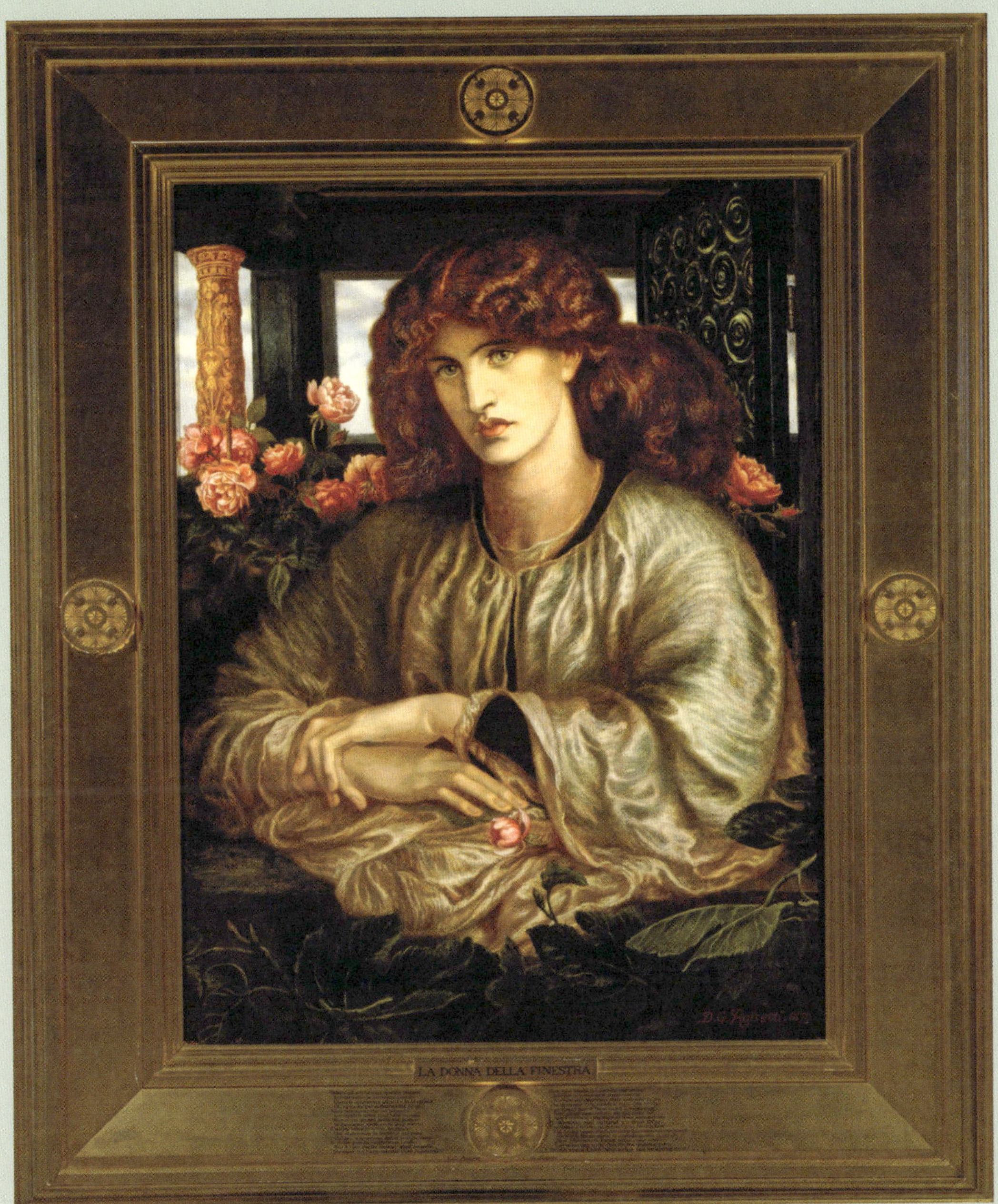
LA DONNA DELLA FINESTRA

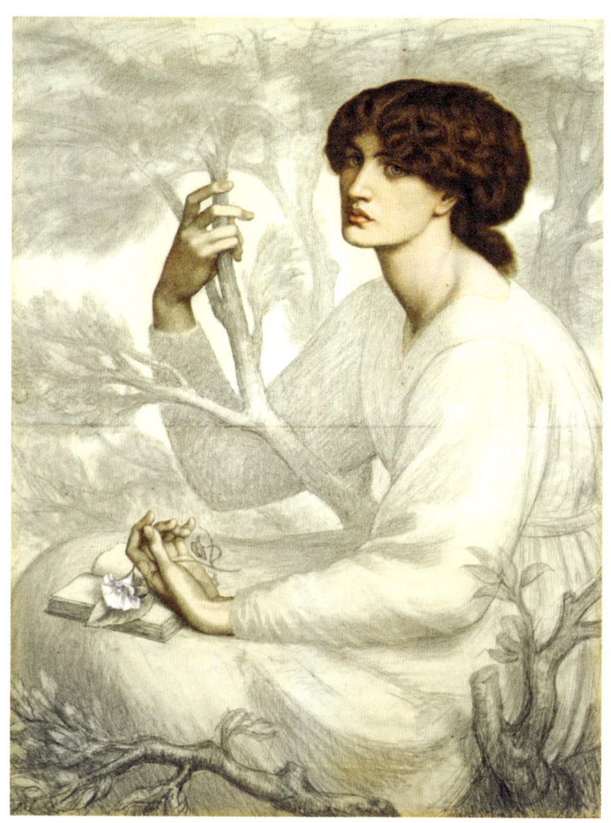

83. *Day Dream*, 1878
Coloured chalks and black chalk
104.8 × 76.8 cm (41⅜ × 30¼ in.)
Ashmolean Museum, Oxford
(WA1939.6)

Rossetti first described an idea to Ford Madox Brown in 1872: a portrait of Jane Morris, seated in a tree with a book in her lap. Seeing this partially finished drawing in 1879 likely prompted the collector Constantine Alexander Ionides to commission what would be Rossetti's last finished painting. At the time, Rossetti called it *Vanna Primavera*, referring to the passage in *La Vita Nuova* in which Beatrice follows Giovanna (Vanna), just as summer follows spring.

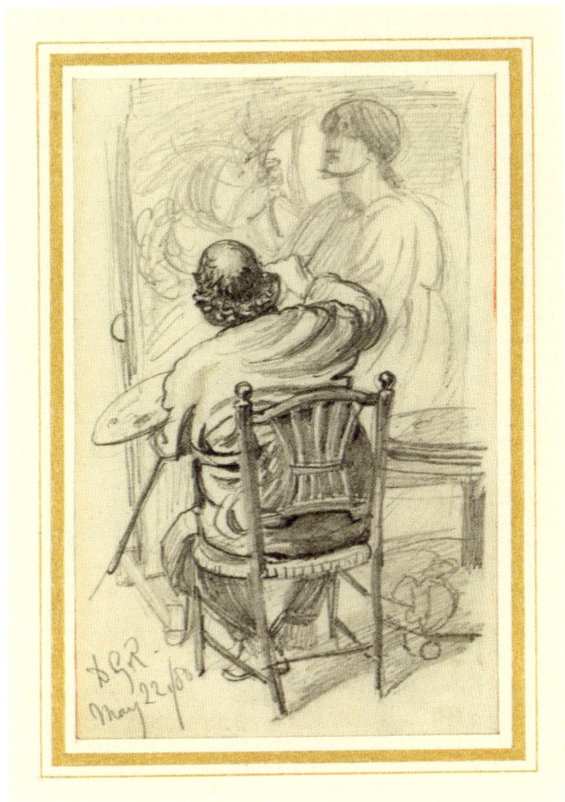

84. Frederic Shields (1833–1911)
Rossetti working on 'The Day Dream', 1880
Pen and ink
18 × 11.3 cm (7⅛ × 4½ in.)
Inscribed, lower left: *DGR/May 22/80*
Ashmolean Museum, Oxford
(WA1978.65)

After visiting his brother on 9 August 1880, William Rossetti remarked in his diary that Jane's likeness in *Vanna Primavera* had been improved: 'more youthful & sweet in expression'. Describing his brother's latest work as 'certainly one of his finest pictures', William noted, as well, that the 'title is now replaced by a better one – *The Day-dream*'.[50] Frederic Shields was also there that night; a few months earlier, he had sketched Rossetti happily engaged in his painting.

The thronged boughs of the shadowy sycamore
  Still fledge young leaflets half the summer through;
  From when the robin 'gainst the unhidden blue
Perched dark, till now, deep in the leafy core.
The embowered throstle's urgent wood-notes soar
  Through summer silence. Still the leaves come new;
  Yet never rosy-sheathed as those which drew
Their spiral tongues from spring-buds heretofore.
Within the branching shade of Reverie
Dreams even may spring till autumn; yet none be
  Like woman's budding day-dream spirit-fann'd.
Lo! tow'rd deep skies, not deeper than her look,
She dreams; till now on her forgotten book
  Drops the forgotten blossom from her hand

'The Day Dream' (September 1880)

85. *The Day Dream*, 1880
Oil on canvas
158.7 × 92.7 cm (62½ × 36½ in.)
Victoria and Albert Museum, London
(V&A CAI.3)

Citing the tree's beautiful foliage, Rossetti set his figure in a sycamore, and in a series of letters to Jane discussed which flower she should hold. Jane suggested snowdrops – one of her favourites – but Rossetti noted that they lacked 'the beautiful play of stem and leaf' of the convolvulus in the 1878 drawing (**83**).[51] Ultimately, he chose a honeysuckle with tattered petals for the 'forgotten blossom' in Jane's hand.

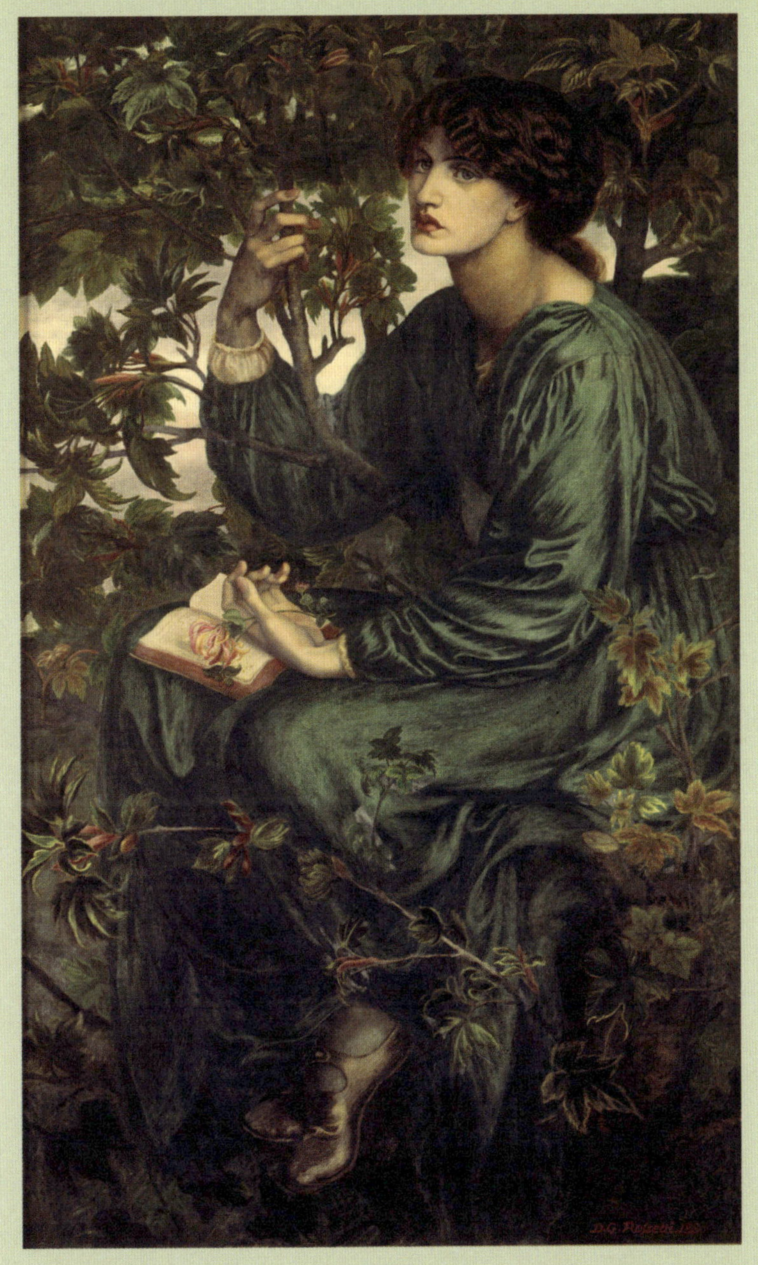

Notes

1. Dated 'Friday' (1880), Surtees 1971, p. 154
2. Written *c.* 1868–9, 'The Portrait' appeared as Sonnet IX in the 'House of Life' cycle in *Poems* (London, 1870). In the 1881 edition and subsequent publications, it appears as Sonnet X
3. Hardinge 1890, p. 2
4. Rossetti reordered his names in late adolescence to be known publicly as Dante Gabriel; his friends called him Gabriel. He dropped Charles, the name of his godfather, the geologist Charles Lyell, a friend and patron of his father
5. Doughty 1949, p. 38
6. W.M. Rossetti 1895, vol. 1, p. 135
7. John Ruskin, *Modern Painters*, vol. 1 (1843), in T. Cook and A. Wedderburn (eds), *The Works of John Ruskin, Library Edition* (London, 1903), vol. 3, p. 624, https://www.lancaster.ac.uk/the-ruskin/the-complete-works-of-ruskin (accessed 21 July 2020)
8. D.G. Rossetti 1902, pp. 29–30
9. Nearly every detail of Elizabeth Siddal's biography, from her date of birth and spelling of her surname, to her profession at the time she began modelling, has been subject to speculation. For the most current critical biography, see Marsh, *Pre-Raphaelite Sisters* (2019), pp. 22–33
10. D.G. Rossetti to Ford Madox Brown, recorded in Brown's diary (10 March 1855), W.M. Rossetti 1899, p. 3
11. D.G. Rossetti to Hall Caine (1880), W.M. Rossetti 1895, vol. 1, p. 135
12. Collinson had already left the group on the basis of religious differences, and in 1852 Woolner emigrated to Australia. By 1853 Millais had been elected to the Royal Academy as an Associate member, and Stephens had given up his aspirations to be a visual artist for art criticism. William Rossetti remained active as an arts writer and editor, while working full time as a civil servant. Hunt and Rossetti continued to pursue their own – and very different – interpretation of Pre-Raphaelite aesthetics and objectives for the duration of their careers
13. Ford Madox Brown, diary entry (6 August 1855), Surtees 1981, p. 101
14. G.B.-J. 1904, vol. 1, p. 163
15. Friends of Morris and Burne-Jones from their university days, Peter Marshall was a trained surveyor and Charles Faulkner served as the company's bookkeeper. Rossetti, Burne-Jones and Ford Madox Brown were the other founding members of The Firm. Morris invested the largest share of money, and when he reorganized the enterprise to create Morris & Co. in 1875, he bought out the other founding members, except for Burne-Jones
16. W.M. Rossetti 1895, vol. 1, p. 225
17. See Surtees 1971, vol. 1, pp. 93–4, for a selection of this correspondence
18. Annie Miller sat as the 'fallen woman' in Rossetti's initial studies for *Found*, replaced by Fanny Cornforth in a well-known version in oil (Delaware Art Museum). A great deal of rumour and embellishment surrounds Annie's life story. For the most recent and reliable biography, see Marsh 2019, pp. 64–73
19. Many details of Fanny Cornforth's biography, from her name (she was born Sarah Cox) to how she and Rossetti met, are impossible to document. For the latest account, see Marsh 2019, pp. 74–85
20. The painting is inscribed, reverse, in Rossetti's hand: *(from the Pourtalès collection)*

Portrait of Smeralda Bandinelli painted by Sandro Botticelli. The property of G. Rossetti, 16 Cheyne Walk Chelsea. It remained in Rossetti's collection until 1880, when he sold it to Constantine Alexander Ionides. The position of the figure, as well as the spatial confinement, typical of later Quattrocento Florentine portraits, influenced his self-consciously Italianate approach to portraiture through the rest of his career. See Mark Evans and Stefan Weppelmann, *Botticelli Reimagined* (London, 2016), pp. 76–80

21. Rossetti first uses the term in a note to George Pryce Boyce, observing that *Bocca Baciata* has 'taken after all rather a Venetian aspect'. D.G. Rossetti to George Pryce Boyce (5 September 1859), Surtees 1971, vol. 1, p. 69
22. Dunn 1904, p. 45
23. D.G. Rossetti to Ellen Heaton (4 July 1863), Surtees 1971, vol. 1, p. 105
24. D.G. Rossetti, 'Genius in Beauty', Jerome H. Buckley (ed.), *The Pre-Raphaelites* (Chicago, 1986), p. 106
25. D.G. Rossetti to Jane Morris (30 January 1870), Bryson and Troxell 1976, p. 33
26. Henry James to Alice James (12 March 1869), Walker and Zacharias 2006, vol. 1, p. 237
27. William Bell Scott to Alice Boyd (17 November 1868), MacCarthy 1995, p. 224
28. These would eventually be included in the cycle 'The House of Life'. Rossetti first published 16 sonnets from the cycle in the *Fortnightly Review* (1 March 1869), as 'Of Life, Love and Death: Sixteen Sonnets'. Between 1870–4 he wrote additional sonnets, a number of which were inspired by and written for Jane Morris, and further augmented the collection for the 1881 version. As the number and order of sonnets was still in flux at the time of his death, there is no definitive version of the cycle
29. 'The Fleshly School of Poetry and Other Phenomena of the Day' by Robert Buchanan, writing under the name Thomas Maitland, attacked the work of Swinburne and Tennyson, as well as of Rossetti, who struck back with 'The Stealthy School of Criticism', in the *Athenaeum* (December 1871). By then, Buchanan had re-released his review as a standalone pamphlet under his own name
30. W.M. Rossetti 1895, vol. 1, p. 244
31. D.G. Rossetti to Ford Madox Brown (22 September 1872), Fredeman 2002–15, vol. 5, p. 276
32. D.G. Rossetti to Jane Morris, Bryson and Troxell 1976, p. 122
33. D.G. Rossetti to Jane Morris (February 1880), Surtees 1971, vol. 1, p. 154
34. W.M. Rossetti, diary entry (6–26 April 1882), Fredeman 1982, p. 239
35. John Ruskin, 'Letter to the Editor', *The Times*, 13 May 1851
36. W.M. Rossetti, V&A Departmental notes http://collections.vam.ac.uk/item/O757490/juliette-print-rossetti-dante-gabriel/ (accessed 26 July 2020). Other illustrations by Rossetti for this particular story have not been found. The facial expression and twisted posture of the female figure in Rossetti's illustration for *Faust: Margaret in Church* (1848, Tate Gallery) is strikingly similar to that in *Juliette*
37. Ford Maddox Brown, Surtees 1991, p. 81
38. Hill 1897, p. 97
39. Hunt 1913, vol. 2, p. 100
40. D.G. Rossetti to Ford Madox Brown (22 April 1860), W.M. Rossetti 1895, vol. 1, p. 206

41. D.G. Rossetti to Ellen Heaton (19 May 1863), Surtees 1971, vol. 1, p. 94
42. D.G. Rossetti to Ellen Heaton (24 December 1861), Surtees 1971, vol. 1, p. 87
43. W.M. Rossetti, *The Art Journal* (1884), p. 167
44. D.G. Rossetti to Fanny Cornforth (29 December 1872), Fredeman 2002–15, vol. 5, p. 374. In a letter written on the same day to Charles Augustus Howell, Rossetti referred to the drawing 'of herself with a fan made lately', as 'one of my best', p. 375
45. D.G. Rossetti to John Mitchell (27 September 1866), Fredeman 2002–15, vol. 3, p. 472
46. D.G. Rossetti to Frederick Leyland, 25 January 1872, Fennell 1978, p. 28
47. Hardinge 1890, p. 405
48. D.G. Rossetti to Jane Morris, 4 March 1870, Bryson and Troxell 1976, p. 18
49. Henry James to Alice James (12 March 1869), Walker and Zacharias 2006, vol. 1, p. 237
50. W.M. Rossetti (9 August 1880), Fredeman 1982, p. 229
51. D.G. Rossetti to Jane Morris (15 February 1880), Surtees 1971, vol. 1, p. 154

Picture Credits

Unless otherwise noted, all works reproduced in this book are in the Victoria and Albert Museum's collection. The other works are reproduced by kind permission of: Mark Samuels Lasner Collection, University of Delaware Library, Museums and Press 10, 27, 45, 72 (top), 91, 122; © National Portrait Gallery, London 12, 21; Courtesy of the Walters Art Museum, Baltimore 15; © National Trust Images/Andrew Butler 18; Courtesy of the London Metropolitan Archives, City of London 24; © Ashmolean Museum, University of Oxford 28, 43, 109, 134, 135; © Tate 34, 36, 37, 56, 60, 86, 92, 125; © Birmingham Museums and Art Gallery 41, 88; © The Trustees of the British Museum 54; © The Fitzwilliam Museum, Cambridge 55; © Gift of James Lawrence/ Museum of Fine Arts, Boston 75; © Amgueddfa Cenedlaethol Cymru – National Museum of Wales 82; © bpk/Hamburger Kunsthalle/Elke Walford 83; © Russell-Cotes Art Gallery and Museum, Bournemouth, UK Supported by the National Art Collections Fund/Bridgeman Images 85; © Delaware Art Museum, Samuel and Mary R. Bancroft Memorial 89; © Samuel and Mary R. Bancroft Memorial/Bridgeman Images 93, 94; © Kelmscott Manor, Oxfordshire, UK/Bridgeman Images 110; © President and Fellows of Harvard College/Harvard Art Museums 113, 126, 133; Courtesy of National Museums Liverpool/Walker Art Gallery 120–1; © Manchester Art Gallery, UK/Bridgeman Images 131

Selected Bibliography

Tim Barringer, *Reading the Pre-Raphaelites* (New Haven and London, 1999)

Tim Barringer, Jason Rosenfeld and Alison Smith, *Pre-Raphaelites: Victorian Avant-Garde* (London, 2012)

Jill Berk Jiminez (ed.), *Dictionary of Artists' Models* (Abingdon, Oxfordshire, 2001)

Odette Bornand (ed.), *The Diary of W.M. Rossetti 1870–1873* (Oxford, 1977)

John Bryson and Janet Camp Troxell (eds), *Dante Gabriel Rossetti and Jane Morris: Their Correspondence* (Oxford, 1976)

G.B-J. [Georgina Burne-Jones], *Memorials of Edward Burne-Jones*, 2 vols (London, 1904)

Stephen Calloway and Lynn Federle Orr, *The Cult of Beauty: The Aesthetic Movement, 1860–1900* (London, 2011)

Suzanne Fagence Cooper, *Pre-Raphaelite Art in the Victoria and Albert Museum* (London, 2003)

Brian Donnelly, *Reading Dante Gabriel Rossetti: The Painter as Poet* (Farnham, Surrey, 2015)

Oswald Doughty, *A Victorian Romantic: Dante Gabriel Rossetti* (London, 1949)

Henry Treffry Dunn, 1904 (ed. Rosalie Mander), *Recollections of Dante Gabriel Rossetti and his Circle – or – Cheyne Walk Life* (Westerham, Kent, 1984)

Francis L. Fennell, Jr, *The Rossetti-Leyland Letters: The Correspondence of an Artist and his Patron* (Athens, Ohio, 1978)

William E. Fredeman, 'A Shadow of Dante: Rossetti in the Final Years', *Victorian Poetry* 20:3/4 (Autumn–Winter 1982): 217–45

William E. Fredeman, Roger C. Lewis and Jane Cowan (eds), *The Correspondence of Dante Gabriel Rossetti*, 10 vols (Cambridge, 2002–15)

William M. Hardinge, 'A Reminiscence of Rossetti', *The Universal Review* 6:23 (January–April 1890): 398–411

Lucinda Hawksley, *Lizzie Siddal: The Tragedy of a Pre-Raphaelite Supermodel* (London, 2004; new ed., 2017)

George Birkbeck Hill (ed.), *The Letters of Dante Gabriel Rossetti to William Allingham, 1854–1870* (London, 1897)

Ford Madox Hueffer, *Rossetti: A Critical Essay on his Art* (London, 1912)

William Holman Hunt, *Pre-Raphaelitism and the Pre-Raphaelite Brotherhood*, 2 vols (London, 1913)

Fiona MacCarthy, *William Morris: A Life for our Time* (New York, 1995)

Debra N. Mancoff, *Jane Morris: The Pre-Raphaelite Model of Beauty* (San Francisco, 2000)

Debra N. Mancoff, *The Pre-Raphaelite Language of Flowers* (Munich, 2012)

Jan Marsh, *Dante Gabriel Rossetti: Painter and Poet* (London, 1999)

Jan Marsh, *The Legend of Elizabeth Siddal* (London, 1989; 2nd ed., 2010)

Jan Marsh, *National Portrait Gallery Insights: The Pre-Raphaelite Circle* (London, 2005)

Jan Marsh, *Pre-Raphaelite Sisterhood* (London, 1985; new ed., 2019)

Jan Marsh, *Pre-Raphaelite Sisters* (London, 2019)

Susan Owens and Nicholas Tromans (eds) *Christina Rossetti: Poetry in Art* (London and New Haven, 2018)

Lona Mosk Packer (ed.), *The Rossetti–Macmillan Letters* (Berkeley, California, 1963)

Leslie Parris, *The Pre-Raphaelites* (London, 1984)

Elizabeth Prettejohn, *The Art of the Pre-Raphaelites* (London, 2000)

Dante Gabriel Rossetti, *Hand and Soul* (London 1902)

Dante Gabriel Rossetti, *Poems and Translations* (London, 1912)

Dante Gabriel Rossetti (trans.), *La Vita Nuova (The New Life) by Dante Alighieri* (London, *c.* 1910)

William Michael Rossetti, *Dante Gabriel Rossetti as Designer and Writer* (London, 1889)

William Michael Rossetti (ed.), *Dante Gabriel Rossetti: His Family Letters, with a memoir by William Michael Rossetti*, 2 vols (London, 1895)

William Michael Rossetti (ed.), *Rossetti Papers: 1862–1870* (London, 1903)

William Michael Rossetti (ed.), *Ruskin, Rossetti, Pre-Raphaelitism: Papers 1854–1862* (London, 1899)

Frank S. Sharp and Jan Marsh, *The Collected Letters of Jane Morris* (Woodbridge, Suffolk, 2012)

Paul Spencer-Longhurst, *The Blue Bower: Rossetti in the 1860s* (London, 2000)

Virginia Surtees (ed.), *The Diary of Ford Madox Brown* (New Haven and London, 1981)

Virginia Surtees, *The Paintings and Drawings of Dante Gabriel Rossetti (1828–1882)*, 2 vols (Oxford, 1971)

Virginia Surtees, *Rossetti's Portraits of Elizabeth Siddal* (Aldershot, Hampshire, 1991)

Julian Treuherz, Elizabeth Prettejohn and Edwin Becker, *Dante Gabriel Rossetti* (London, 2003)

Janet Camp Troxell (ed.), *Three Rossettis: Unpublished Letters to and from Dante Gabriel, Christina, William* (Cambridge, Massachusetts, 1937)

Pierre A. Walker and Greg W. Zacharias (eds), *The Complete Letters of Henry James, 1855–1872*, 2 vols (Lincoln, Nebraska, 2006)

Stephen Wildman, *Visions of Love and Life: Pre-Raphaelite Art from the Birmingham Collection, England* (Alexandria, Virginia, 1995)

Stephen Wildman, *Waking Dreams: The Art of the Pre-Raphaelites from the Delaware Art Museum* (Alexandria, Virginia, 2004)

Andrew Wilton and Robert Upstone, *The Age of Rossetti, Burne-Jones and Watts: Symbolism in Britain, 1860–1910* (London, 1997)

Acknowledgments

For their encouragement and advice in the initial conception of this project I would like to thank Tom Windross, Head of Content at the Victoria and Albert Museum, and Julian Honer, Editorial Director, Museum Publishing, at Thames & Hudson. I am deeply grateful to Hannah Newell, Development Editor at V&A Publishing, for her perceptive guidance throughout the writing and editorial process, and to Susan Owens, formerly Curator of Paintings at the Victoria and Albert Museum, for her discerning comments on the manuscript. Also at the V&A, I very much appreciate the assistance of Ana Debenedetti, Curator of Paintings, in verifying details of works in the collection. Also at Thames & Hudson, my thanks to Elain McAlpine for her insights and steady hand guiding the later stages of the project, and to Isabel Roldan and Avni Patel for designing this beautiful book. As ever, I thank the Newberry Library for supporting my ongoing research as a Scholar-in Residence. Daniel Greene, President and Librarian, Keelin Burke, Director of Fellowships and Academic Programs, and D. Bradford Hunt, former Vice-President for Research and Education, were especially supportive. For their interest and insights I thank my colleagues Sarah Lea Burns, Tim McGee, Michal Raz-Russo and Margaret D. Stetz. And with heartfelt gratitude for his generous contribution to this project, and to the field of Pre-Raphaelite studies, I dedicate this book to Mark Samuels Lasner.

Author's Biography

Debra N. Mancoff, Scholar-in-Residence at the Newberry Library, Chicago, has written extensively on the Pre-Raphaelites, including *Danger! Women Artists at Work* (2012), *The Pre-Raphaelite Language of Flowers* (2012), *Jane Morris: The Pre-Raphaelite Model of Beauty* (2000) and *Burne-Jones* (1998). Her articles have appeared in such journals as *Art Quarterly*, *Journal of Pre-Raphaelite Studies*, *Museum Studies/Art Institute of Chicago* and the *Princeton Library Journal*, as well as the exhibition catalogues *Love Revealed: Simeon Solomon and the Pre-Raphaelites* (2005), *Pre-Raphaelites and Other Masters: The Andrew Lloyd Webber Collection* (2003) and *Julia Margaret Cameron's Women* (1998), and she edited the essay collection *John Everett Millais: Beyond the Pre-Raphaelite Brotherhood* (2001). Her most recent book is *The Face: Our Human Story* (2018).

Front cover image: Detail of *The Day Dream*, 1880 (p. 137)
Back cover image: *Aglaia Ionides*, 1870 (p. 115)
Opposite title page: *Mrs William Morris, The Blue Silk Dress*, 1868 (p. 110)
Opposite contents page: Detail of *Veronica Veronese*, 1872 (p. 94)

First published in the United Kingdom in 2021 by
Thames & Hudson Ltd, 181A High Holborn, London WC1V 7QX
in association with the Victoria and Albert Museum, London

First published in the United States of America in 2021 by
Thames & Hudson Inc., 500 Fifth Avenue, New York, New York 10110

British Library Cataloguing-in-Publication Data
A catalogue record for this book is available from the British Library

Library of Congress Control Number 2021931494

ISBN 978-0-500-48071-7

Printed and bound in China by C & C Offset Printing Co. Ltd

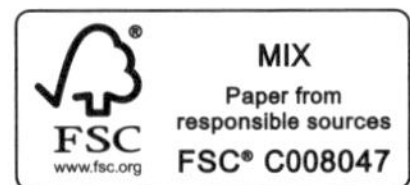

V&A Publishing

Supporting the world's leading
museum of art and design,
the Victoria and Albert
Museum, London